*f*P

THE BOARD OF EDITORS

Men of international artistic standing
and achievement offer the books
in this brochure for your reading pleasure...

W. H. AUDEN — One of the great poets of the English language, Mr. Auden is generally considered the most influential poet of his generation. An anthologist of note, a translator of distinction, and the co-author of several plays, Mr. Auden brings to the Society a versatility not often found in a master poet.

JACQUES BARZUN — This critic, translator, historian, and teacher of eminence has devoted his life to writing, lecturing, and travel. He is now Dean of the Faculties and Provost of Columbia University. His most recent work *The House of Intellect* is a best seller in its seventh printing.

LIONEL TRILLING — In England as well as in the United States, Mr. Trilling is acknowledged to be the most influential of the American literary critics. A superb stylist, he is author of a number of celebrated books, most notably *The Liberal Imagination*. He is Professor of English at Columbia University.

A Company
of Readers

Uncollected Writings of
W. H. Auden, Jacques Barzun,
and Lionel Trilling *from*
The Readers' Subscription and Mid-Century Book Clubs

Edited with an Introduction by
Arthur Krystal

Foreword by
Jacques Barzun

THE FREE PRESS
NEW YORK   LONDON   TORONTO   SYDNEY   SINGAPORE

THE FREE PRESS
A Division of Simon & Schuster, Inc.
1230 Avenue of the Americas
New York, NY 10020

For information regarding special discounts for bulk purchases,
please contact Simon & Schuster Special Sales at 1-800-456-6798
or business@simonandschuster.com

Designed by Charles B. Hames

Manufactured in the United States of America

10 9 8 7 6 5 4 3 2 1

Library of Congress Cataloging-in-Publication Data
A company of readers: uncollected writings of W. H. Auden,
Jacques Barzun, and Lionel Trilling
from The Readers' Subscription and Mid-Century book clubs / edited with
an introduction by Arthur Krystal; foreword by Jacques Barzun
p.   cm.
I. Krystal, Arthur. II. Auden, W. H. (Wystan Hugh), 1907–1973. III. Barzun,
Jacques, 1907–. IV. Trilling, Lionel, 1905–1975.
AC5 .C7317 2001
081—dc21   2001023188

ISBN 0-7432-0262-7

Poets and Professors and all those whose love of books exceeds their love of automobiles will welcome a chance to save in excess of 50% on their book purchases.

W. H. Auden

Contents

Foreword: Three Men and a Book

Jacques Barzun

THE BOOK CLUB is not a twentieth-century invention, unless turning a thing upside down is inventiveness. In the eighteenth and nineteenth centuries, small groups of people clubbed together to buy books because they were expensive. In colonial New York, for example, five or six men formed The New York Society for such a purpose in 1754, and it has had an uninterrupted existence to this day. It is now a large collection open to the public. Around the same time, the Boston Library Society thrived, and by joining another society became the present Boston Athenaeum, which combines a grand museum with a vast library and is now expanding its quarters.

The book club of the mid-twentieth century was no such grassroots affair with a noble future. It started from the business end of things, its purpose being to increase the sale of books. This need had been made acute by the practice of letting booksellers return to the publisher any unsold copies. With the enormous output of books annually and the competing agencies of film, radio, and television, the publishing industry found itself producing more than it could distribute in the ordinary way of chancy announcements through reviews. Advertising is too expensive to waste on works that do not take flight on their own. The result is that by far the greater number issued—good, bad, or indifferent—are hustled to the remainder house. Incidentally, the book jacket is a by-product of this return policy; it protects the object on its multiple comings and goings. The simple days are over when the printer-publisher sold his wares on a stall outside the press, direct to the passerby.

In this country, The Literary Guild inaugurated the distribution of popular novels to people who agreed to buy every month—or nearly—a book chosen for them by the Guild. Next, the Book-of-the-Month Club offered in the same way works of a more intellectual cast, and several other organizations catered to the tastes of people interested in a single subject, such as history or popular science. In England, the Book Society was for the generalist, and the Left Book Club for Soviet sympathizers. All these enterprises succeeded in materially extending the dissemination of new books. In both countries, such success showed up the publishing industry's incapacity to sell what it made; the buyers were there, but nobody had found the means of reaching them steadily as individuals.

Book clubs achieved this purpose by offering each month a fairly wide choice of books, together with a share of the usual publishers' discount. This lowered by 25 to 30 percent the list price of books, which fifty years ago ranged from six to eight dollars. If a club member did not return the card enclosed in the bulletin by a certain date, he received the main selection automatically. Consent and absent-mindedness were on a par.

AMONG THE AMERICAN CLUBS serving the public in this way, one had a different origin from all the rest. Instead of being the offspring of salesmanship, the Readers' Subscription was founded in September 1951 to create an audience for books that the other clubs considered to be too far above the public taste. The Book-of-the-Month Club had somewhat lowered its original goal and the specialist caterers also looked for the safely popular. The idea of going beyond these limits and supplying readers with books of solid intellectual merit arose in a conversation between Lionel Trilling and his former student in Columbia College, Gilman Kraft. He was the brother of the future political journalist Joseph Kraft, who had been a student of mine and who vouched to me for Gilman's intelligence and integrity.

Trilling and I were then teaching together a seminar for Ph.D. candidates, and when he asked me to serve with him as coeditor of the venture, I agreed. But I urged that we needed a third, not only to resolve possible differences in making the selections, but also to offset the appearance of exclusively academic judgment. I suggested a poet and proposed W. H. Auden. He and I shared a strong interest in music and used to go together to Richard Franko Goldman's classical band concerts in Central Park. Auden accepted "editing" with us, and we were off with controlled enthusiasm.

Gilman Kraft was a good organizer. He found the needed resources and used them prudently: no large staff or sumptuous offices, but two modest rooms on Broadway, a typist, and a handyman, a charming, gentle, efficient soul, who turned out to be the brother of the novelist James Baldwin. To help Kraft write the briefer notices of alternative choices and occasional recordings, we had young Leo Raditsa, later a distinguished scholar and teacher at St. John's College. The mailing of materials and other relations with members—the shipment of books, billing, and bookkeeping—were handled by one of the two or three firms that called themselves "fulfillment" companies, a title that soon took on the hue of irony.

The name Readers' Subscription was chosen after a long discussion in the Trillings' living room on Claremont Avenue. Gilman Kraft was present but not Auden. It was Diana Trilling who coined the formula; I thought it inaccurate: a club member is not locked in like a magazine subscriber; he can choose a substitute for the month's offering or refuse it altogether. This disagreement was, I am happy to say, the last on any important matter. At that same session, it was Gilman Kraft who baptized the future bulletin *The Griffin*. The body of a lion and the head of an eagle is perhaps an apt description of the species Critic.

At the first editorial meeting, the three judges tackled a large pile of books that Kraft had solicited from publishers or that had been sent after the public notice of our existence. We each chose half a dozen for reading at home and briefly scanned and discussed possible others. We did this every month, or rather, every four weeks, making a year of thirteen months and thirteen books. At a second meeting each month, we reported, chose the main selection and several alternates, and decided which of us would write the lead reviews. The discussions were remarkably urbane. I recall no dispute, not even unpleasant vehemence. Nor was there ever a 2-to-1 decision.

By good luck, we were all three incredibly punctual and faithful. It took the flu to keep one of us away, and this happened only a few times in the 139 months of our service. Wystan Auden, who may have begun with a little apprehension about trading literary opinions with a pair of professors, soon saw that Lionel and I had long forgotten our Ph.D.s and were at ease with each other—as shortly were the three of us.

This good understanding was desirable, because each review was mailed by its author to the other two and changes or additions freely suggested by phone. Sometimes the book that one of us particularly favored had to be postponed one month to make room for another; timing was governed by the need to offer a book as soon as possible after publication. On occasion, we were outbid by the Book-of-the-Month Club, where Clifton Fadiman, the highly qualified judge, evidently shared our estimate of a new work and persuaded the rest of his panel.

It goes without saying that the tone and twists of blurbery were automatically avoided. The reviews were indeed always favorable; the book would not have been chosen if it had not pleased us all. As to our range, it had no preshrunk limits about viewpoint or subject. We offered E. M. Forster's essays on politics and society and the plays of Bertolt Brecht, the poems of Cavafy and Proust's first novel, *Jean Santeuil*. *The Griffin* might in addition feature a letter from an author, or a poem, or a guest reviewer for a second book. Among these visitors I recall Peter Gay, Alan Pryce-Jones, and Edmund Wilson. Forster dropped us a line when working on the libretto of *Billy Budd*. First and last, we recommended works by authors as far apart in opinion as Günter Grass, James Baldwin, Lawrence Durrell, Eleanor Clark, William Golding, Norman O. Brown, Harold Rosenberg, James Agee, William Burroughs, Caesare Pavese, Lévi-Strauss, Muriel Spark, Iris Murdoch, and J.R.R. Tolkien.

Some of our authors were at the start of their renown, but to bring out Flaubert's *Bouvard and Pécuchet* (with its annex, *The Dictionary of Accepted Ideas,* for the first time in English) or Berlioz's dramatized music criticism, *Evenings with the Orchestra,* was tantamount to offering our readers unknown "first works." It was not surprising that some who enjoyed our painstaking essays (each of us had two critics always at his elbow) should suggest reprinting the best pieces. Lionel Trilling yielded to the entreaty and made from among his reviews the now well-known *A Gathering of Fugitives,* published in 1956.

But there hung over us another obligation, unexpected and, unlike the rest, a chore. That hopeful word "fulfillment," applied to the mechanics of distribution, turned out a delusion and betrayal. Fairly soon, friends, colleagues, or strangers who knew us through our writings sent us pathetic or indignant letters about their running battle with Fulfillment. They had received no book or the wrong book or the main book when they had declined it; they had been billed for it or billed twice or the wrong amount—or rather, they had been unable to get these misdeeds remedied after repeated letters and phone calls. We the editors were the court of last resort and we had to reply, expressing regrets coupled with promises we hardly believed in. We switched firms, but errors continued to bedevil us.

THE READERS' SUBSCRIPTION succeeded beyond the editors' expectations—we had been a trio of cultural skeptics. But after eight years the club did not meet Gilman Kraft's financial hopes or needs, and one day in early 1959 he told us that he had reluctantly decided to leave for greener pastures. He gave us time to find his replacement. For his new venture he bought *Playbill,* made it profitable, and enlarged it while improving its literary quality. We missed him. He was always calm, friendly, and solicitous about our wants. He never offered an opinion on books unless asked for one, as we did from time to time, for he was a thoughtful person whose Columbia College education had given him a solid grounding in literature and history.

Remembering those book-centered discussions tempts me to suggest the atmosphere in which they took place. We enjoyed ourselves. We expressed our preferences, our prejudices, freely, often turning them into sources of entertainment. No tricks of thought or manner were frequent enough to annoy, even though we were strongly marked characters, forced to meet face to face every two weeks and settle points of style and literary judgment by phone in between. Our work was, in fact, a long conversation heading toward endless decisions. But unlike the Supreme Court soberly weighing wire-drawn arguments, our discussions were interwoven with jokes, puns, and parodies. We behaved like friends talking over what to recommend to other friends.

To make a point about something—I no longer remember what—Lionel invented *A History of English Literature from B. O. Wulf to Virginia Woolf* and parodied the textbook style. Wystan would utter a clerihew he thought apposite, and he and I got into the habit of matching clerihews by way of touching off the proceedings. For those who do not know what a clerihew is, here are one of his and one of mine: "Joseph Haydn / Never read Dryden, / Nor did Dryden / Ever hear Haydn." "Henry James / Did not name names, / But all the Bostonians knew / Who was who." Later, Auden published two collections of these ink-spot biographies. About one element of our work we all groaned in unison: the galleys. In those days, books were circulated before publication in unpaged proofs on sheets nearly two feet long and unbound. Turning over these streamers, carrying them folded in half in a duffel bag (a briefcase would not hold six or eight sets), and marking one's place or trying to find an earlier passage were as irritating as locating the set wanted, since it bore no mark on its back.

As critics we had one trait in common: none of us applied a theory or system. Apart from this unifying mode, our tendencies and backgrounds differed widely, surely a desirable diversity for the purposes of the club. Trilling has latterly been dubbed a disciple of Matthew Arnold because he wrote a classic work on the subject, but it is a misjudgment. In youth Lionel had been a Marxist, later he was a good Freudian, and although something of these influences remained visible in his work, he was nobody's follower; his original thought outweighs the derived elements, as is true of every genuine thinker. What is more to the point than influence, he knew no foreign languages, but drew all his critical principles from absorption in English and American literature, including the great critics.

This happy single-mindedness set him apart from his two colleagues. Au-

den, partly because of his pride in ancestry, which his given name Wystan sig-
nalized, felt deep interest in things Germanic. He and I had had a classical education strongly colored by Greek and Latin, but he rejoiced that Oxford had
compelled him to learn Anglo-Saxon. During his years with the club he was
reading the Icelandic Eddas and detailing their merits to us. After many sum-
mers spent in Italy, he came to prefer life near Vienna, and he died there. His
intellectual rapport with Hannah Arendt confirmed this sympathy with Germanic culture, as did his coolness toward French literature and ideas. For
some reason he hated Racine almost as much as he hated the works of A. A.
Milne.

That Wystan and I were good friends was no doubt a tribute to my Amer-
icanization. My antecedents contrasted with those of my fellow reviewers.
The intellectual imprint of a French lycée should have made me a disciple of
Descartes and a devotee of seventeenth-century literature, but early in life music had been an antidote and made me value the Romanticists in art and letters, this in the teeth of contemporary opinion, both French and American.
Since I had grown up among the artists of the next wave, the Cubists and
their peers, I was resistant to those currents of thought. My masters in criticism were Gautier, Hazlitt, and Poe, Goethe and Nietzsche. Trilling being untouched by them, and Auden disdainful of things French, our reviews in *The
Griffin* were in an effortless way independent.

WHAT EMERGES from this sketch of our inclinations is the principle of what
Trilling was the first to call "cultural criticism," that is, criticism inspired by
whatever is relevant to the work. Its genesis, form, and meaning have roots in
the culture where it appears, and it is also unique through its author's own
uniqueness. To us, none of this was new. We were cultural critics with no
need of a doctrine, for the essence of culture is inclusiveness. And here
Matthew Arnold properly enters again. It was he who said: "The men of culture are the true apostles of equality. They have a passion for diffusing, for
making prevail, for carrying from one end of society to the other, the best
ideas of their time."

It is clear in retrospect that not we alone but the mid-century as a whole,
particularly in the United States, made a many-sided effort to carry out the
Arnoldian mandate. The hope of a collective enjoyment of the best in thought
and art was still strong. It was manifest in the drive to send the young to college, in the foundations for the advancement of one or another cultural good
and in the free public libraries, in the many series of classics in cheap, well-
edited form, and not least, in the book clubs.

Ours continued without a break after Gilman left us. Trilling found a successor in Sol Stein, another former student. He was Kraft's opposite in temper—buoyant, expansive, and as a budding novelist, consciously literary. He had found a sponsor for buying the Readers' Subscription, the well-to-do Arnold Bernhard. Soon we were in more spacious offices emphatically on the East Side, served by a larger staff, including the elegant and businesslike Patricia Day, who later formed with our executive the publishing firm of Stein and Day.

Aware, perhaps, of the pressure of the times, we chose as the name of our second club The Mid-Century. It was that of the monthly bulletin as well. The kind of books we chose and the way we presented them remained the same, but nearly everything else about the society was different. I have already mentioned Sol Stein's princely ways and the classier offices. The atmosphere changed with them. For one thing, Stein took part in our discussions, which lengthened them to little perceptible advantage, because he introduced considerations of pricing and of favors to and from publishers—elements we had known nothing about before and from which we firmly remained aloof.

We were happy to have, in replacement of Leo Raditsa, a recent Harvard Ph.D., John Simon. He was a highly cultivated young man with whom it was a pleasure to work. His career since then as a leading critic of theater, film, music, and language confirms the judgment that brought him into our midst forty years ago and made him so congenial a helper.

In this new incarnation of our purpose, I remember fewer appeals from distraught readers angry about bills. Fulfillment had gained somewhat in its Manichean battle with Frustration. But not long after the change-over, a worse preoccupation began to cloud our work. It started with a suggestion from Sol Stein that the editors should become part owners of the society, on what terms was not clear. My fellow editors expressed interest, coupled with a vague alarm, which I shared. I was reluctant, both because I thought a financial interest inappropriate to our role as judges and because I foresaw additional time being used up for present negotiations and future business meetings.

They began right away and proved a kind of commitment. We were soon spending afternoons in parleyings. Then came what we had all half-detected: the society was in financial trouble. Overhead and costs exceeded revenue. When the truth was out, we became well acquainted with our backer, whose emergency help Sol Stein was soliciting. Arnold Bernhard was the founder and head of ValueLine, the highly regarded and profitable financial newsletter. Mr. Bernhard was a cultivated gentleman, whose intentions in entering our small domain were entirely altruistic. His interest was in literature and, as head trustee of the University of Bridgeport, in the spread of general education. He straightened out our current troubles and was further intent on making the editors part owners at no cost to them.

But Mr. Bernhard made one mistake, as he was the first to say when the collapse occurred. His rescue of the company had given him in double measure the right to oversee its operations and he thought of delegating the task to one of his aides at ValueLine. But he deferred to Stein's assurances and forbore, leaving the ship to its fate. After a lapse of twenty years, in November 1985, just before his death, Arnold Bernhard and I met at lunch, and soon our conversation turned to the old subject. Without any word from me, he mentioned his deep regret that he had not set a watch on the Mid-Century.

THE END OF THE CLUB in 1963 was not a decline and fall. The membership had risen from about thirty-five thousand to a little over forty thousand. This formidable surge was attributed to advertising. Arnold Bernhard believed that with the company's proper handling and publicity this number could be at least doubled. The Readers' Subscription had used only mailings. Now readers of the *New York Times Book Review* and the *Herald-Tribune Books* could see the three editors in arranged poses that showed the intensity of their conferrings; journalistic realism was at work in our behalf. We also appeared on television on David Susskind's program, *Open End,* meaning that once we started talking, nothing could stop us. We forgathered one evening about eleven o'clock, and after a vague briefing went on the airwaves, seated on camp chairs and divided by a table on which were several pots and mugs. Lionel and I had coffee pots, Wystan one for tea, but the brownish liquid that flowed from his was whisky.

Our host Mr. Susskind had collected a good many reviews of our published works and arranged them, folded, in three little piles. He took up one at a time, glanced at it, and with a rising inflection quoted a sentence or two. Thus goaded we were presumably to start a discussion, but after two or three such prods from the little piles (our host looked as if he were playing solitaire) nothing really got going. We had to jerry-build a conversation, unavoidably leaving him out. His voice, though, cut in at short intervals with ads. One of them touted a brokerage firm: "I tell you, these people are integrity-ridden." Some of our listeners, half asleep, took this encomium to be about us. Kenneth Tynan reviewed our session adversely, and quite right he was. We had tried hard to be serious and had been defeated. Trilling, in his later review of Tynan's *Curtains,* rose to our defense, claiming jocularly that Tynan "deals with [our] performance with no comprehension of its genre: he takes it to have been a problem drama, when actually it was wild, grim comedy."

That second half-life, I hasten to add, was not wholly spoiled by money matters and legal confabs. Besides the reading-and-choosing, which continued to spark good conversation, there were Wystan's birthday parties. These were held on February 21 at his apartment on St. Mark's Place. The house was a fine old specimen, really old. The floors curved downward, and when his thirty or forty guests stood on them, glass in hand, anyone who walked could test the degree of flexibility underfoot.

Wystan's invitations were formal, typed and multigraphed, and they bore in the lower left corner: "Carriages at eleven." About that hour on one of these occasions, the Mid-Century gang went in a body to the back room where the overcoats were piled on a couch. It was a freezing cold night and powdery snow was falling. Arnold Bernhard could not find his coat. We helped him to search again: it was gone. Arnold made no comment, thanked Wystan without mentioning the loss, and walked out with us as if all parties ended this way. Fortunately, several of us had mufflers, we wrapped them around his throat and torso, and he suffered no harm. A couple of days later a muffler arrived in the mail.

The end came suddenly, by telephone and without details. The new deficit was greater than Arnold Bernhard cared to make up. When the three of us met again for mutual solace, we agreed that there would have come a time, not indefinitely far off, when we would have wanted to cease and desist. And any successors of ours would have made something different of the society, perhaps more popular but not so ecumenical. The title Readers' Subscription had in fact been acquired for a club still in being today.

The close of ours, although abrupt, should not be called premature. In our eleven years and six months of existence, we had made a point about books and readers, publishers and their methods. For my part certainly, I was glad to be free of the burden of reading, meeting, and writing; but at the time I had a special cause of annoyance: my ultimate review, for February 1963, got lost in the breakup of the office. Wystan had sent it in after phoning me to say that he particularly liked it because of the parallels in it. The book was Henry Miller's autobiographical *Tropic of Cancer,* which I had compared with *Werther* for its hero and with Henry James's *Ambassadors* for its setting, which is Paris. The terms of these comparisons, like the loss, I have magnanimously forgotten.

Introduction: Club Work

THE LOVER OF BOOKS is a disgruntled beast. If it's not Horace shaking a fist at multiplying poets in Ancient Rome, it's Dr. Johnson groaning under the weight of superfluous Authors in eighteenth-century London; if it's not Goethe denouncing book reviewers in nineteenth-century Weimar, it's Randall Jarrell lacing into supercilious critics in twentieth-century New York. For every season there is a time under heaven for complaining: "[I]n the degree that we have come to take literature with an unprecedented, a religious, seriousness, we seem to have lost our pleasure in reading. More and more young people undertake the professional study of literature; fewer like to read." A pretty fair description of the current state of literature studies in the academy, wouldn't you say? If you did, you'd be wrong. The words appeared in a 1952 review of Edmund Wilson's *The Shores of Light,* and the reviewer, Lionel Trilling, seemed put out that reading, "which used to be an appetite and a passion, is now thought to be rather *infra dig* in people of intelligence." There is something else out of place about these sentences: they appeared in the publication of a book club whose stated purpose was the dissemination of the very books that Trilling despaired of ever being savored.

In 1951, Trilling, Jacques Barzun, and W. H. Auden had been enlisted by Trilling's former student at Columbia, Gilman Kraft, to form the editorial board of a fledgling publishing venture to be named the Readers' Subscription Book Club. Their duties would entail choosing books and writing monthly columns for the club's bulletin, *The Griffin.* Why would someone who believed that readers were becoming insensible to the pleasures of literature take on such work? For one thing, Trilling probably believed it less than he made out; for another, he knew that however small the audience for books, it needed looking after. His bolder, more prescient point concerns the relation between the professional study of literature and the love of reading. Shortly after the founding editors departed from the book club in 1963 (by which time it had been reincorporated as the Mid-Century Book Society), the deconstructionist gale blew in from across the Atlantic, upsetting the historic balance between readers and texts, between literature and criticism—thereby casting the book-club essays by Auden, Barzun, and Trilling as some of the last examples of literary criticism aimed at a general audience by professional critics. Indeed, the fact that two professors in the humanities and a poet famous for his learning once deigned to head such a club speaks volumes, as it were, about the difference in the literary culture then and now.

One such difference, more felt than acknowledged, has been the almost complete bifurcation of literary criticism into the academic and the journalistic styles. Until the early 1960s, literary prose was roughly divisible, as Cyril Connolly suggested, into the Mandarin and the Vernacular. The former rejoiced in complex sentences that took their sweet time to get to the point (the point may well have been the eloquent unfurling of one dependent clause after another), while the latter depended on familiar speech patterns and the brisk rhythms of journalism. Unalike in sensibility and syntax, the two styles nonetheless shared an unwavering belief in the transparency of the written word. This faith in language, however, would soon be tested by continental philosophers and semioticians, who concluded that the problematic nature of mind and language required a style of discourse emblematic of this difficulty. Instead of borrowing from—and contributing to—the language of literature, academic critics began to generate an alternative parlance that, for want of a better word, became known as the Theoretical—a style whose tortured syntax and profusion of technical terms purportedly mirrors the socio-psychological conundrums that underpin cognition. An implicit tenet of the new style was that everything written in the old style was somehow innocent of its own deeper implications. This, in turn, had the unintended effect of placing an intellectual barricade in front of any new lettristic movement, and so the progression of Classic-Augustan-Romantic-Victorian-Modern came to a standstill with Postmodernism, which has little to do with literature and everything to do with rapidly changing theoretical models: structuralism, deconstruction, reader-response theory, New Historicism, post-colonialism, culture studies, gender studies, queer studies.

How all this will play out in the university is anyone's guess. One thing, though, seems self-evident: the Theoretical style showcases by default the organic relationship that once existed between literature and criticism. Whereas the Theoretical essay was never meant to be taken for a category of literature, the lettristic is an extension of the literary experience—is, in fact, in the right hands, a species of literature. One has only to think of Samuel Johnson, Hazlitt, De Quincey, Stevenson, Arnold, Ruskin, Orwell, and Henry James of the Prefaces. The literary essay, or more accurately the essay about literature, reached its highest elevation during the second quarter of the last century, with the prestige conferred on it by T. S. Eliot, whose own efforts were models (certain of his opinions notwithstanding) of clarity, discernment, learning, and persuasiveness. With Eliot, the critical essay not only fed on the work of poets, it enhanced it, providing an exegetical frame to set off the poem's colors and shadings. And modern literature, because it was complex and disturbing, because it openly equated form with function, brought forth critics intent on measuring the tension between the cultural implications of rhetoric and the autonomy intrinsic to unique works. Twenty years after the publication of *The Waste Land*, we had reached, as Randall Jarrell famously said, "The Age of Criticism," an age that relied on literature's preeminence in order to emerge.

An age of criticism naturally serves up critics unhappy with the age, and Jarrell's designation wasn't meant as an honorific. Criticism, he pointed out, "which began by humbly and anomalously existing for the work of art, and was in part a mere by-product of philosophy and rhetoric, has by now become, for a good many people, almost what the work of art exists for: the animals come up to Adam and Eve and are named—the end crowns the work." Jarrell was being disingenuous; criticism was never so humble, and he knew it. His anxiety preceded the age; and it was only after his death that his cautionary remarks bore fruit. In fact, it was the Age of Criticism because most critics would not have bothered to state that literature was more important than how they spoke about it: "Books were our weather, our environment, our clothing," Anatole Broyard recalled about his days in Greenwich Village in the 1950s. "We didn't simply read books; we became them. We took them into ourselves and made them into our histories." The only thing that mattered was the life of the mind, and everything important to that life—God, sex, politics—had to pass through the centrifuge of literature.

All this is to say that the literary critic labors under a burden that critics of the other arts do not. Unlike those who write about music, painting, or architecture, the literary critic relies on the same instrument used by the poet and novelist. No one asks that the critic's prose be equal to the writer's, only that it display a passionate advocacy of—or considered opposition to—the poem or novel's own heightened language. Passion can be mute, inarticulate, eloquent—it can even be polemical—but it cannot be jargon-ridden or willfully obscure. Awkward, even clichéd prose is forgivable, but to come to literature with the theorist's pride in complexity and obscurantism is like encountering a slightly demented lover who lavishes all his time and effort on a letter rather than on the person the letter is intended for.

IS THERE A RIGHT WAY to write about books? Edwin Denby, the dance critic at mid-century for the *Herald Tribune,* perhaps came close when he stipulated: "It is not the critic's historic function to have the right opinions but to have interesting ones." What Denby meant by this is something more than might first suggest itself. "Interesting" is not a terribly interesting word; it is, however, a deceptively transparent one. To tweak a phrase, serious is easy, interesting is hard. But in the absence of a universal template, how does one go about being interesting? In a 1955 talk, slyly titled "On Not Talking," Trilling pronounced that the "most discouraging element in American cultural life was "a lack of innocence and ready human respect, a fear of being wrong, an aspiration to *expertise.*" (Isn't this the genome of the postmodernist?) Trilling, who was perhaps our most sophisticated reader of novels, sensed that knowledge itself is subject to hesitancies and uncertainties, and that perhaps literature is ground too fine to be poured into any one theoretical, or porous, vessel. What Trilling was getting at was a definition of sophistication that did not preclude openness on the part of the critic. Let the critic stumble, reverse himself, question his own motives—why not? Isn't a critic surprised by his own response to literature preferable to one who thinks he has all the answers? We may want a critic whose reading has been seasoned by experience, and whose experience is better informed for having read seriously, but we also want that critic to invigorate us, to clear the mind of unruly shrubbery, to broaden our perspective, not by being right, but by getting close enough to make us intuitively think about what is right.

It was a hill, really, that Montaigne lived on and drew his name from: it is only the Essays that are mountainous.

As a man grows older it is likely that the new books to which he forms a permanent attachment are reference books.

The House of the Dead is not Dostoevsky's greatest work but it is, perhaps, his least irritating.

For years I resisted every recommendation to read her. Her name conjured up for me the conventional anglo-saxon images of Paris as the city of the Naughty Spree . . .

One of my college teachers said that the day comes to all men when they no longer delight in reading novels.

There is probably no literary career in America today that matches James Baldwin's in the degree of interest it commands. The reason for this is as deplorable as it is obvious.

Thus begin some of the reviews and essays that Auden, Barzun, and Trilling contributed to *The Griffin* and *The Mid-Century.* In the post-Derridean classroom, one might argue that these particular writers, through no fault of their own, read books with a certain culturally inbred naiveté, insufficiently aware of an author's cultural assumptions or the tie-in between semiotic and social structures. Of course, this is somewhat like condemning all those who died before the coming of Christ for never getting the chance to accept Him. However inadequate as social scientists and semioticians the editors might have been, their own work displays that *informal* expertise that is second nature to the habitué of books. The innocence embraced by Trilling is an innocence predicated on the expectation that the primary purpose of literature (and criticism) is the communication of artistic vision, without which "obscurity," as Auden once put it, "is mostly swank." None of the editors would have claimed, as does a recent advertisement for the *London Review of Books,* that the club was "unashamedly intellectual." The book club was not only not unashamed, it was clearly in the Arnoldian mold of bringing intellectual news to all those who were, as Arnold observed, "interested in the advance of the general culture." Its legitimacy was fact because it remained unstated.

Which is not to say that the editors were absolutely convinced that such a club would work. It may have been the Age of Criticism, but it was also the end of the age (naming always foreshadows endings), and though "literary" and "intellectual" were still spoken of in the same breath, what guarantee that a club offering good books and only good books would find an audience? Braiding the commercial with the intellectual has never exactly been a sure-fire way of getting to the top of the publishing heap. Still, if you're going to throw the dice—the fuzzy literary kind—better to do it when men and women of letters are actually standing around the table. In 1950, Edmund Wilson presided over the book section at *The New Yorker;* Lincoln Kirstein was the Fine Arts editor of the *New Republic;* and Malcolm Cowley was a contributing editor of the *Nation.* That year the *Partisan Review* had ten thousand subscribers, and, as Auden had dryly observed: "Our intellectual marines / Landing in little magazines / Capture a trend." To be sure, a few marines such as William Empson and Kenneth Burke were beyond the pale of the nonspecialist reader, but that still left Desmond McCarthy, Alfred Kazin, Leslie Fiedler, Mary Mc-Carthy, Cyril Connolly, Randall Jarrell, and George Orwell (who died in 1950) as well as critics of a more pronounced academic stripe—F. O. Matthiessen, Frederick Dupee, Allen Tate, R. P. Blackmur, Cleanth Brooks, M. H. Abrams, W. Jackson Bate, and Harry Levin—all of whom wrote for places the general educated reader could visit without a graduate school visa.

But were there enough such interested travelers? Who made up this pool of potential customers who could be enticed by Santayana's *Letters* or the epistolary humdingers that flew between Richard Strauss and Hugo von Hofmannsthal? Not a fan of letters? Well, the club could ship you David Riesman's *The Lonely Crowd*, the *Selected Writings of Sydney Smith*, Caesare Pavese's *Diaries*, Hannah Arendt's *The Human Condition*, or a spanking new biography of the young Sam Johnson. The secret word was "eclecticism": E. M. Forster's memoir of his great aunt, the latest translation of Molière's *Misanthrope*, George Sansom's *History of Japan*, the *Oxford History of English Literature*. All for you, all at special savings. Of course, the book club was offering more than books at reduced rates, it was granting access to highly respected critics. To put it indelicately, Barzun, Auden, and Trilling were trading in—literally banking on—their reputations. Trilling was already the author of a classic study of Matthew Arnold and had just published *The Liberal Imagination;* Barzun had six books under his belt, including *Berlioz and the Romantic Century;* and Auden, too, had a sizable body of work behind him, including *The Age of Anxiety* and *Nones*. Discerning readers joined the Readers' Subscription for the same reason they shopped at the neighborhood butcher instead of the supermarket. The butcher chose and cut his own meats and offered only the marbled and most tender. You not only trusted his expertise, you felt he was looking out for you.

BY THE TIME the Readers' Subscription reemerged as the Mid-Century Book Society, in 1959, the literary climate was beginning to change. As more and more books tumbled into view, and as publicity mills began pumping up the volume, the Mid-Century was put into a bind. It needed subscribers, but it didn't want to carry those nominally serious works that Dwight Macdonald dubbed "Midcult," whose proliferation, Macdonald warned, would lead to an irrevocable muddling of highbrow and middlebrow. He needn't have worried. High culture would soon relocate lock, stock, and barrels of books to the university, leaving the public arena to Midcult and later PopCult (whose significance, oddly enough, would require the erudition of these same self-exiled highbrows). But without benefit of focus groups, polling methods, and questionnaires, the editors could only speculate about the audience—how few, how fit?

In statements prompted by the incorporation of the Mid-Century Book Society, the editors attempted to identify the people they were writing for. Barzun spoke of readers who might appreciate the very books that the editors would choose for themselves; Trilling spoke of those who "stand at the middle level of taste" and mentioned giving his dentist a copy of Norman O. Brown's *Life Against Death*. Auden was both more direct and more dreamy. Unlike his two confreres, he acknowledged the less-than-intellectual nature of the exercise; it was marketing strategy pure and simple. Their real rivals, Auden speculated, were not the Book-of-the-Month Club and the Literary Guild but paperback series such as Anchor Books and Penguins, which traded in intellectual wares. Our goal, he wrote, is "to turn our members not into highbrows, but into intellectual dandies." The highbrow, apparently, belongs to a cell of intellectuals (the cell "may be only a Little Social Beast, but a Social Beast it is"), whereas the intellectual dandy is unique and opposed to cells of all kinds. This leads to a problem: How are you going to appeal to the person who would never dream of joining a book club in the first place? It's about the advertising, stupid, Auden declaimed—or words to that effect—and since advertising "is based on the proposition that unique persons do not exist, only social beings with socially conditioned and predictable desires," the only way of promoting the club, he counseled the front office, is: "Be modest. Keep your voice low. Remember that you are selling books, not authors. Be brief. Be ABSOLUTELY HONEST. NEVER EXAGGERATE. Be witty if you can, but remember that nothing is more awful than a bad joke." What was he thinking? This isn't practical advice for advertisers, although it makes good sense when reviewing books.

During the eleven years that they wrote for the book clubs, Auden, Barzun, and Trilling turned in some 173 reviews and essays, covering novels, poetry, letters, anthologies, histories, and biographies, as well as books on natural history, music, theater, the arts, society, and civilization. Some are patently book reviews; others, full-length essays; a small number began life as introductions to books; others as homages to authors alive or dead. There are solemn and not so solemn essays; essays of an Olympian judiciousness and others of a casualness that almost borders on whimsy. In the main, they were occasional pieces, which meant that the editors' loftier concerns—Auden's religiosity, Trilling's Freudianism, Barzun's Pragmatism—were reined in. But they were also pieces occasioned simply by enthusiasm for a particular book or author; and given the editors' cosmopolitan backgrounds, neither the books nor the reviews reflect a peculiarly American sensibility: French, German, and English authors are touted as regularly as American ones.

Each of the editors naturally had his own field of expertise—"domain" might be the better word—yet any one of them could have stepped in for another and, in a manner of speaking, often did. If Barzun got the nod to write about Virginia Woolf's *Diaries* for *The Griffin* (July 1954), Auden might turn around and review it for *The New Yorker,* which he did (March 1954). The great thing was that they'd been handed a bully pulpit to write about what interested them and even, on occasion, what they had an interest in. Barzun's translation of Beaumarchais's *Marriage of Figaro* is praised by Auden, while Trilling pushes the *Poems of Cavafy,* which is published with an introduction by Auden. But at least this vested interest was out in the open; subscribers could take a recommendation or leave it. The point of the book club remained one of trust: if the book was good enough for the editors, it was good enough for the subscribers.

This trust was confirmed monthly by the clubs' publications, which in size, format, and number of pages were more like the little magazines of the day than the standard blurblike communiqués from other book clubs. Aside from one or two reviews by the editors, one might find an article by Mark Van Doren, E. M. Forster, Saul Bellow, or Richard Poirier. In one issue of *The Griffin,* Elia Kazan reminisced about directing *A Streetcar Named Desire* (1951, vol. 2, no. 6); in another, Trilling's "The Early Edmund Wilson" (1952, vol. 1, no. 9) is followed by Wilson's own piece, fetchingly titled "A Modest Self-Tribute." On occasion, the unwary subscriber could stumble across a passage from Baudelaire's letters, an excerpt from Nietzsche's reflections on Schopenhauer, or a sketch by Leslie Stephens.

But it was Auden, Barzun, and Trilling the subscribers paid to read, a fact not lost on the trio. While the reviews and considerations they generated could be as short as a thousand words, the usual entry was around thirty-five hundred words, sometimes as many as five thousand. Moreover, they shared the work, often reading the same books and blue-penciling one another's drafts. Each had a hand in what the others wrote, but not so you'd notice more than one set of fingerprints. Auden's contributions, understandably, are the least academic in spirit; Trilling's, the more serious and reflective (except on those occasions when they're not), and Barzun's are at once plainspoken and rich in detail. A hasty generalization derived from their respective styles: Auden delights in the world and occasionally finds himself annoyed by the world in which books play a large part; Trilling is delighted or annoyed by books in which the world plays a large part; and Barzun, enamored of order but wary of systemization, seems the most comfortable in the world and in his own skin. And all three seemed at ease doing what they were doing. The book club was *their* club too, where they could kick back, light up a cigarette (Auden and Trilling smoked like dragons), go through the publishers' lists or parcels of manuscripts, and divvy up the goods. Barzun gets Shaw, Proust, Montaigne, Molière; Trilling gets Bellow, Baldwin, Dickens, Nabokov; Auden gets Sydney Smith, Marianne Moore, John Betjeman, Ford Madox Ford. And *we* sometimes get surprises. It's not Auden who draws Kenneth Tynan's *Curtains,* but Trilling; not Trilling who wades into the Faulknerian underbrush, but Auden.

No less than his uptown accomplices, Auden had a pedagogical streak, though he pretended otherwise: "Criticism should be casual conversation," he remarked when it was suggested that he oversee a volume of his collected prose. He also liked to play down his reviewing assignments. His review of Muriel Spark's three novels begins: "It is all too easy for a reviewer to confuse his job with that of the literary critic. A reviewer must remember that his audience has not read the book which he is discussing; a critic starts with the assumption that his audience is fairly familiar with the work or author he is reexamining." No doubt this is so, but it is also more than just a matter of switching hats. Book reviewers come and go, and most of them depart without causing us undue distress. But every so often one appears who makes us want to read more of his own work than the book under review. Auden may have slighted his criticism publicly, but he took it seriously. James Fenton goes so far to say that "in Auden's work, prose and poetry interpenetrate to a far greater extent than in the work of any other English-language poet of this century." Auden may have written prose for lucre and poetry for love, but, as Auden's executor Edward Mendelson shrewdly observes, Auden was a poet who dramatized the tension between public responsibility and private desire, whose poems speak in "the voice of a citizen who knows the obligations of his citizenship." Could his other—his prose—voice do less?

THIS MAY BE THE PLACE to say that of the three editors, it is Trilling who, at times, seems the least characteristic. His vaunted prose style, commonly described by his detractors as baroque, complex, and opaque, is less in evidence here than in his other essays. Although not everyone finds his mature style troublesome, it is tough to reconcile the Trilling of the book clubs with the Trilling of the *Partisan Review,* a distinction he himself made in the preface to *A Gathering of Fugitives,* which captured (among others) a dozen of his book-club pieces. Because the clubs' subscribers amounted to what was essentially a captive audience, Trilling could say that he was led "to write less formally than I usually do, and more personally, even autobiographically. . . . Writing frequently and regularly for the same audience relaxes the manner of address," he wrote a tad formally. And while his penchant for going into things could not always be stifled by the quick turnaround required by monthly reviewing (witness his pieces on Lawrence Durrell's *Alexandria Quartet* and Saul Bellow's *The Adventures of Augie March*), there are also some fine examples of Trilling Light (see "Practical Cats More Practical Than Ever Before").

Mark Krupnick makes much of this division in *Lionel Trilling and the Fate of Cultural Criticism,* characterizing him as both avant-garde intellectual, "alienated, agonized, intransigently adversary in temper," and book-club editor, "relaxed, comfortable, at ease in the world." But why the dissection? Trilling was as much a teacher of literature as a writer, and as much a writer of literature as a critic; and all three personas took on the work of the book clubs. In an eloquent memoir, written a year after Trilling's death in 1975, Barzun drew a connection between the book club's genesis and Trilling's intellectual makeup. When Trilling mentioned his interest in a proposal "to disseminate good books," Barzun took it in stride. He knew the man, knew that he "was not a 'humanist' against science or social science, or a 'critic' against 'scholarship.' Nor did he look down on the general public as an undifferentiated mass of barbarians: all his remonstrances were directed in the first place at professionals who could fight back."

If Trilling's prose is complicated, it is also accessible; if he seems, on occasion, indecisive, he is persuasively so. Literature worried him; it worried at him. In essay after essay, he seems to be asking: "What is it that literature depends on for its effect?" The cultural complicity of literature, about which ideologues make such a fuss, Trilling took for granted: Because culture traps us and envelops us, because even the ways that we reject it are culturally determined, no judgment can be entirely devoid of a certain inquisitorial tension. This isn't ambivalence or uncertainty but the intuition that decisive formulations about art must be extracted from a mess of antinomies. "What is it that literature depends on for its effect?" Trilling's answer, or at least one variation of it, expressed in a characteristic dialectical trope, stresses both "the aesthetic effect of intellectual cogency" and "the *primitive* which is of the highest value to the literary artist." "Intellectual power and emotional power go together," he wrote in "The Meaning of a Literary Idea"—a statement that goes a long way toward explaining why aesthetic judgments are allergic to one or another theoretical blanket.

Barzun, who began to teach with Trilling in 1934, took a different approach to the complexity which all thoughtful people sense when taking stock of their surroundings. As Barzun remembers: "Trilling was bent on developing the large consequences of the often hidden relations and implications for life that he found in literature. I was trying to compress great batches of fact and opinion into descriptions and conclusions that the reader of history could grasp. . . . The excess on my side that Lionel reproved was, therefore, a characteristic unwillingness to 'go into it.' Some decisive formulation of mine would make him curious, raise his antennae for the complex, and he would say, 'Open it up—that sentence deserves a paragraph . . . that paragraph, a page.'" But whether it is Barzun's shorter, more direct sentences, or Auden's elegantly casual prose, or Trilling's undulating elaborations, it is ultimately the high state of awareness each brought to the work that repays our investment.

CIVIC-MINDED CRITICISM is neither moralizing sentiment nor sermonizing cant. Criticism is an aid, not an answer; and the book club, as envisioned by its board, embodied a tending-to-the-flock mentality, shepherding readers, so to speak, toward nutritious leaves of grass. In more urban terms, the editors, albeit self-appointed, were the public's proxy, investing its capital in literary markets that would pay out. They may not have always walked a fine line between high-handed and high-minded, but in writing for the general educated public they wrote as themselves, not as a committee, and certainly not in the service of any one ideological cause. Matthew Arnold would have approved. In a little-known essay, "The Bishop and the Philosopher," Arnold noted that there are some books, however specialized or scholarly, which seem to require the critic's attention, for the obvious reason that not everyone "is a theologian or a historian or a philosopher, but everyone is interested in the advance of the general culture." He may have been reaching, but even if there were only one interested party, it would be enough to justify the critic's intervention. The book Arnold had in mind was one of biblical scholarship, a subject in which he lacked the requisite academic credentials. But as he explained, "[A] work of this kind has to justify itself before another tribunal." The editors *were* that tribunal, and the book club was their excellent Arnoldian adventure.

In retrospect, there is something wonderfully optimistic about the whole enterprise. Maybe it's because we live in a time when literature, pinioned by criticism and overshadowed by media, makes the idea of starting such a book club so improbable that the first meeting of the Readers' Subscription begins to blend with one of those MGM movies in which Judy Garland and Mickey Rooney get the bright idea of putting on a show. This is not to suggest that the book club wasn't serious; it certainly was, but the boys were having fun, and they let you know it. They were like those classical musicians who, upon leaving work at the symphony, head downtown to play jazz all night in a smoky club. Did they go downtown on books? In a loose sense, yes—not during every set, of course, but every so often one or another of the trio would launch into an uncharacteristic riff that signaled the pleasure they derived from playing together; and surely no small part of that enjoyment lay in the knowledge that they were performing for a literate audience who had come expressly to hear them.

Biography and Belles Lettres

As Uncomfortable as a Modern Self

Jacques Barzun

On Virginia Woolf's *A Writer's Diary*

WHAT WE ASK of a writer in the first place is a unique voice. We ask for the rest later, and we may even pretend that it is only the later things we require— no personal, individual, induplicable quality, just pure art. But that this is pretense appears from our readiness to say apropos of even the most ancient and most classical author that some modern translator or interpreter has failed to catch his tone.

By this standard of the unique voice, Virginia Woolf is a contemporary whom critics will continue to scan, until they decide whether she possesses the remaining qualities needed for a permanent place in literature. There can be no doubt that she wrote like no one else. And this is not, of course, a mere matter of vocabulary, syntax or style. The characterizing element is: what she found it imperative to say; it is the singularity without strangeness of what she remarks. Even at her simplest, in *To the Lighthouse,* one enjoys the double satisfaction of feeling the claims of common reality and of wondering, "How did such a view of things ever get born in a human mind?"

It is to answer that question that we go to criticism and biography, and more especially to letters and diaries. To be sure, the question never receives a direct, much less a full, answer; but the documents from life fill out gaps of conjecture and exclude wild surmises. Virginia Woolf's *A Writer's Diary* has been especially designed to do just this. It is a volume of modest size—350 pages—which brings together all that the novelist wrote in her journals about writers and writing in the years from 1918 to within four days of her death.

This is not to say that the book is not also full of personalities. Virginia Woolf was nothing if not personal, and the interest of her day-to-day jottings is not in the main technical and professional. For one thing, she talks a great deal about herself and about the few intimates on whom she relied for criticism and counsel—her husband, Leonard Woolf; her sister and brother-in-law, Vanessa and Clive Bell; and among others: Lytton Strachey, E. M. Forster, Roger Fry, David Garnett, John Maynard Keynes, and G. Lowes Dickinson.

Again, Mrs. Woolf was a writer who reads. Partly from taste, partly from financial necessity, she made a place for herself as a critic, and some people who cannot "go" the novels relish and admire the two *Common Readers* as well as *The Moment and Other Essays*. The diary naturally contains by-products of all this tasting and testing of literature; so that together with the inevitable clinging bits of domesticity, visiting, the affairs of the Hogarth Press, and the business dealings with editors and publishers, this compact volume gives a well-rounded view of the productive life as it was lived by the unusual woman whom her husband and editor rather sadly introduces as "a serious artist."

Her own definition of herself is still more saddening but incomparably more vivid: "What a born melancholic I am!" says she apropos of revising *A Room of One's Own.* This is at a time when she feels she has just established herself, not so much in literature as in domestic finance: money is an important subject in the diary as it was in her life. No doubt Virginia Woolf's melancholia had deep roots in the soil of family affection and family oppression, but the surface manifestations that we glimpse in this conscious record have critical and social importance. One of these was her view of money as the means of liberation from masculine tyranny. Three guineas, the twelve-pound look, and down with the tyrant male. Without wanting to pry, one wishes there were inside or outside the diary a clearer explanation of the Woolfs' domestic economy. She apparently pledged herself to pay her way, from the kitchen to the buying of whole houses, and it preyed on her mind while causing her both pleasure and resentment. The sums are always rather small, and one involuntarily thinks of Balzac at the extreme opposite, juggling with millions while sweating over his work in a similarly contrasted way.

For Balzac's work was at once the expression and the glorification of the Will, whereas Virginia Woolf's shows on the contrary the struggle of sensibility to overcome a deficiency, or perhaps one should say rather an unhappy division, of the Will. This does not contradict the fact that Virginia Woolf's career represents a single-minded and strenuous devotion to art. It *was* strenuous—and one feels the strain. Her health, her duties, and her doubts would certainly have stopped a less determined woman. One marvels at her productivity and one infers a kind of will power. But the achievement does not spring from any sort of abundance, whether of life or of thought. At one time she finds she cannot write more than one hour a day, and she can read scarcely longer. By doggedness she does cover many pages of first draft, but she hates the looseness and she parboils the mass to quintessential strength. This at times yields but fifty words a morning.

One is free to say, "Better fifty words of Woolf than a cycle of Balzac." One great issue of modern culture is wrapped up in this preference, and that issue obsesses Mrs. Woolf. As an admiring reader of Scott, Defoe and Byron, and even more as the daughter of a Victorian notable, she was directly aware of what creative power is. Her aunt Miss Thackeray (Ritchie) once told her that of the moderns only Shaw had a touch of the robust qualities—what Shaw himself alluded to when he said that "great art is either easy or impossible." Virginia Woolf and the moderns generally choose to find it impossible. They take creation hard and make it a virtue to stop at pearls. Universes are a fad of the past.

This limitation is due in part to the moderns' position as late comers in a long line of creation accompanied by systematic criticism. The critical sense, inherited by us in sharpened form, keeps saying: "No, not that; no, not this. *This* is merely Dickens done over; *that,* the public learned from Jane Austen or Chekhov, or whoever." Hence no free writing. Instead of tapping the rock for a clear bubbling spring, the artist fears that he is only squeezing the sponge: the water comes out colored. The new novel or poem must then be written on the margins of those first drafts that come straight out of the traditional fund. Flaubert was among the first to experience the hardship and became the first of the groaners. Mrs. Woolf was not the last.

But she suffered from a further handicap—that of her upbringing in the house of the masterful Leslie Stephen, which somehow generated in her a special distress at being a woman. On her father's birthday she writes: "He would have been 96, 96, yes, today; and could have been 96 like other people one has known, but mercifully was not. His life would have entirely ended mine. What would have happened? No writing, no books;—inconceivable." As to the status of women, her views are well known. She expressed them or alluded to them repeatedly in her novels and essays. What strikes us in the diary is her habit of isolating literary qualities as masculine. She even makes a category of them and speaks of Milton as "the first of the masculinists," going on quite unjustly to deny to *Paradise Lost* any psychological truth in depicting the relations of man and woman.

The doubtful word here is "truth," for it could reasonably be argued that it is we of the twentieth century who keep missing the truth of this and other human relations. Clever, analytic, deep-diving through layer after layer of ill-assorted intentions, we may well be; but the returns in feeling and action do not cast great credit on the enterprise. We learn the truth, it seems, only in order to justify our worst instincts. "The truth is," says Mrs. Woolf, "people scarcely care for each other. They have this insane instinct for life. But they never become attached to anything outside themselves." Is it really so? Virginia Woolf was herself full of generosity and affection. She is moving in her grief at the death of her friends because she herself is moved. And yet in keeping with her "principle" above, many of her observations about people are tinged with the hostility of overinterpretation. One is too often reminded of the exchange of letters between her and Logan Pearsall Smith which he published some years ago in volume two of *Orion*—not the masculine in literature, nor the feminine either, but the androgynous feline.

One cause of this puny hatred infecting our age lies in the same radical self-consciousness which makes great art "impossible" rather than easy. Disseminating critical views of society, the emotions, and the arts has made all impulses and attitudes suspect, particularly to oneself. Friends are a bit fiendish: one knows it by looking into one's own heart. Or, again, is it really so? Mrs. Woolf is bedevilled by the pros and the cons of this debate and she tells herself, about writing and about living, that the great rule is not to think about oneself. But this is to mistake the premise for the conclusion. Introspection is and remains a fine thing, especially for a writer. Only, the external, anthropological outlook must not prevent the two halves of the self from being glued back together. Here is our diarist, aged thirty-seven and legitimately scanning herself: "If Virginia Woolf at the age of 50, when she sits down to build her memoirs out of this book, is unable to make a phrase as it should be made, I can only condole with her and remind her of the existence of the fireplace." But here is the illicit sequel in the next entry: "I have written to Hester but how I doubt the sincerity of my own emotion!"

And again: "If one is to deal with people on a large scale and say what one thinks, how can one avoid melancholy?" Or about work considered as an extension of the self: "Is the time coming when I can endure to read my own writing in print without blushing—shivering and wishing to take cover? . . . The worst of writing is that one depends so much on praise."

There we have it. Praise means approval, regard, love. Since one can't bestow this boon on oneself one starves for it, and a company of praise-starved writers and friends discover that on the whole people are attached only to themselves. It follows that their instinct for life is insane and Mrs. Woolf ends (in a rare moment of self-praise) by referring to "that terribly depressed woman, myself." The vicious circle should have been more firmly broken by a healthy vice, such as vanity. Instead, the novelist hung breathless on the words of half a dozen friends who seldom gave her what she hungered for. True, her claims were large—she wanted to be remembered as a writer, to win fame, just like the masculinist Milton in his last infirmity.

But he ascribed it to noble mind, and in doing so made peace with himself. Virginia Woolf could be at peace neither with the lack of fame nor with the longing for it. There is pathos in her repeated anguish and confession. One would suppose that after twenty years of writing and introspecting an intelligent woman would accustom herself to the critical free-for-all, or else accept her own imperfections. There must be fresher things to observe than old flaws and scars. But no. She cannot let go. When she visits Thomas Hardy (who had endured far worse neglect and abuse) she is astounded by his philosophic calm, the coolness of his regard for literature, and his assurance that to be sociable and a poet at the same time only calls for—physical strength.

The effect of Virginia Woolf's utterly different conviction on her novels is beyond the scope of these descriptive remarks, but the reader will not fail to notice that her comments on the writing of *To the Lighthouse* resemble none of the rest. "I am now writing as fast and freely as I have written in the whole of my life; more so—20 times more so." Whether this was due to the familiarity of the subject matter, the pleasure of recreating the scenes of childhood and the figure of her father, or whether the form and the substance came happily together as a result of unchartable coincidences, the fact remains that Virginia Woolf seems to have taken most pleasure in writing the book that has given the most to her readers.

If in reading the diary her admirers dwell on the making of the novels they will weep and groan by turns to see the writer torturing herself, first into working and then into liking her work. The spectacle could not be borne if one did not also see every year or so the products of such flagellation. Mrs. Woolf had a great ambition to be a social critic and to put all of life and death into stories. What she undeniably put there is the travail and the duplicity of the modern ego. The desire to overcome the sense of powerlessness drives the mind, the heart, the pen, and one novel after another, one more essay, then a book of essays, are added to form an output which is remarkable for bulk in a writer who started relatively late and who did not reach her sixtieth year. Like all exhibitions of persistence in work, it is a gratifying and mouth-stilling sight.

Yet there is more to be garnered from these pages than the history of a writing career and the fears and frailties of an unhappy, dauntless woman and artist. The obiter dicta about other writers are precious too, and may even give a truer view of Mrs. Woolf's critical judgment than her deliberate essays.

She is by nature tentative and needs three tries to reach a just decision: she often generalizes with too little imagination for the opposing negative; but when she has pondered, her thrust is quick and her verdict is embodied in a good phrase:

> *On Peacock's novels:* "Fantasticality does a good deal better than sham psychology. One touch of red in the cheek is all he gives, but I can do the rest."

> *On "the masterly Scott":* "I'm in the middle and have to put up with some dull sermons; but I doubt that he can be dull, because everything is so much in keeping—even his monochromatic landscape painting. . . ."

> *On Vernon Lee's writing:* "Her ligaments are too loose for my taste."

> *On Joyce and T. S. Eliot:* "And Tom, great Tom [Eliot] thinks *Ulysses* on a par with *War and Peace!* An illiterate, underbred book it seems to me; the book of a self-taught working man, and we all know how distressing they are, how egotistic, raw, striking, and ultimately nauseating. When one can have the cooked flesh, why have the raw? But I think if you are anaemic, as Tom is, there is a glory in blood."

A Writer's Diary, as these quotations show, is not written in the same prose as the novels, but the author of both need not have worried at 37 that at 50 she would need the fireplace to devour her phrases.

—JULY 1954

Man Before Myth

W. H. AUDEN

On James Clifford's *Young Sam Johnson*

ONE CANNOT HELP wondering if the shades of Dr. Johnson and Boswell are still on speaking terms, for what could be more painful to an author's vanity than to know that for one person who still reads his books there are ten who read the biographer whose efforts have created for him a peculiar public. The Johnsonian is not—as the Doctor, surely, must wish he were—someone who reads and re-reads *Rasselas, The Vanity of Human Wishes, The Lives of the Poets* etc. with ever growing admiration, but someone who wishes to know every detail of their author's private life, including those details and traits of which he himself was most ashamed. If, in a prophetic dream of a bookshop two hundred years hence, I were to see a new volume about myself, I should, of course, at first be delighted, but how, I wonder, should I feel if, on looking at the index, I were then to find such entries as the following:

> laziness; lessons, method of getting; masochistic traits; melancholia;
> memory; negligent pose; outsider, feeling of being; physical handicaps

I do not honestly know what we can say to appease Johnson's indignant and unwieldy ghost except: "We can't help it. Our curiosity about you is stronger than our sense of good manners. It's your fault for having been in life so continuously and diversely fascinating." *Young Sam Johnson* deals with the first forty years of his life, ending, that is, just before his meeting with Boswell, while he was still a struggling and relatively unknown writer. (Incidentally, how typical of his peculiar position in literature it is that his latest biographer, Mr. James Clifford, should be described on the jacket as the only Johnsonian who has been an engineer.)

Mr. Clifford writes clearly and simply, is scholarly without being heavy and, where Johnson's nervous peculiarities are concerned, has very sensibly preferred to give the historical facts so far as they are known and let the reader interpret them for himself instead of indulging in any fancy psychology.

Any man who has managed to rise from obscurity to eminence must, on looking back, acknowledge that success owes as much to chance as it owes to talent that—had he not met certain people or read certain books at certain moments and in certain places, had he not experienced, even, what, at the time, seemed failure or defeat, he would never have gotten where he has—and when we inquire into the history of such a man it is the providential elements about which we are most curious to learn.

After reading *Young Sam Johnson,* it seems to me that he was much luckier in his father than he himself realised. At a time when libraries were an aristocratic luxury, what better choice of parent, short of a lord, could a future man-of-letters have made than a bookseller? Indeed a bookseller was perhaps better than a lord, since it was not considered becoming in a gentleman to show more than a dilettante's interest in literature. Even Michael Johnson's love of making his precocious child perform, a trait which Samuel resented and modern psychologists deplore, did him more good than harm. It may have been partly responsible for the bouts of accidie from which Dr. Johnson suffered all his life—sloth is frequently the result of a conflict between a high standard to which the sufferer feels he is expected to conform and a fear that his accomplishment will fall below it—but it also certainly implanted that sense of superiority and desire to excel without which there would have been no Johnsonian prose, no Johnsonian repartee.

Again, not many adolescents living in the country have had the good fortune to find such intellectual stimulus as the young Johnson found in the at-once scholarly and worldly-wise company of his first cousin, Cornelius Ford, and the witty lawyer, Gilbert Walmesley. The public, familiar with a famous writer's work, are apt to forget that there was once a time when he had written little or nothing, but every writer himself knows what an eternal debt of gratitude he owes to the first person who took a chance on him and gave him work to do, even if it was sheer hack-work. Knowing how lucky Edward Cave was in having Johnson on the staff of the *Gentleman's Magazine,* we must not forget that there was a moment when the luck seemed all Johnson's. Moreover, Johnson was not one of those dedicated geniuses like Wagner or Proust, in whom the notion of the exact kind of work they wish to create and the passion to create just that kind and no other, at whatever cost, are so strong that, audience or no audience, published or unpublished, they go ahead and complete it; aside from the poems and the unreadable *Irene*, there is scarcely a page of Johnson's which was not commissioned. Given the multiple stimulus of a prescribed task, financial need and a deadline, he could write with great fluency and speed; without them he was in danger, like all melancholics, of day-dreaming about an infinity of projects and executing none, or of dissipating his imagination and talent in the intoxicating immediacy of talk. It is always an ominous sign when the list of works which a writer thinks he might some day do is large and heterogeneous, and Johnson's list was both.

As the years progressed, his "designs" grew until there were almost fifty titles. There was a history of criticism from Aristotle to the eighteenth century, a history of the Revival of Learning in Europe, an edition of Chaucer from manuscripts and old copies, "with various readings, conjectures, remarks on his language," a translation of Aristotle's *Rhetoric* and his *Ethics,* a translation of Machiavelli's History of Florence, translations of Herodian, Claudian, Cicero, editions of such English writers as Oldham and Roscommon. In a separate category, he listed possible works of the imagination: a "Hymn to Ignorance," "The Palace of Sloth—a Vision," "Prejudice—a Poetical Essay," "The Palace of Nonsense—a Vision." Not one was ever completed in the exact form originally planned.

Johnson does not appear to have been seriously tempted to go drinking or whoring, but for someone of ready wit who is afraid of his own society, conversation can be an even more dangerous form of debauchery. A man who succumbs to it must, however innately respectable, soon find himself in disreputable and Bohemian society, for only in such circles are fellow talkers available at all hours. Many of Johnson's closest friends during the first forty years of his life were rascals: there was Richard Savage, a paranoid drunk, there was Samuel Boyse who could "spin verses as fast as most men write prose, but he only worked when he could not sponge off forgiving patrons and friends. (He made use of the most disgraceful experiments to excite charity, sometimes raising subscriptions for nonexistent poems, and sometimes having his wife report that he was dying.") There was George Psalmanazar who "as a young man pretended to be a native of Formosa and actually had gone so far as to invent an elaborate alphabet and grammar of the language and even to publish a historical and geographical description of the island. (So little was known at that time about Formosa that he was invited to spend some months at Christchurch in Oxford teaching his pretended language to a set of gentlemen who planned to go out to convert the natives to Christianity.") Johnson himself was anything but a rascal and far more talented than any of his cronies but they all shared one temperamental trait which can all too easily deny to talent any lasting achievement, a trait which nobody has described better than Johnson himself.

> As soon as I enter the door of a tavern, I experience an oblivion of care, and a freedom from solicitude: when I am seated, I find the master courteous, and the servants obsequious to my call; anxious to know and ready to supply my wants: wine there exhilarates my spirits, and prompts me to free conversation and an interchange of discourse with those whom I most love: I dogmatise and am contradicted, and in this conflict of opinions and sentiments I find delight.

Mr. Clifford does not go in for detailed criticism of Johnson as a writer but by skillful documentation he shows in a most interesting way how early in life both his critical attitudes and his style were formed. The unknown hack-writer in his twenties who, on reading the line "Which of pure seraphim consumes and nourishes the soul?" commented thus: "Mr. Crousaz is so watchful against impiety, that he lets nonsense pass without censure: Can anything consume and nourish at the same time?" and who could compose such a period as the following:

> Here are no Hottentots without religion, polity, or articulate language; no Chinese perfectly polite, and completely skilled in all sciences; he will discover, what will always be discovered by a diligent and impartial inquirer, that wherever human nature is to be found, there is a mixture of vice and virtue, a contest of passion and reason; and that the Creator doth not appear partial in his distributions, but has balanced, in most countries, their particular inconveniences by particular favors.

is temperamentally and stylistically little removed from the Grand Old Dictator who castigated *Lycidas* and wrote of Pope's incursion into landscape-gardening: "Where necessity enforced a passage, vanity supplied a grotto."

It is only Johnson the poet whom one can imagine developing otherwise than as he did. On the evidence of his poetic juvenilia like the hymn for the feast of St. Simon and St. Jude, and of later occasional poems like the memorial verses for Dr. Lovett and "Long-expected one-and-twenty," one is curious to know what he might have produced had he had the time and the inclination to depart more often (and for more serious subjects) from the heroic couplet.

The reader will find in *Young Sam Johnson,* if not all that he would like to know, all that is certain knowledge, and the value of the book is greatly enhanced by the excellent illustrations, not least the end paper map of Lichfield in Johnson's time.

It is to be hoped that one result of reading it will be to send him back to Johnson's own writings, and not to *The Lives of the Poets* only. An author's valuation of his work is never to be ignored. Johnson thought *The Vision of Theodore, the Hermit of Teneriffe* the best thing he had ever written. How many people alive to-day have read it? It cannot be too strongly emphasised that Johnson and Boswell are not the same person and that Johnson is much too good and interesting a writer to be left to the Johnsonians.

—APRIL 1955

"The Blest Group of Us"

Jacques Barzun

On Henry James's *Autobiography*

THE GOOD FORTUNE of bad health, it is well known, saved from the blight of the Civil War the two oldest sons of the amazing James family. William and Henry, first and second born of Henry, Sr., were respectively nineteen and eighteen as the war broke out; and when two years later their younger brothers Wilky and Robertson were in the Union Army, William was studying comparative anatomy at Harvard and Henry had begun to publish fiction.

Thus began the careers of two geniuses whom the American pantheon could ill afford to be without, for they are of the first rank. And although the stature and influence of each have gone through the usual variations of estimate caused by our changing culture—now one, now the other being deemed the superior mind—they are best thought of together as transcending equally the categories in which they made their name. Novelist and Philosopher seem too narrow for men who were at the same time complementary and self-sufficient in their unique role, that of the artist as thinker and thinker as artist.

Apart from their abundant works, their unforgettable letters, and the growing literature about them and their father, the place where one can best recover their essence and quality is in the volumes that the survivor, Henry Jr., began to compose after the death of William in 1910. *A Small Boy and Others, Notes of a Son and Brother,* and the unfinished *The Middle Years* take us from the beginnings of the James family in Albany, N.Y., to Henry's first entrance into British literary society—George Eliot, Tennyson, and Lowell's friends—in 1870, that is, in the recorder's twenty-sixth year. These volumes, long out of print and increasingly expensive when come upon, have now been reissued in one book of six hundred large pages entitled *Autobiography*.

This title, one soon sees, is at once necessary, appropriate, and misleading.

The work is perfectly consecutive in reminiscence, like any usual autobiography, and no other term would as simply unite the three parts. But it is surely an uncommon autobiography that covers only one third of a life and breaks off precisely when things of public interest are beginning to happen in it. And although the indispensable "I" is prominent from the outset, it is clear also from the outset that the subject of the book is much larger than the "I": it is a pair of minds, a family, a time, a series of places, and the peculiar atmosphere with which the observer colors them in his recollection. This autobiography, in short, reminds one of a novel and a history much more than of a biography. It is, after all, a work by Henry James, and as such it has to be "taken" and interpreted after being attentively experienced.

This does not mean that facts of biographical importance are absent or obscured. Indeed, the most important of all such facts in James's life is to be found chiefly here. It is that the later novelist's relation to Europe began in infancy, began even before the small boy set foot in Europe. It began, really, with his father's easy acceptance of an almost entire alienation from the forms and tendencies of contemporary American life. Of independent means and mind, the elder Henry James had no business, no profession, no visible, protracted occupation. He wrote books and articles, to be sure, but they were little attended to; he held religious and philosophical ideas, but they squared with no orthodoxy and no namable heresy. In the home his beliefs and motives were regarded with affectionate amusement as "father's ideas"—a natural phenomenon that was somehow outside the order of nature. Henry Sr. was on most friendly terms with Emerson, Oliver Wendell Holmes, Horace Greeley, and other notables, but he did not become one of them; he never tried to. He may therefore be said to have led, on this continent as on the other, a visiting existence—and this in spite of the solid connections and propertied anchorage he successively made use of in Albany, New York, Newport, and Cambridge.

The upshot of this Ariel-like relation to the mundane earth—a relation which the son renders with his usual virtuosity of innuendo—is that the family's departure for five years of Europe when young Henry was twelve was far less a breaking of what are commonly called roots than would have been true of any but a vagrant's household. This last contradiction in terms expresses the facts: the boys by then had been through four or five schools, had already been to Europe in their nonage, had met and given their hearts to dozens of relatives and neighbours and strangers, had in a word accepted the restless comings and goings of the paternal mind and the paternal plans as the very principle of existence.

The image, therefore, of a middle-aged Henry James with an established literary reputation "abandoning" his native country in order to indulge his snobbish instincts by settling abroad is worse than inaccurate. It substitutes a newspaper cliché for the remarkable odyssey of a man who for the first twenty-five years of his life was nowhere at home, and who during that time forged for himself an ideal of life which Europe was then still in a position to countenance and which America then positively denied. Europe was to the younger Henry James what the elder had blandly assumed the United States ought to be: the theatre of man's achieving perfected form.

These unpredictable motions of their hearth, the two James boys met differently. William developed versatile gifts of adaptation and a passion for the tangible; Henry withdrew into an inner world of treasured sensation and subjective fancy which robbed him—as he long thought—of any capability whatever. Even so, William and Henry were deeply and permanently attached to each other. The whole family was in fact frighteningly close, and to their overabundance of mutual love and conscious blessedness may be attributed the various lesions, moral and emotional, from which every one of the five children (Alice being the only girl and the youngest) sooner or later suffered. But Henry's autobiography closes before any of the crises took place, and is therefore all picturesque delight, unless one considers his description of remembered childhood as a record of dull, inexplicable pain.

I do not believe this is what he meant it to be. Rather, the book sounds like a manly though unwitting self-vindication. Its impetus comes from the thought of William recently dead, always worshipped as the elder brother who could do things, who always went first, blazed the path, and could be seen striding in the shining distance far ahead. "Yet all the while," Henry seems to say, "I too was growing, thinking, feeling, developing powers. And though I could never do arithmetic, never cared for microscopes, I had my curiosities and insights just the same; I missed nothing of significance, which I hereby prove in giving you portrait after portrait, impalpable atmospheres of friendly houses and foreign hotels, visions of obscure emaciated schoolmasters and forgotten stage celebrities. This was our life, of which facts are but the raw material, and life in this sense was ever my domain."

We must of course, in reading this autobiography, keep separate from the raw material and its native emotion the sometimes wonderful and sometimes pointless elaboration which James the writer supplies with an occasionally regrettable ease. An example of the felicitous sort will show that there are three layers to distinguish—the small bare fact, the remembered feeling it evoked, and the bulk of meaning it assumed when looked at through the lenses of masterly age:

The then pre-eminent figure of the group was a very big Newfoundland dog on whose back I was put to ride. That must have been my first vision of the liberal life—though I further ask myself what my age could possibly have been when my weight was so fantastically far from hinting at later developments. But the romance of the hour was particularly in what I have called the eccentric note, the fact that the children, my entertainers, riveted my gaze to stockingless and shoeless legs and feet, conveying somehow at the same time that they were not poor and destitute but rich and provided . . . and that their state as of children of nature was a refinement of freedom and grace. They were to become great and beautiful, the household of that glimmering vision, they were to figure historically, heroically, and serve great public ends; but always, to my remembering eyes and fond fancy, they were to move through life as with the bare white feet of that original preferred fairness and wildness. This is rank embroidery, but the old surface insists on spreading—it waits at least with an air of its own. The rest is silence.

For the daily actuality less richly embroidered one must go elsewhere—to Mr. Edel's biography, *The Untried Years,* or to accounts given by James's brother, nephew, or other unimpeded witness. Though the passage above and many like it distil Henry's humor through Henry's vision and exaggeration, we need a few touchstones, such as the following, to make his preciosity appear precious as well: here is Edward Emerson's firsthand report of the James family in action:

Mealtimes in that pleasant home were exciting. "The adipose and affectionate Wilky," as his father called him, would say something and be instantly corrected or disputed by the little cocksparrow Bob, the youngest, but goodnaturedly defend his statement, and then Henry (Junior) would emerge from his silence in defence of Wilky. Then Bob would be more impertinently insistent, and Mr. James would advance as Moderator, and William, the eldest, join in. The voice of the Moderator presently would be drowned by the combatants and he soon came down vigorously into the arena, and when, in the excited argument, the dinner knives might not be absent from eagerly gesticulating hands, dear Mrs. James, more conventional, but bright as well as motherly, would look at me reassuring, saying, "Don't be disturbed; they won't stab each other. This is usual when the boys come home." And the quiet little sister ate her dinner smiling, close to the combatants.

Of such particulars pure and simple, Henry's recollection is chary. He does name and picture his parents, brothers, sister and cousins; they live for us vividly, but in his way, not theirs; for their recorded acts do not serve generalization so much as impressionism. In this matter of meals, for instance, we will get the admirable but disembodied reflection: "We are everything in those days by the bushel and the barrel, as from stores that were infinite; we handled watermelons as freely as cocoanuts, and the amount of stomach-ache involved was negligible in the general Eden-like consciousness."

As for Henry himself, since he is of necessity the unchecked narrator, we have of him multiple presences who demand a like discrimination. There is the old man who repeatedly remembers—or as he says "recovers"—this or that bit of the past; there is the "small boy" who scarcely changes (James tells us why) from six to twenty-six, and there is the adolescent who constitutes the small boy's defense against a bewildering world of brandished dinner-knives, omnicompetent brother ("*I* play with boys who curse and swear!"), benevolent paterfamilias—Jove with a grin and a wooden leg—above which orchestra of egos there resounds a medley of voices representing home and foreign schools, native and foreign tongues. That adolescent James who seemed impervious and was biding his time can be glimpsed in a letter that William, already at Harvard, writes to the family after a visit of Henry's: The "radiance of it," says William, "has not faded yet, and I come upon gleams of it three or four times a day." But William's affectionate longing for them all is unabated, "the more so as the abovementioned H[enry] could in no wise satisfy my craving for knowledge of family and friends—he didn't seem to have been on speaking terms with anyone for some time past, and could tell me nothing of what they did, said, or thought, about any given subject. Never did I see a so-much uninterested creature in the affairs of those about him. He is a good soul, though, in his way, too."

Allowing for the Jamesian banter and exaggeration, this early Henry is one with the creature who appears in almost the last phrase of the autobiography as the "brooding monster that I was"—monster in this only, that he could seem completely detached from those about him while actually preparing himself for the art of the searcher and knower par excellence. His was to be a special kind of knowledge, the knowledge of a willing Tantalus: "It literally seems to me that there was more history and thereby more interest recoverable as the matter stood than if every answer to every question about it hadn't had a fine ambiguity. I like ambiguities and detest great glares."

Now this highly original view of "history" to which James dedicated himself and to which he bent the exuberant family idiom, has its origin, as we say, in temperament. And this particular temperament appears to have been molded to its characteristic shape by what Henry calls the "fatalistic philoso-phy" with which he took his total circumstance—that of having an admired older brother so able to cope with difficulty as to break the younger's spirit of emulation. That it didn't break his spirit *tout court* was due to "the general sense that almost anything, however disagreeable, had been worth while; so unable was I to claim that it hadn't involved impressions." Impressionism in him, then, grows out of a partial inhibition, but it is one that doesn't damage the will to live and to love. Henry comes to see himself healthily as matching (though not equalling) his genius-brother. For a time, when learning anything seemed such an insuperable task, he thought that "life and knowledge were simply mutual opposites, one inconsistent with the other. . . . There was to come to me of course in time the due perception that neither was of the least use—use to myself—without the other."

We have here a chief difference between James's impressionism and the ni-hilistic one of some of his contemporaries. The famous description (also in these pages) of the great nightmare in which James, then an adult, turned upon the Hidden Thing against which he had but a moment before tried to hold the door shut, and routs It with "straight aggression and dire intention," was assuredly the symbol of many earlier last stands bravely converted into forward motion, many an "act indeed of life-saving energy." This act in the dream took place in the long picture gallery of the Louvre, and the conjunc-tion of energy and art is noteworthy. For all his memories of paralyzed gaping given in these pages, and all the infuriating avowals of modesty visibly mis-placed, James belongs, exactly like his brother William, with the believers in the energies of art and life, not with the refugees of the first and contemners of the second.

Unless this is borne in mind, it comes as a paradox to find what artistic in-fluences were strongest on young Henry's mind and later: they are: Dickens, melodrama, Balzac. A dozen years ago, I tried to show that like the work of these two authors, James's was reducible to the middle term, melodrama. And this, too, seems a paradox if one confuses surface with subject. This is not the place to argue the point anew with the aid of a redefinition of the melodra-matic, but only to draw attention to the living manner in which James sum-mons up the clear sight of the old thrilling mid-century theatre as it existed in every great city including New York. The child was far from uncritical, as the amused reporting shows, but the moral impress then given is obviously that reproduced in the novels, just as the acknowledgement of Dickens's pervasive moral force implies the objection James was to advance against the impassiv-ity of Flaubert and the realists: that impassivity meant the divorce of knowl-edge from life. James wanted both and for *use*. His favorite masters in literature were flanked by Titian, Rubens, and Veronese in painting—life and knowledge in exuberant form and color.

True as all this is, the reason for restating it is more than to guide new readers through the Gothic vastness and flamboyant tracery of the *Autobiography;* it is that the opposite view, which made of James a sublime or reprehensible escapist, prevailed until not very long ago and was obviously not a pure fabrication. It built upon the evidence of a style which is symptomatic of a philosophy. For James philosophizes with every phrase, and those who have maintained that his mind was too fine to be violated by an idea cannot have pondered his adverbs. The very rhythm of James's best sentences is a rebuke to the social and intellectual pretensions of a class, while his mixture of colloquialism with circumlocution is virtually a political platform—that on which stands the Tory Democrat.

Indeed, it is only a little frivolous and fanciful to recall the infant "liberal" astride the Newfoundland dog and to say that his admiration of naturalness in the form of bare feet was soon reflected in the limpid style of his early stories. A Dickensian humor then played about certain characters in them, but without Dickensian exuberance. Everything shone in its own light by virtue of smooth surface and polished edge. James's style was in its Realistic phase, and if Impressionism is to be found already at work in him it is the solid Impressionism of Manet. Later, the impressions crowd out the desire to be understood and a new exactitude prevails, with a new extravagance: the Realist-Impressionist becomes the Impressionist-Neo-Romantic, and we begin to see the phantasmagoria of life through the stream of images spun out by the "brooding monster" no longer held in check.

Of this later style one must say that it pays for its felicities by being not only difficult but also often bad. James the "finished" artist is now capable of being as turgid as Dickens, as careless as Shakespeare, as mechanical as both of them put together. It is a mistake to pretend otherwise and take it all as the perfection of subtlety, though it is indeed necessary to *take it all,* for as in Shakespeare and Dickens the whole easily sustains the parts. In this every fit reader of the three great last novels will concur. But a word must be added for readers of the book in hand, because, its subject not being completely of James's fashioning, the disharmonies of matter and style are more frequent and jarring. Again and again, if one did not know better, one would conclude that James was immorally shrinking from the truth, genteelly cowering or snobbishly pretending. For example, he wants to say that during his family's sojourn abroad, the panic of 1857 occurred and affected them. He calls it "a 'financial crisis' of great violence to which the American world, as a matter now of recorded history, I believe, had tragically fallen victim." Those quotation marks, those "I believe" and "tragically" are as many offenses against manliness and sense. And since there may be a mithridatic virtue in knowing the worst at once, I classify and illustrate these faults here, if only to give the reader assurance that he will suffer nothing worse.

The most venial of James's faults is obsessive repetition: "scant" and "note" reappear hundreds of times, while the serried ranks of adverbs ending in -ly, preceded or not by "so," fall on a seemingly deaf ear. Somewhat graver is the Dickensian periphrasis—"my infant participation," "the gustatory process," or—about an ancient actress—her needing "for the low-necked ordeal, less osseous a structure." At times this habit tempts James to write pure Micawberish, as when he says that he mentions Poe "not so much because he was personally present (the extremity of personal absense had just overtaken him)—" that is, Poe had just died.

It has been said that James's later style suffered from having been dictated, not written. But no one has said that the typescript was sent to the printer without revision. The presence of confused images and halting rhythm and vague equivocation must therefore have been either intentional or deemed unimportant—the careless line of the old artist, due not to blindness but to indifference. This accounts, no doubt, for such things as: "The more I squeeze the sponge of memory, the more its stored secretions flow"; and "that near presence of rank cheese which was in those days almost everywhere, for the nostril, the note of urban Switzerland"; or yet again (to encompass eye, nose, and throat in my examples) the unsayable: "Of what, at the same time, in those years, were the great rooms of the Louvre almost equally, above and below, not the scene, from the moment they so wrought, stage by stage, upon our perceptions?"

None of this, though, is as deplorable as the effect produced by certain passages in which the words sound abysmally hollow and the emotion therefore sentimental. I close my catalogue of horrors with one such passage, ludicrous—almost obscene—and certainly inexplicable otherwise than as a sign of James's recollected embarrassment and vicarious pain. The occasion was his first call on George Eliot:

G. H. Lewes was absent for the time on an urgent errand: one of his sons, on a visit at the house, had been taken with a violent attack of pain, the heritage of a bad accident not long before in the West Indies, a suffered onset from an angry bull, I seem to recall, who had tossed or otherwise mauled him, and, though beaten off, left him considerably compromised—these facts being promptly imparted to us, in no small flutter, by our distinguished lady, who came in to us from another room, where she had been with the hapless young man while his father appealed to the nearest good chemist for some known specific.

After two pages of complex impressions, the "distinguished lady" accepts Henry's post-Impressionist offer to go and fetch the surgeon whom Lewes had planned to call in, and the incident apparently closes in real life with none of the wretched affectation that James imbued it with in the telling.

Here and only in a few similar places was James "betrayed by what is false within." When emotion did not merely stir him unpleasantly but shook him to the depths, he spoke out. It is of the loved Minny Temple that he writes: "She burned herself out; she died at twenty-four." But everywhere, surrounding and quite overwhelming the blunders and blemishes, flows the current of the most virtuoso prose of the Impressionist era. It can wrap itself with the same close-fitting sinuous embrace around every kind of fact or feeling, from the memory of the ladies of the house returning from the department store "with the familiar Stewart headache from the prolonged strain of selection" to the vignette of Thackeray who, as he laid on the boy's shoulder "the hand of benevolence, bent on [his] native costume the spectacles of wonder"; to the description of Henry's fruitless early studies as "the handful of specimen dust . . . extracted from the scratched soil of my intelligence"; and it can further reach out like a molten spreading medium into the involutions of an entire character, his own, which he resumes in these poignant lines about the family's return from Europe in 1860:

> I had had cousins, naturally, in the countries we were quitting, but to a limited degree; yet I think I already knew I had had companions in as full a measure as any I was still to know—inasmuch as my imagination made out one, in the complex order and the colored air, almost wherever I turned; and inasmuch as, further, to live by the imagination was to live almost only in that way, so . . . I buried my associations, which had been in a manner till lately my hopes as well, with all decent dignity and tenderness.

I need hardly add that the true and subtle in this kind, the delicate, the controlled in thought and expression, predominate in this book as in the rest of James. But the wise reader will not pass from my uneven sampling straight to the text: he will first pause to read Mr. Dupee's Introduction, which in my reading I left to the last because I always find him so cogent and persuasive about James that I am tempted to echo his words rather than summon up my own. Here his sobriety and point will perfectly attune the reader's mind, just as the Notes will bring it light.

—JUNE 1956

The Man-Mountain

JACQUES BARZUN

On *The Complete Works of Montaigne,* translated by Donald M. Frame

IT WAS A HILL, really, that Montaigne lived on and drew his name from; it is only the Essays that are mountainous. Like mountains they tower along the horizon, vaguely known except to a few climbers, though generally admired as decorative, in the mistaken belief that they are what they seem from a distance.

The murmur of tradition, which one is likely to overhear and trust before the mind is fully awake, is that the Essays are a bedside book, the work of a humane skeptic who remarkably anticipates the doctrines of liberalism. Living in fanatical and dangerous times, he preached tolerance and desired progressive education, confessed to doubt and contemplated death, with the aid of multitudinous quotations from classic authors. One is supposed to go to him for random reflections on life, as Shakespeare is said to have done, and if it is to the French text or to Florio's English that one goes, one finds the reflections quaint as well as shrewd. Montaigne thus survives in conventional criticism as a sort of prose Chaucer or discursive Horace reiterating the religion of sensible men.

Any tameness in this is felt to be redeemed by extensive and candid self-revelation, some of it titillating; so that as autobiographer and explorer of the human condition (the phrase is his), Montaigne becomes IMPORTANT. If only he had had the gumption to put his—ah—er—insights into systematic form, if he had produced a *philosophy* susceptible of close analysis, the contemporary examiners of credentials such as the *douanier* Eliot would assign him a higher place. But then he would not be a bedside book. The *Essays* would be moved to the study and eventually to the public rooms, where they would impress the neophytes and supply them with topics of disputation.

Now, it may be too late to shake off the curiosity hunters; they do little harm as long as they remain a murmuring minority. But it is essential to give the rest, and especially the newcomers, a chance to see Montaigne for what he is; and for this Donald Frame's new translation of the entire canon—Essays, Letters, and Journal—comes remarkably apropos.

The first sight of the volume is in itself tonic: these eleven hundred large pages cannot possibly be turned into a bedside book—they crush dilettantism and shame impertinence; while the merest glance at the sinewy modern prose dispels quaintness and brings before you, speaking and gesticulating, a subtle mind at the service of a powerful will. Though Montaigne's long paragraphs have been broken up to please our modern eye, the prevailing impression is that of an irresistible continuity of thought.

The greatest of Montaigne's readers, who was Pascal, felt this pressure of mind most deeply and forged his own philosophy by leaning against it, as many jottings and allusions in the *Pensées* testify. What is more, Pascal's ultimate triumph in the unwritten work projected in the *Pensées* was to rest on the same base as Montaigne had solidly erected in the Essays. Pascal uses the chart of existence that Montaigne has drawn, but adds to it the realm of Transcendence. And even the arguments for giving faith and primacy to that realm derive from the premises and conclusions common to both thinkers. When, therefore, Pascal says that in reading Montaigne one finds a man and not an author, the reference is not to the autobiographical details—that Montaigne was below medium height, walked briskly, wore only black and white, had a keen sense of smell, loved conversation, and hated beer—it is to the fact that the Essays embody knowledge and not learning.

The presence of the many quotations is in fact as misleading as the tradition of the wise old skeptic: it was only after Montaigne's death, in the first posthumous edition of 1595, that the bulk of the Latin insertions occurred. True, Montaigne had been gathering them during the last four years of his life, but who shall say that his motive was not the familiar one of seeking confirmation by parallels? The more independent and imaginative a writer is, the more in retrospect he is likely to find his novelties consonant with recorded reality. It is not as tags or as proofs that Montaigne multiplies classic instances; it is as a means of establishing an historical span for the truth of his observations. That is why he says "Historians are my meat," knowing that he was not compiling an anthology: "I speak others' minds only to speak my own the more."

WHOEVER WANTS to know Montaigne the discoverer, Pascal's Montaigne, and very likely Shakespeare's, had best begin with the very last essay, the thirteenth of the third book, "Of Experience." It is a culmination, to be sure, but thanks to it we are soon on a height from which we can survey the other parts of the range with less danger of mistaking their relations. And first we must know: Why these tumultuous essays? "I love order and clarity," says Montaigne earlier. Yet not one of his chapters or books gives the least semblance of what a publisher's reader would call order. The first paragraph of "Experience" contrasts Experience with Reason; the second takes up the relation of civil codes to independent judges; then we are asked to consider the limitations of language that affect government, religion, and natural philosophy, only to come upon the great subject "Montaigne" that the author uses as a touchstone when the diversity of schools and rhetorics makes him suspect the errors of declared Reason and reported Experience:

> I study myself more than any other subject: this is my metaphysics and my physics too. . . . In this universe of ours, I ignorantly and carelessly let myself be pushed about by the general tendency of things: it will be knowledge enough when I feel its effects. My knowing it would not change its course; it will not change for my sake. It would be folly to hope so and greater folly to regret the fact, since it is necessarily uniform, public, and common.

Thereafter all the subjects I have named, and others besides, intertwine into a great tapestry of ideas, facts, memories, and associations. To read the essay is not to follow with the mind but to participate with the senses. And this exemplifies the continual appeal from books and theories to nature and conviction: "I would rather understand myself at first hand than through Cicero. In the experience I have of myself I find enough to make me wise, if I only am a good pupil: whoever recalls the excesses of his past anger and how far this fever carried him, sees the ugliness of this passion better than in Aristotle, and conceives a more justified hatred of it."

The key to Montaigne's "method" (to use our modern jargon) is in this word *justified*. The open, fearless mind that our liberal theory posits finds the world raucous with doctrines—Scholastic and Humanist, Protestant and Catholic, naturalist and mystical. Indoors, learning always keeps a full attic—rarities and rubbish mixed, from the ancient poets and philosophers to their latest commentators or contemners, the Utopians and ideologists. Each written or spoken word is made the basis of a creedlet, in whose name force and folly disport themselves. Everyone is summoned to believe or surrender some or all of life—two forms of self-abdication, which is to say, two forms of lying. In this mêlée Montaigne clings to the evidence that comes to him direct and that survives his relentless scrutiny. That is why he never drops a subject, no subject is cut off and disposed of, all subjects become himself; he has knowledge by carnal possession—as we have of food. This ruminating, by the time of his fullest strength in the essay "Of Experience," has become a passion:

> Judgment holds in me the master's seat; at least it tries to with infinite care; it lets my appetites go their way, and my feelings—both hate and love, even the love I bear myself—without being changed or corrupted thereby: if it cannot reform my other parts in keeping with itself, at least it does not let itself be deformed by them; it plays its own game, apart.

What a world of difference between this pertinacity, this jealous autonomy of mind, and the "free inquiry" which the "independent thinker" of any age follows chiefly in the editorial columns of his chosen radical weekly! Troubled by the wars of set ideas and brutish parties, Montaigne did not want merely reassurance and comfort—the warmth of partisanship, the joys of indignation, or the solace of being small and harmless. He wanted mastery over reality. For this he took risks, political as well as spiritual, far greater than has been recognized. The political risk was to be suspect to all parties and fall a victim to any by chance. This danger threatened more than once, in the open country, during the guerrillas, and once again in Paris, on orders of the Catholic League, as a member of the "brain trust" of Henry of Navarre, the future Henry IV.

But greater still was the spiritual danger, of which we have heard so much in these last years of the decay of liberalism. To reject dogma, sniff at ideologies, and erect one's intellect as the judge of the universe brings mastery only if one can be persuaded to include oneself in this lordly review. Montaigne's strength was to perceive this, which gives his "skepticism" and his "tolerance" an entirely different character from that shown in the acts of his supposed disciples in latter days. Skepticism in Montaigne is not a rhetorical precaution in arguing with opponents, but a condition of solid knowledge. For if *Que sçay-je?* implies only that he knows nothing, the question mark is an impertinence. In reality the motto means: "Don't be too sure," which ranks qualities of belief and keeps the way open for future truth. Truth is not all paid in and on deposit for the stockholders. Indeed, the game that Montaigne's judgment plays "by itself, apart" is the pragmatic Truth from Consequences, as against the rationalist game of Truth from Antecedents, from enunciated ideas, however advanced. Montaigne's punning objection to all rationalists is that "they give up things to run after causes" (*Ils laissent les choses et courent aux causes*).

But what are "things"? It can be argued against the pure empiricist that he rejects the tested knowledge of all humanity (to say nothing of divine revelation), in order to enjoy the conceit of his own error. Montaigne's rebuttal lies in his study of himself, which any man can emulate:

> When I find myself convinced by somebody else's reasoning that my opinion is false, I do not merely learn the new thing he has told me and my particular ignorance—that would be but a small gain: I learn my general weakness and the treacherousness of my understanding, from which I draw the reformation of the whole mass. . . . To learn that one has said or done a foolish thing is nothing: one must learn that one is a fool—an ampler and more important piece of instruction. The blunders that my memory has so often led me into, even when it is most sure of itself, are not useless and wasted, for now it can swear to me its complete certainty, I turn a deaf ear: and the first resistance that anyone makes to its testimony will give me pause. I will not dare rely on it about any weighty thing, nor guarantee it in someone else's behalf. And were it not that what I do from bad memory others do still more often from bad faith, I should always take a matter of fact on another's word rather than my own. If every man watched closely the effects and conditions of the passions that rule him as I have done with those whose victim I am, he could see them coming and moderate their impetuous course.

So much for the conduct of the understanding in a world of over-articulate sophomores. The conduct of those very passions which not only limit a man's judgment but also define his spiritual complexion is no less important if we are to accept (as Montaigne wishes us to do) the human condition. Today the phrase has come to stand for "the damnable human condition," which means that we do not accept it at all; we flail about us, impotent and angry. Because one of the early essays bears the classic title "That to Philosophize is to Learn to Die," it is sometimes assumed that Montaigne anticipated our response, though with better grace, fashioning stoical virtues out of evil necessity. The Saint-Bartholomew, we are told, had on him the effect that Lidice or Dachau had on us; the long continuance of senseless war can only have lowered the estimate of man's estate in a thinker who denied mundane certainty and declined supernatural consolation.

The Essays themselves tell another story, and do so from the beginning. War is one of men's diseases, and death is one of life's conditions. Both are limiting but not crippling, nor are they breaches of any contract guaranteeing man's happiness. "Death is indeed the end, but not therefore the goal, of life;

it is its finish, its extremity, but not therefore its object. Life should be an aim unto itself, a purpose unto itself." One might have foretold this teaching from Montaigne's passionate resolve to try all things and from his repugnance, too little noted, for the chief proponents of ready-made ends, the Aristotelians. That sect was still powerful and as ever in love with boxes, circles, and systems. Montaigne will have none for himself or for the mind he would educate: "Let him put everything through the sieve and lodge nothing in his head on mere authority or faith. Let Aristotle's principles be no principles to him, no more than the stoic or epicurean. Let him be offered this diversity of judgments: he will choose if he can. . . ." Whereupon Montaigne quotes Dante (*sic*) on the desirability of doubt.

Tastes, feelings, instincts, come into play and incite the passion for diversity. Montaigne finds in himself a taste for books, but not for bookishness; he can think and write for weeks or months together without reading. He loves travel and the immediate sensation of things. Truth being his delight, he loathes the life of a courtier. Yet its opposite, the philosopher's, should not be withdrawn or vexatious by design. Philosophy is a gay science, to which the satisfaction of the senses is a proper minister. Money is to buy pleasure, and Montaigne "hates poverty as the peer of pain." But human condition or no, there are terms on which alone it is fitting to live: "by right and authority not by permission or as a reward."

Thus revolting against his century, Montaigne expects its disapproval. He might have suffered more had it been less busy with mutual extermination. And then, too, the form of his thought protects him: he writes neither for glory nor for the reader's benefit, but only because he discovers himself in composition and enjoys it, and because his descendants might like to know him as well. This enables him to develop his criticism of the age: ruined by false subtlety, it ignores nature and does not know simplicity: he speaks of the learned theorists of love and says:

> My young page makes love and understands it: read to him Leon Hebreo or Ficino—their words are about him, about his thoughts and acts—and he understands nothing. I cannot recognize in Aristotle my ordinary doings: they have been covered and cloaked with strange garments for the use of the schools. God grant that they did right! If I were a man of the trade, I should naturalize art as much as they artificialize nature. Let us drop Bembo and Equicola!

Yet neither nonsense, folly, crime, nor the worst of all states, that in which "unjust evil comes to be legitimate and just," can make Montaigne mistake his present condition for "the human condition." As a student of history he knows that times have been worse and better too. He knows what man is capable of in both directions. Hence he "hates the glum and surly spirits that slide over the pleasures of life and fasten and batten on its woes, like flies which cannot grip a smooth polished surface, but must cling to rough and uneven places, or like leeches that suck and crave only bad blood." For his part, he has enough resilience and strength to wax ironic about his times: for thirty years "every Frenchman has lived each hour under threat of death or ruin," but "let us give thanks to fate for making us live in a century that is neither soft nor idle and languishing: many a man who would never have achieved fame in any other way will now go down in history through his misfortunes."

Paradoxically, the strain of reality proved harder to stand when order was finally restored. In the century of Descartes and Pascal, Montaigne had to be expurgated. When Descartes wanted to make a clean sweep of chaotic teachings and a fresh start in thought, he felt bound to disregard experience and to begin with a close union of reasoning with the supernatural. When Pascal wanted to discredit cant and acknowledge the diversity of life, the "order and clarity" of Louis XIV's settled society was not enough for him: he wanted a more authentic resolution of conflicts hereafter. Though he had gone to school to Montaigne he could not, like him, "accustom his imagination to the continual variation of human things," and along with variation he rejected what Montaigne named as the handmaidens of his hard-won philosophy: health, wealth, physical beauty, leisure, and liberty.

REGARDLESS OF THE RANK accorded him, Montaigne has always caused astonishment and a kind of awe for the naturalness with which he writes about himself: no vanity and no false modesty, despite an abundance of statements creditable and disparaging; no weariness or disgust in the reader, despite many details of the most trivial and least scandalous privity. The literary tour de force by which this is accomplished is an object of pleasure in itself, though the explanation lies on the surface: in the meanders of his frequently mistitled essays Montaigne gives us the strictest kind of thought-pursuit, the absolutely original stream of consciousness. Our moderns—Proust or Joyce—seem apprentices in comparison.

Montaigne edits himself, to be sure, for the interior monologue or therapeutic confessional would distract us by its grammatical false starts and unmeaning repetitions. But the suppression of these stammerings does not change the substance. We see the growing thought turn and twist, grapple with an image, drop it half way for lack of a fitting close, pick up an earlier thread or spin a new one, return to the comparison and cap it with the image that will lodge it in the thinker's memory—it is a magical and unique inspection of another's mind, for it approaches the immediacy of introspection.

The prose that renders this has all the virtues that prose can have, including the faults of inattention that mark spontaneity. Balance, rhythm, rounded periods are never there when an abrupt stop, a redoubling of epithets, a mismating of clauses, actually occurred in response to the sudden sight of the object. It is this unrhetorical rhetoric, and not his antiquated vocabulary, that makes Montaigne hard to translate. Since Florio, who was in tune but inaccurate, the Essays have generally passed into a monotone English that destroyed a part of their veracity. The mountain ruggedness became all road, and in being straight and smooth it often became dull. Donald Frame has changed all that. He knows his Montaigne as a cultural historian and critic, not merely as a linguist and translator. He divines, that is, the unwritten context and can thus render the intention. He can see an epigram or a play on words (for Montaigne is an habitual wit), and give them to us again in equivalents that preserve the salt; and just as important, he does not make epigrams when Montaigne is simply turning his back on elaboration.

One could argue, of course, about particular phrases, and especially about the always difficult choice of modern words to reproduce the easy crudity of Latin and French dealings with sex and the body generally. But all such hagglings and carpings disappear in the magnitude of the success achieved. That it should be matched by an exquisite tact in the supplying of notes and critical judgments shows that once in a while he who can do the greater can also do the less. No other proof of the translator's understanding and skill is needed than the way he preserves the differences between the Essays and the Journal, and between both and the Letters—differences which attest in the original author a natural complexity that only heightens our wonder at the conscious artist: Montaigne the traveler was a sober self-communer who, transfigured, embodies in the Essays the extravagance of man thinking, and who in the Letters stiffens into the dignity of the public man—a man of property, wearing a ruff, Mayor of Bordeaux, twice elected for his pains, though a trifle ridiculous in solid citizens' eyes for letting his otherwise respectable name appear in print.

—NOVEMBER 1957

The Artist as Scapegoat

Jacques Barzun

On Frank Harris's *Oscar Wilde*

FRANK HARRIS'S *Oscar Wilde* is one of the great biographies in the language. Looking back on it after half a century, during the greater part of which it has been out of print, one can see that the book has the fundamental requisites for permanence; it has the ring of finality. Perhaps it was "scandal" and "daring" that gave it notoriety when it first appeared, but now it is the intellectual solidity and the form, the immediacy and the emblematic truth of the narrative, that commend it to our judgments.

When I say that this biography has the fundamental requisites of greatness, I have first in view the author's direct knowledge of his subject. Turn the pages and the dialogue is there to assure you, as in Boswell's *Johnson,* that the portrait is from life. Pass from the dialogue to the unbroken paragraphs and you see that the writer is moved by the desire for truth. He may err from ignorance or invincible bias, but he has striven—he is striving, with ease and success—to disentangle the natural confusion of life. And in any passage you may light on, he demonstrates his genius for exhibiting through words the once-living present.

It is of course a proper question, and in our day a likely one, whether Oscar Wilde is also a great subject, worthy of these great powers. If the answer is based on common knowledge, which is to say the spoken tradition about Oscar Wilde's wit, arrogance, and degradation, the verdict will probably be adverse: Wilde is usually deemed less than great by the tests of either Victorian or modern opinion—not a great poet or profound thinker, not a noble character or a vengefully debased one. That is the very reason for reading this life by Frank Harris and rediscovering precisely what Oscar Wilde was.

The story opens with the Dublin trial in which Wilde's father and mother—noted characters both—were rather scandalously implicated. Lime-light and the defiance of opinion were Oscar's inheritance, together with wit, breeding, intellect, and a talent for literature. His schooldays, Oxford, and the undergraduate eccentricity and merits that brought him early fame; his triumph in London by means of the stage and snobbish society; the defiance of the lesser and the greater gods through vanity and cowardice combined; his downfall, incomplete expiation, and abjectly ugly death—these are the moments of the journey which the biographer has chosen to recreate with self-effacing art in pursuit of his double object—to show Wilde from far and near and to explain him.

Frank Harris, himself an eccentric and self-willed writer, besides being an explosive Irish-American and a power in fin-de-siècle London, is persuaded, and seeks to persuade us, that Wilde was brought down by the English public because he was an artist. Certainly he was one who made it his study to typify for his generation *the* artist, taunting the educated Philistine in every possible way—by insult, by the externals of dress and speech, by the affectation of social eminence, by the reality of charm of manner, by popular success, and finally by transgressing the ultimate prohibitions of the sexual code.

And it is equally true that by reviving the mode of the dandy and borrowing as well something from the Byronic formula of hauteur and simple charm, Wilde made his loftiness unforgivable. He played the part too deliberately and, in the end, deceived himself even more than others. Yet it took the manic Marquess of Queensberry—the legislator of the boxing ring—to destroy the imposture and at the same time blazon to all the world what before only London knew—the most vivid and plausible impersonation of the modern artist, enemy and victim of society.

I say impersonation and not embodiment, for Wilde was a very limited artist. He produced one fine poem, *The Ballad of Reading Gaol,* one fine fiction, *The Happy Prince,* and one undoubted masterpiece, *The Importance of Being Earnest.* If it is possible to find a common element in these, it is the moral and critical intelligence raised to the self-sufficiency of art. Shaw and others since his day have been quite right to say that *The Importance of Being Earnest* is disturbingly heartless: it is in fact what people think Shaw's plays are—all intellect and no humanity. But that is because the animus throughout *The Importance* is purely analytic: read the first two pages of dialogue between master and servant, before anything of moment has happened, and what you find is a definitive exposure of the class system. Later, every joke is a capsule of social or literary criticism. No humor or indignation, hence no satire; no "feeling" or plausibility, hence no comedy; but the greatest critical farce ever written.

Wilde was a very great critic who used his gift to define the place of art in nature and modern society. He can be excused for trying to act out his precepts and exemplify them in verse, stories, and plays: he had genius—though not the genius that creates. Even in prose, Wilde is original and great only when he is doing nothing tendentiously "beautiful." Not that his conscious efforts seem strained; they do not smell of the lamp, but—which is far worse—they smell of purple patchouli. They would cast doubt on his literary judgment altogether, if one did not have the excellent simplicity of his reviews in the *Pall Mall Gazette, The Speaker,* and other periodicals of the eighties and nineties. These short essays abound in just and original views, some of which were later elaborated into dialogues or condensed into epigrams, and they teach us that in the later opinions and aphorisms one must continually sort out the crystalline truths from the paste. Like many a verbal improviser, Wilde was often on paper a rather mechanical imitator of himself.

What we could not know without Frank Harris is that in conversation with his friends Wilde sustained his best genius, that of simplicity and truth, as in his critical work. His talk was a masterpiece in speech; his manners were exquisite; his language held, for the moment, the purity and force of his intellect. It followed naturally from what he talked about that Wilde should seem the standard-bearer of art.

And in retrospect, despite the rubbish and the wreckage, that glory cannot be taken away from him. Pater, Henley, Davidson, Aubrey Beardsley, Wilfred Scawen Blunt, Dawson and the drugged poets, George Moore, Shaw, Frank Harris himself, though all more gifted and better craftsmen than Wilde, could not hope to rival him in the Nero-like power of making the figure of the artist explicit, commanding, unforgettable.

His is no longer the image of the artist that we give our regard to; but brush aside the trimmings, and his impersonation still shows enduring elements: think, for example, of Baudelaire, Stefan George, and Ezra Pound, merely as figures, and it is clear they exhibit identical traits which it is fair to call distinctively professional. They pose, curse, and legislate in the same way. In so far forth they remind us of Wilde, and this says something about the modern artist as an institution.

Frank Harris's life of Wilde makes no analysis of this role and its mask any more than it discusses Wilde's literary works, or follows his footsteps to America and elsewhere. It sticks to portraiture and expends all its critical force on the characters portrayed. It spares no one, Wilde least of all. His vanity and lack of depth in friendship, his irresolute, womanish will, his fitful glimpses of the common life and quick retreat into verbiage or sensuality, his specious reasonableness in defence of homosexuality and Greek utopias—all this is set down in brief, deft words that never impede the movement of time or the gestures of the actors of the tragedy. For it is a tragedy even if one does not share Harris's view of the motives at work in contemporary English society. One cannot but perceive that greatness fell by its own fault and also by the working of inalterable law.

The design of the retelling is, as I have said, perfect, not excepting the insertion of two splendid fragments by other hands—Shaw's Memories of Oscar Wilde and the famous long letter from Robert Ross on Wilde's last days.

—JULY 1959

Life Into Words

Jacques Barzun

On *Two Gentle Men* by Marchette Chute

IF THE PUBLIC did not always count on being rightly informed by the mere noise that books make or fail to make, the name of Marchette Chute would be better known than it is. A new work in her characteristic genre would then be eagerly awaited by the considerable body of educated readers, instead of remaining the special delight of those who have by luck or cunning discovered who and what she is.

Who then is Marchette Chute and what does she write? To call her a biographer does not say enough. To suggest that she has the virtues of a novelist, though this is a fact, would be misleading. To affirm that she is a first-rate scholar is also true, but possibly alarming to that skittish public which caters so blindly and so poorly for its own tastes. Let me say simply that Miss Chute is a student of lives and times. She has up to now taken three of the great English poets—Chaucer, Shakespeare, and Ben Jonson—as the occasion for as many original depictions of mingled character and history. She composes a lifelike narrative without ever straying from the strictest truthfulness, but her aim is to reproduce the sensations of contemporaneity. She is—if only one word must be used—an Impressionist.

She divides her palette by the simple expedient of treasuring the telling little fact—*le petit fait vrai,* of which Stendhal was so fond. But she avoids the fallacy for which Lytton Strachey has received much praise, the fallacy of making the presentment a mosaic not of telling but of telltale facts. Miss Chute's books are not brief caricatures. They are panoramas, in which the immediacy of life is conveyed by the abundance of details—and of course by the hidden art with which they support and supplement one another. Any dramatic quality arises from the whole, the sheer weight of what was, and not from some trick of lighting, some twist for emphasis, such as we still find in the remote followers of Strachey. The admirable tone Marchette Chute employs with subtle variation to record the passage from the prose to the poetry of existence has its root in curiosity about the matter of fact. Her model is the all-embracing Herodotus, not the tight-lipped Thucydides. Here is a page from her *Shakespeare of London:*

> During these successful years of working with the King's Men, Shakespeare moved his residence again and returned to the London Side of the Thames. The exact date when he left Southwark is unknown, but it may have been about the time of James' accession that Shakespeare left the Liberty of the Clink and took lodgings on Silver Street.
>
> Silver Street was in St. Olave's parish, an aristocratic neighborhood on the northwest side of town that stood next to the parish in which John Heminges and Henry Condell had their homes. It was a district of handsome houses, and Shakespeare lived there as a lodger in the home of a French family named Mountjoy. Christopher Mountjoy was one of the many Huguenots who left France after the Massacre of St. Bartholomew, and he had prospered in London as a maker of head-dresses for women. . . .
>
> The Mountjoys had an only child, Mary, whom they had educated in the intricacies of silver wire and the art of using a twisting wheel until she knew almost as much about the business as they did. They also had an apprentice, Stephen Belott, who completed his seven years' service with them and in 1604 had just returned from a trip to Spain. A marriage between the two young people seemed both obvious and desirable, and Mrs. Mountjoy turned for assistance to her friend and lodger, William Shakespeare.
>
> A marriage agreement was a serious matter because of the property settlement involved, and it was Shakespeare's responsibility to work out an arrangement on the dowry that would be agreeable to both sides. A married couple who were friends of Belott went formally to Shakespeare to discuss the size of the marriage portion that Mountjoy had offered, and as Shakespeare himself testified there were "many conferences" on the matter. The family servant, Joan Johnson, remembered eight years later how the lodger, "one Mr. Shakespeare," had made the arrangements whereby Stephen Belott consented to marry Mary Mountjoy. . . . The wedding took place in the midst of the Christmas season at Whitehall, just nineteen days after the King's Men had opened the season with a performance of Shakespeare's *Othello.*

It is easy to see from this passage the truth of what I said about Miss Chute's combining the virtues of a novelist and a scholar: she understands relevant irrelevance. The combination keeps her from being merely gossipy, like a garrulous woman writing fiction, or from reproducing all that she has found, like a sciurine scholar to whom a book is a place to hide his hoard.

Miss Chute has in fact quietly fashioned for our pleasure and instruction a distinctive literary form. If one does not want to call it a new biographical genre, one must at least say that her way of writing lives is hers alone and that it commands and furnishes a special kind of knowledge. The clue to her secret is that she is at home both with her characters and with herself. I mean by this that Miss Chute does not feel the modern need to decry mankind and dissociate herself from the specimens before her. She can be critical but she never plays the biographer's game of siding with the public against her subject in some witty form of ridicule or censure. She has so firm and natural a grasp on the principle of life that she has no need to be "lively."

It is by virtue of all these talents, native and acquired, that Miss Chute has been able, most recently, to make a book out of the lives of two other—though lesser—English poets, George Herbert and Robert Herrick. She calls them Two Gentle Men and it would seem axiomatic that if the appellation is correct, biography is at a disadvantage. Just as happy nations have no history, gentle men have no lives. This is where Miss Chute's special mode of weaving character and contemporary fact triumphs over inherent impossibility, like Gainsborough painting the impossible "Blue Boy."

Indeed, our narrator produces a greater surprise than Gainsborough and achieves a higher drama. For she can trade on our conception of English history from Elizabeth to Charles II to make us unceasingly aware that times and lives need not form a unison or even a discord; they can join and part in a fluid counterpoint. Her gallery of portraits is in itself a demonstration. We begin with the Herberts, whose name evokes Charlemagne, the Wars of the Roses, and the Tudor dynasty, and brings us to Elizabeth's court, to Bacon and Donne, to the philosopher Herbert of Cherbury, brother of the poet, and to the poet himself—a sort of Saint Francis who started life in justified pride and ended it in deliberate but at last easeful humility.

Thus revisited, George Herbert appears as akin to Pascal—many-gifted but restlessly driven to make an offering of all he had to God and, in the course of finding the way, leaving an imperishable record of the search. A gentle man, yes, when compared with his warrior kinsmen and his plotting and persecuting contemporaries. But a fierce man also, whose preoccupation with his soul and his verse expressed passion and ambition and selfishness in saintly form. It is perhaps lucky for the world that the gentle poets and mystics of this particular breed are so appalled at what they find within themselves that they turn to God and good works. They would otherwise make simple characters like Attila seem philanthropists by comparison: Pascal and Herbert were potential Napoleons.

The skill with which the biographer uses Herbert's poetry to show the growth of his impulse to withdraw from the great world and then the increasing concentration of his power in the density of his verse is a notable feat of criticism, all the more admirable for drawing no attention to itself. We are very far, here, from the pretentious gestures of the "serious" critic washing his hands in public and sterilizing his mind for the laborious surgery to come. In biography everything must contribute to forward motion, time must pass perceptibly, and Miss Chute is too good a craftsman ever to forget it, though the particles of fact and idea may separately seem slight:

> It was a period when the sense of separation from God weighed with special heaviness upon Western man. . . . As long as Herbert was sheltered by an orderly career and the conviction that he was spending it in God's service, these winds of the mind had less force. As long as [he] lived a tidy and limited existence his verse was relatively commonplace. There was nothing to restrain and therefore no necessity to exert the kind of strength that is indispensable to a poet. It was not until his life was formless that form became a vital necessity. . . .
>
> He experienced many times, for instance, a furious sense of having been trapped into giving his life to a service in which he could not succeed and from which he could not escape. All the worlds of love and courtliness and learning were open to him as an aristocrat. . . .
>
> > Full of rebellion, I would die,
> > Or fight, or travel, or deny
> > That Thou has aught to do with me.

This is the truth of fact but it [is] not yet the truth of poetry. It is hardly more than a rhymed statement. Yet the idea it expresses is a reality—one of the foes that Herbert encountered in the house of his mind—and therefore it remained with him until he brought it to complete expression in that most beautiful of poems, 'The Collar.' [It begins:]

> > I struck the board, and cried, No more.
> > > > I will abroad.
> > > What? Shall I ever sigh and pine?
> > My lines and life are free; free as the road,

> Loose as the wind, as large as store.
> > Shall I be still in suit?
> Have I no harvest but a thorn
> To let me blood, and not restore
> What I have lost with cordial fruit?
> > Sure there was wine
> Before my sighs did dry it: there was corn
> Before my tears did drown it.
> Is the year only lost to me?
> Have I no bays to crown it?
> No flowers, no garlands gay? All blasted?
> > All wasted?
> Not so, my heart: but there is fruit,
> > And thou hast hands. . . .

In coupling Herrick with Herbert, the biographer not only extends (and in a sense completes) her timespan, but also redoubles the dramatic contrast established at the beginning: Herbert breaks away from family tradition and Elizabethan high life to end prematurely as a poor parson in a small rural parish. He leaves a book of poems studiously pruned and composed, to be treasured ultimately by a special audience of ardent Christians and critics fed on Donne; yet *The Temple* was an immediate best-seller. Herrick, contrariwise, is a long-lived Jonsonian, a pagan profuse of his words and smiling upon all the manifestations of the senses. He too is a clergyman, but one who can stand the imputation of having fathered an illegitimate child, and whose book is an unorganized collection of lyrics and epigrams, supplemented with pious pieces mostly manufactured to make the luscious "Hesperides" pass the censor. But this jumble, on publication, falls stillborn from the press, in part because it was offered as a work of divinity.

The year was 1648 and the time no less harsh for poets than when Herbert had died fifteen years before, but the difficulties were of a different order. Herrick was caught in the civil wars and had to ride out the storm. He survived into the Restoration, the last among poets, certainly, who could call himself an Elizabethan.

With this background, it would have tempted a worker in crude contrasts to represent Herrick as in fact a rollicking satyr and wine-bibber. The *Hesperides* and some vague traditions might have afforded plausible reasons for such a portrait. But Miss Chute is not to be tempted. Or rather, there was before her a more delicate temptation, which as an artist and a scholar she saw she had no right to resist. This was the opportunity of portraying the sentimental hedonist. I mean by sentimental here the working of belief without passion. Herrick's verses in praise of virgins and bridal beds and wine are neither false nor second-hand. They are not mere exercises: there is feeling, but it is feeling remembered in what is almost an overdose of tranquillity. The imagination at work is genuine but not, as it were, immediate. One has only to think of Villon, or even of Swinburne, to perceive the difference. It has nothing to do with what the poet himself experienced. Herrick could have had a dozen illegitimate children and Swinburne led the life of an anchorite, Herrick would still write like one who distils emotion not for voluptuousness but in secret self-defense against it. He belongs not to the tribe of Ben, though he revered and was befriended by the older poet, but to the commoner tribe of bachelor uncles.

That makes his verses no less enchanting, though it spoils almost all his epigrams. They have not enough anger to bite, even when they make rude noises. It is one thing, however, to descry all this in the work; it is another to make it play its part in the story of an uneventful life, especially when it is clear that one passion did rule that life—the passion to write. Add that the stage is in turmoil and the entrances and exits made by men in boots—James, Charles, Archbishop Laud, Cromwell, and another Charles, and you have the measure of Miss Chute's triumph.

If anyone wants to look for blemishes in the rendering, or slight miscalculations in the proportions, he can find them. The diction here and there is a little tainted with contemporary jargon (e.g. "successful marriage"). And here and there, too, the tone slips momentarily into the didactic. But one has to be a pop-eyed reviewer looking for trouble to even notice these microscopic irregularities of texture. The entire book is a superb fulfilment of a right intention. Nor is it only the more spacious life of the times depicted that gives us a sense of freedom; it is also the easy movement with which the author has conceived, selected, and composed.

—SEPTEMBER 1959

History and
Social Thought

The Sense of History

Jacques Barzun

On Hugh Trevor-Roper's *Men and Events* and Jacob Burckhardt's
Judgments on History and Historians

SOMEWHERE IN HIS denunciations of the modern mass man Ortega describes that unhappy, over-anatomized creature as having been "emptied of his own history." This is at best a half truth. It may be true if it means that modern men are less likely to ruminate on their own and their neighbors' past, to form or perpetuate local legends, and to resist change by citing their grandfathers' satisfaction as grounds for their own. But as against these, so to speak, instinctive forms of the historical sense which have been lost, men today have almost everywhere acquired a habit of historicism which in its excess has alarmed good observers. Nietzsche, for one, thought that the invariably historical outlook killed originality and courage, and he compared the unhistorical cow in the field with historical man, concluding to man's disadvantage.

Certainly, when one thinks of the indigestible bulk of data that we collect about every patient and pupil, every applicant and every piece of business, every army post and every movie star, every act of government and every word uttered in court, every fleeting opinion and every sexual fancy, when—in short—whatever is off the record is sure to be also on the record and somehow taken account of, one is tempted to turn Ortega's complaint upside down and say that modern man is choked with his own history. No longer does he come to experience fresh and eager and confident, but timidly asking for its credentials in the form of garrulous antecedents. When perchance a new idea occurs, the first thing it does is to generate not action but a file—a set of false grandfathers on paper, which will soothe everybody's irritable sense of history.

This is not to say that industrial democracy at large knows or cares much for genuine History, that is, for verified and coherent knowledge about men and events in the past. But then no society has shown any great penchant for true learning. Popular history has always been an irregular web of legend, error, and indifference, just like popular science. We can blame "the schools" as much as we like, it remains so far an empirical truth that the love of history as a serious and systematic passion is an individual affair dependent on native gift, like the love of birdlore or of music. All of them are distributed unpredictably and perhaps more widely than one thinks, but this still leaves a gulf between the connoisseur and the layman.

In recent times, to be sure, certain systems of history have been taken up with such vociferous acclaim as to cast doubt on the generality that History is a special taste. Marx, Spengler, and Toynbee seem to have broken through the barrier of indifference and given whole classes and peoples an understanding of history. But far from being an exception to the rule, this vogue of systems confirms it. For systems are by definition a denial of the reality of history. They do not exhibit but use history, confounding the historian by showing that what he takes as reality is but appearance, a phantasmagoria needing a clue found only in the system. And being a riddle with a key, following a law, History necessarily repeats—repetitious evolution through class struggle in Marx; growth and decay of culture forms in Spengler, challenge and response according to a spiritual plan in Toynbee. In other words, all systems assert or imply that history is fated, that the mind of man does not make history but is made by it.

In these plans and clues the student of history properly so called takes only an incidental interest; for they destroy at once the substance and the problems he clearly sees. And it does this by mechanical tricks which on close scrutiny appear culpably crude—as, for example, when Toynbee calls the Thirty Years' War and that of 1939–45 "secondary wars" because they do not fit into his preestablished scheme.

History proper, then, is equidistant from the casual historicism of the man in the street, from the haphazard images of popular history, and from the formulas of the system maker. Though all three are obviously related to his work, it is the historian's business to refute them and to replace their provincial views and ways by two positive creations—an ordered narrative and a running interpretation, both methodically tested.

The best way to know real History is of course to read it, and of all living historians I can think of none more enticing and more rewarding than H. R. Trevor-Roper whose *Men and Events* has just appeared in this country. Under this modest title the author reprints some forty essays originally published in the English press, and which together demonstrate not only what history is, but also what it is for: it is for pleasure and instruction. The book also proves that success in conveying both depends on the historian's power to seize the fact and the word and compel them into a marriage that shall seem unforced. No one can doubt that Mr. Trevor-Roper possesses this power as a birthright. But to draw and hold the unprofessional reader's attention to some period chosen by the writer for his own reasons calls for a different gift, still rarer than the first—the gift of establishing relevancies between past and present without falsification or vain moralizing. Once again, the marriage must seem unforced; and this gift too belongs to Mr. Trevor-Roper.

By chance or design, his period is the best in modern history for combining novelty with closeness to our troubles, the period of the great social, religious, and political revolution that occupies the fifteenth, sixteenth, and seventeenth centuries. We gaze there upon a death and a birth to which we cannot be indifferent, for much of what was born then is dying now. The death of feudal Christendom therefore moves us, as does the spectacle of our birth—the birth of the modern western world, with its national state and diverse religions, with capitalism and empire and the culture of the printing press. All this, thanks to our historian, we witness in the minute detail of personality and also on the large scale of persistent issues.

How Mr. Trevor-Roper manages to do this in essays sometimes written as book reviews, and often no more than six pages long, remains a secret of his art—and of his artfulness in arranging the sequence. But one thing that can surely be said of this collection is that the author's prefatory claim of an underlying philosophy unifying the parts is altogether true. The philosophy, be it understood, is a philosophical outlook and not a system; its consistency is the flexible one of a living organism capable of adapting itself to the varieties of fact, and not a robot-like contrivance of bolts and angle irons. If one had to characterize Mr. Trevor-Roper's philosophy one would call it liberal conservative; but perhaps these words are no longer capable of raising any but blurred images. It is therefore best to give examples of his judgments and of the facts his mind dwells on: Listen to his words on the Jesuit mission in England under Elizabeth:

> The function of the Jesuit missionaries was not to excite direct political opposition, it was to create and maintain a potential fifth column. How that fifth column should be used would be determined not by them, but by the enemies of England. Understandably, they protested that they had no poli-

tics, they only preached a gospel. Understandably, the English government failed to make that distinction. When the Cominform preaches war, local communists vainly, even if genuinely, insist that they mean peace.

Again, in the superb portrait of Clarendon, witness and historian of the English Civil Wars and Chancellor under the Restoration, we hear Mr. Trevor-Roper defining the ideal historian "who, having tasted, in equal measures, the alternating extremes of fortune, had arrived at the magnanimous philosophy which alone can judge the complex revolutions of human politics." And still speaking of Clarendon: "he could never have entertained the academic error of determinism. He understood, as modern doctrinaires do not, that economic interests are abstractions which cannot mobilise themselves. . . . Every character was to him half an agent, half a victim in the avalanche so imprudently set sliding, and every character therefore required—and received—a just and careful portrait."

Mr. Trevor-Roper, who is known among historians for his just and careful portrait of Archbishop Laud and among a wider public for his awe-inspiring account of the last days of Hitler, is persuaded (rightly, as I think) that historical knowledge cannot be had, let alone communicated, without an intuitive grasp of political reality and human character. Perhaps the two are one. At any rate, men and the framework of society are the irreducible elements of history. Other kinds of facts exist—the history of art, of war, of prices, of marriage, of games, is true history, but each lacks form and intelligibility when divorced from the political and private lives of men.

This does not mean that Mr. Trevor-Roper turns his back on current controversies that are couched in abstractions. On the contrary, he tackles them vigorously, bringing the categories which "cannot mobilise themselves" down to the ground on which men do move. Thus, in discussing the social causes of the English Civil Wars, he rejects alike the theses of the Marxists and of the Weber-Tawney school. "I conclude," he says, "that the Great Rebellion was not a 'capitalist' rising, nor did it 'succeed' in any sense, nor in any way directly forward the advance of capitalism in England. It was the blind revolt of the gentry against the Court, of the provinces against the capital: the backwash against a century of administrative and economic centralisation."

Applying the same test of concreteness, Mr. Trevor-Roper destroys the pretensions of Marxist scholars to being historians at all and of Marx himself to being in any sense whatever the creator of an historical or sociological method. This is done so expertly and quietly and definitively that it will leave breathless the many good people who still think that although Marx was wrong in general, he must be credited with a revolution in men's views of history. This, says Mr. Trevor-Roper, agreeing with all those who have examined the facts, is "a strange perversion of intellectual history." And he winds up his case with the obvious yet still obscured fact that "disproved by all intellectual tests, it is Russian power alone which now sustains and irrationally seems to justify the Marxist interpretation of history.'"

Outside his period, Mr. Trevor-Roper's admirations and rejections are equally firm and judicious, being based on that almost bodily sensation of rightness which for any craftsman clinches and crowns the labor of research. One is not surprised that for our author Lytton Strachey is no historian at all and Macaulay a very great one. Indeed, setting aside Macaulay's excessive delight in material progress, one could say that Mr. Trevor-Roper is a fortunate re-embodiment of Macaulay's spirit. We find again that extraordinary narrative art, didactic without being pedagogical; that unshakable common sense, undeflected by even the strongest currents of political, esthetic, and other fashions; that power of putting much observation in little space which is frequent in the great historians, but which rarely seems so spontaneous, so matter-of-course, as in Macaulay and Trevor-Roper. I cannot forbear quoting again from these delectable essays:

> For historical knowledge, like other knowledge, is advanced by theory and only disciplined by facts.

On the English aristocracy in the age of Louis XIV:

> As a class it had no time for the pen. Only its casualties turned to literature.

> To Strachey historical problems were always, and only, problems of individual behaviour and individual eccentricities. He read big biographies and wrote little biographies.

> Marxists have not yet been able to decide whether the economy of the medieval Italian cities was 'capitalist' or 'feudal', and it has now become a major industry among Marxists to discuss the real meaning of the terms they have invented.

> And yet, behind that solidarity of ignorance and prejudice which so often unites governments and people, the greatness of Machiavelli was never forgotten.

And to close with a contrast, let me give first what is perhaps the most compact and luminous phrase in the volume: "that prosperity upon which any
liberal culture must rest"; and then the ampler period which by means of
three words reaches the grand style: "Raleigh and Essex, famous as courtiers,
sustaining on the spoils of church lands, court offices, and war their ambitions, their retinues, their dependent poets, their elaborate gestures, were nevertheless not court figures only."

It may seem, after so much excellence, as if the critical spirit would retreat
discomfited from any encounter with our historian. Unfortunately for our
hope of perfection, this is not so. Mr. Trevor-Roper's work shows a defect:
this is in itself no curious discovery. What is curious is that in a man so alive
to the interplay of mind and circumstance, and so "magnanimous" about
doctrines, the protean life of ideas should occasionally escape him entirely.
Thus the article on Hobbes's *Leviathan* expresses only our historian's detesta-
tion of absolutism. That wonderful book is called "a fantastic monster . . .
without ancestry or posterity: crude, academic, and wrong." Surely every epithet here is a misfit for a work which springs from the spirit of science, which
inaugurates British empiricism, which is beautifully, not fantastically, shaped,
and which is as far from academic as genius itself. Mr. Trevor-Roper grants it
style, yet he calls the book "dead by 1680" as if it were not demonstrably
alive in his pages and mine. As for its wrongness, it is that of any classic, the
error of premises and affirmations, which yet leaves the central thought untouched. And lo and behold, Mr. Trevor-Roper himself sees this distinction
and tells us what it means: by his work Hobbes "had cleared political thought
of its ancient, biblical cobwebs, and set it firmly on the secular basis of human
psychology."

The best thing a man in error can do is obviously to contradict himself. I
regret that in speaking of Hobbes and Carlyle, Mr. Trevor-Roper does not go
even farther in self contradiction. He evidently fears them both as would-be
fascists: he deplores Hobbes's awareness of fear and competition, and he has
no use for Carlyle's sense of awe in the face of the miracle of government.
This is being too rationalistic to be reasonable, just as it is too ingenuous in
him to say of Machiavelli's *Prince* that its message is neutral and scientific.
Why scowl at Hobbes and smile at Mac? Ideas are never quite so much in
and of themselves as Mr. Trevor-Roper pretends. Their raison d'être is to
drive against other ideas, and their intent is half their meaning. Hence I prefer
the usual horror-struck interpretation of *The Prince* (though I do not share it),
or else the latest reading given out by Mr. Garrett Mattingly, who finds in the
work an elaborate irony.

In any case, Mr. Trevor-Roper rejects moral dualism in political theory as hateful while he maintains unimpaired his judgment of political practice in which that dualism obtains. This possibly explains why he is an enthusiastic admirer of Jacob Burckhardt, whose *Judgments on History and Historians* have just been translated by Mr. Harry Zohn. Mr. Trevor-Roper's introduction to the volume is an expansion of the essay which the reader will find in *Men and Events* and it seeks to explain why Burckhardt, little regarded in his own day, has come to mean much to us. Burckhardt was among the first to prophesy political and cultural doom for Europe after the revolutions of 1848. He did so not through system, like Gobineau, but in telling comparisons of and reflections upon the historical periods he knew best—the Italian Renaissance, the age of Constantine, and his own. Moreover, as Mr. Trevor-Roper points out, Burckhardt was a humanist. It might be added that Burckhardt was Nietzsche's friend and that both gained in wisdom from the friendship.

These personal circumstances and philosophical broodings account for Burckhardt's present vogue: he pleases intellectuals because he dislikes the modern world and loves art. But these are dangerous grounds for admiration: they leave us in our self-conceit, forgetting that to think like Burckhardt in the nineteenth century is to be a seer, and to repeat his words with unction in the twentieth is to be a blind echo. The present collection of Burckhardt's lecture notes should provide the thoughtful with a corrective to this contemporary infatuation. God forbid that a man should be judged by his lecture notes, yet these are so abundant and consecutive that one may be forgiven for using them as indications of Burckhardt's weaknesses as well as his strength.

In the first place, Burckhardt is only a moderately good prophet, and we do his memory harm whether we overrate him in this role or are disappointed at his poor showing in what is after all not the historian's business. Burckhardt was undoubtedly right about the coming threat of dictatorship, but the "enduring tyranny" he prophesied for Germany lasted only a dozen years. In the second place, his critique of the masses and materialism is neither original nor sufficiently concrete; it is vague and often querulous. He comes back again and again to the oppressiveness of the period 1830 to 1848, which under an apparent stoicism he seemed to take as a personal affront. Life may indeed have been hard to bear in Basel at that time, and, as we knew from other artists, elsewhere also. What then? We are entitled to ask by what criterion historical periods are justified, and when we do so we find Burckhardt and his modern devotees applying the criterion of art, or to be more precise, the criterion of art history: a period, it seems, a place, a people, should be lovely and productive of loveliness. And this loveliness should be continually apparent to its contemporaries. Which is absurd.

In his best moments, Burckhardt knew better: "It is our task [the historian's] simply to observe and describe objectively the various forces as they appeared side by side or one after another." He was wise, by this same rule, to reject the doctrine of progress and even wiser to concentrate upon what he could be most "magnanimous" about, namely cultural history. As we can see even in these fragments, the esthetic part of life is what makes him vibrate and ring true. On genius and art he is passionate and impeccable, and when he has to describe the social and political conditions of high culture, his zeal makes him an admirable historian. The rise of the sixteenth century, the work of Camoëns, the soul of Loyola, inspire him to great passages even in lecture notes. But when the subject is man's life unlighted by "mighty, expressive people," or worse, when it is darkened by bald political necessity, Burckhardt loses interest and wanders distressingly. The portrait of Queen Elizabeth is unrecognizable, and of her father the apprehensive foreseer of dictatorship can write:

A mixture rare among princes: Henry VIII is at once a lout and a devil. Yet in the face of terrible special forces which could break forth again out of the dark it can be highly desirable for the general welfare that one person wield the rod. And such a person can then behave as he pleases, circumstances permitting.

In reading these notes, then, allowance must be made for Burckhardt's unpolitical nature and mode of life: two rooms over a grocer's shop in Basel may be the right platform for metaphysics as it was for art history, but—genius apart—it was not a setting conducive to just views of the worldly world, past or present. Nor must Burckhardt be judged with finality on the basis of this book alone, both because it is fragmentary and because the translation is less than adequate. I have not collated it with the German original, but it is easy to detect crudities and to note that several of the passages in French and Latin are followed by erroneous translations, which culminate in the egregious rendering of *in anima vili* as "in a spirit of wickedness."

The limitations of Burckhardt carry the mind back to the concluding essay in Mr. Trevor-Roper's collection, "Arnold Toynbee's Millennium." It is a magnificent piece of textual criticism, which has shocked many readers (and will, I hope, shock many more) by its proofs of Toynbee's literal messianic pretensions, feebly disguised as historical revelations. The accusation is grave, but so is the offense; and a large part of the offense is chargeable as well to the ruling intellectuals of the day who, whether in Toynbee or in Burckhardt, in Spengler or in Marx, find a pseudo-historical justification for their culpable love of doom. Mr. Trevor-Roper uses an even stronger word and calls it hateful:

> For Toynbee does not only utter false arguments and dogmatic statements, calling them 'scientific' and 'empirical'; he does not only preach a gospel of deliberate obscurantism; he seems to undermine our will, welcome our defeat, gloat over the extinction of our civilisation, not because he supports the form of civilisation which threatens us, but because he is animated by what we can only call a masochistic desire to be conquered. If Hitler or Stalin rejoiced in the prospect of destroying the West, theirs at least was a crude, intelligible rejoicing. They smacked their lips because they looked for plunder. Toynbee has no such clear interest in supporting a conqueror. He hungers spiritually not for this or that conquest but for our defeat. . . . Like many intellectuals, Toynbee seems fascinated by brute power and longs to surrender to it. And since he identifies himself with the History of the world, . . . he wants the whole world to surrender to it too.

There is, of course, no such thing as the Voice of History; but the voice of an historian who can think otherwise than obsessively is at all times inspiriting, for it speaks in the knowledge that nothing in human affairs is cut-and-dried and "scientifically" predictable, nothing final, inevitable, and irresistible. For—to leave Mr. Trevor-Roper his own last words—"the irresistible is very often merely that which has not been resisted."

—May 1958

Thinking What We Are Doing

W. H. AUDEN

On Hannah Arendt's *The Human Condition*

THE NORMAL CONSEQUENCE of having read a book with admiration and enjoyment is a desire that others should share one's feelings. There are, however, if I can judge from myself, occasional exceptions to this rule. Every now and then, I come across a book which gives me the impression of having been especially written for me. In the case of a work of art, the author seems to have created a world for which I have been waiting all my life; in the case of a "think" book, it seems to answer precisely those questions which I have been putting to myself. My attitude toward such a book, therefore, is one of jealous possessiveness. I don't want anybody else to read it; I want to keep it all to myself. Miss Hannah Arendt's *The Human Condition* belongs to this small and select class; the only other member which, like hers, is concerned with historical-political matters, is Rosenstock-Hussey's *Out of Revolution*.

Possessiveness is, of course, an immoral emotion and, if the following remarks misrepresent or fail to do justice to Miss Arendt, at least they have been a moral discipline for me.

Nobody, I fancy, feels "happy" about the age in which we live or the future which even the living may know before they die. At all times in history men have felt anxious about their own fate or the fate of their class or community, but there has seldom been a time, I believe, when the present and future of the whole human endeavor on this earth has seemed questionable to so many people.

Miss Arendt is not, of course, so foolish or presumptuous as to offer saving solutions. She merely asks us to think what we are doing which we can never manage unless we can first agree about the meaning of the words we think with, which, in its turn, requires that we become aware of what these words have meant in the past.

It would not be inaccurate, I believe, to call *The Human Condition* an essay in Etymology, a re-examination of what we think we mean, what we actually mean and what we ought to mean when we use such words as nature, world, labor, work, action, private, public, social, political, etc.

Consequently, the best way to approach it might be by discussing some of its definitions as if it were a dictionary.

Nature

MAN IS PART of nature in that he is a biological organism subject, like all other creatures, to the laws of nature and the temporal cycle of generation. From the point of view of nature, man has no history, only the proto-history of the evolutionary processes by which the human species came into being. For nature, every man is an anonymous member of his species, identical with every other, or, at most, divisible into male and female. For nature, therefore, so long as the human species exists, there is no such thing as death, only life, and terms like growth and decay have no meaning, for these are only relevant to individuals of whom nature knows nothing. This natural biological man is, like some but not all animals, *social*—the survival of this species requires that its members associate constantly with each other—and he is a *laborer*. Miss Arendt defines as *labor*, any behaviour which is imposed by the need to survive. Thus, a tiger hunting its prey, can be said to be laboring. Man, however, is the laboring animal par excellence—the bee runs him pretty close—firstly because his particular needs and his numbers require that he spend a much greater part of his time in acquiring or producing what he needs to survive, and secondly, because he seems to be endowed with both the capacity and the instinct to produce a surplus over and above his immediate needs of consumption.

Man the laboring animal does not act; he exhibits human behaviour, the goal of which is not a matter of personal decision, dictated by the natural instinct to survive and propagate life. His motive, if the word can properly be used at all, is pleasure, or rather the avoidance of pain. Though he is social, the experiences of the laboring animal are essentially *private* and subjective. What he experiences are the unshareable experiences of the body. He needs the presence of his fellows not as persons but as bodies, another set of muscles, a fertile member of the opposite sex.

To man the laboring animal, past and future have no meaning. All that is temporally real to him is the present point on the biological cycle. For this reason he has no need of *speech*. If he uses words, he uses them as bees use dance-movements, as a code for conveying necessary information.

Lastly, man the laboring animal does not and cannot ask what his behaviour means for life as life is something given, not made. It is like asking whether we live to eat or eat to live.

World

IN ADDITION to being a member of the human species, every man is, what no other animal is, a mortal individual, aware that, though the race may be immortal, he and every other human individual must die.

At the same time he is aware—or was aware until modern science has made him doubt the evidence of his senses—that the realm of nature is made up not only of mortal creatures, but also of things, the earth, the ocean, the sun, moon and stars, which are always there.

Out of this double awareness, of human mortality and the everlastingness of things, arises the desire and hope of transcending the cycle of natural birth and death by *making* a *world* of things which endure and in which, therefore, man can always be at home.

As Miss Arendt says:

> Birth and death presuppose a world which is not in constant movement, but whose durability and relative permanence make appearance and disappearance possible, which existed before any one individual appeared into it and will survive his eventual departure. Without a world into which men are born and from which they die, there would be nothing but changeless eternal recurrence, the deathless everlastingness of the human as of all other animal species.

The mortal individual who is man the maker is not social, that is, for the process of fabrication he requires the presence, not of human beings, but of the various materials out of which he fashions a world. The objects, he makes, on the other hand, require the existence of a public community of human beings to use them and enjoy them. The fabricated world has an objective reality which is lacking in both human behaviour and human action.

> Against the subjectivity of men stands the objectivity of the man-made world rather than the sublime indifference of an untouched nature. . . .

Only we who have erected the objectivity of a world of our own from what nature gives us, who have built it into the environment of nature so that we are protected from her, can look upon nature as something "objective." Without a world between man and nature, there is eternal movement but no objectivity.

What distinguishes working from laboring is that the results of labor are immediately consumed by the laborer, while the products of work, whether use-objects like tools or enjoyment-objects like works of art, once they are completed, persist as they are unchanged and, ideally, for ever. A tool may wear out or be replaced by a better one, but this is an accident, while the notion of a loaf of bread that lasts for ever is absurd; if it is not consumed, it is worthless.

The attitude of the worker or maker towards time, therefore, is quite different from that of the laborer. The past and future have a meaning for him but in a special way. What he assumes is that the future will be like the past; time for the maker, that is, has neither the cyclical motion of nature, nor the unilinear irreversible flow of history—like space it does not move but is there. All he knows about time is that it takes time to make an object so that he can only define it to himself as that which must not be wasted.

While the laborer always remains the servant of nature upon whose fertility his survival ultimately depends, the worker regards nature as raw material which has no value until he confers value upon it by transforming it into a world of objects.

To the degree that these objects have enjoyment value as well as use value, they may be said to be forms of speech. A beautiful temple "addresses" us no less than a beautiful poem. But it is the thing that speaks not its maker. While the laborer cannot even ask the question "what does life mean," the worker can say "life itself is meaningless but it provides the opportunity for making a meaningful world." He does not desire glory for himself but immortality for the things made with his hands.

Action

IN ADDITION to being a member of the human species, subject to natural necessity, and a mortal individual who can transform mortal life into immortal objects, every man is a unique person. Though all must die, the birth of every human being marks the beginning of the existence of a being the like of whom never existed before and will never exist again. To be a person is to be able to say "I" and to have a biography of one's own, and the sum of all human biographies constitutes what we call history. While the laborer may require the society of other members of his kind and the worker the existence of others to use or enjoy his works, only the person requires a *public* realm of other persons to whom through his *actions* he discloses who he is. For human action, as distinct from human behaviour, speech is essential, the means by which the person identifies who he is, what he is doing, has done, and intends to do.

Labor is recurrent, work comes to an end when it has completed its task (which can be undone), but action is unpredictable, unrepeatable and irretrievable. The name of the actor, even the act itself, may be forgotten, but it will affect the actions of others till the end of time. Action tends to be as boundless as the freedom in which it is grounded and would destroy us if we did not voluntarily set limits to what we do. The three principal limitations are law, forgiveness and promises. By laws we establish a common agreement to prohibit certain actions and to punish offenders rather than take unlimited vengeance. By forgiveness we dismiss an error for the sake of the person who committed it. In an admirable sentence, Miss Arendt indicates the relation between law and forgiveness:

> Men are unable to forgive what they cannot punish, and they are unable to punish what has turned out to be unforgivable.

By promises we set a bound to our actions in the unknown future. Promises are always specific, valid for an agreed purpose; a general promise like saying "I promise to be good" is meaningless.

IN HER HISTORICAL REVIEW of these notions, Miss Arendt starts with the Greeks.

It is hard to say which is the most astonishing, the Greek pride which identified the human with the human person who acts out of freedom not necessity and relegated all that men do with their bodies or their hands, all that is necessary or useful to a sub-human status, or the Greek clearsightedness which saw exactly what, in their age, such a premise must involve. The truly human person can only exist if there are semi- or sub-human beings who will supply his necessities and build his world for him. But no human beings exist who will do this of their own free will; they must be compelled. The necessary pre-political condition for the free community of persons is violence and slavery. It is to their credit that the Greeks never pretended, as some later upholders of slavery have done, that certain kinds of human beings are happier as slaves than they would be as free men; on the contrary, they argued that a slave must be a base fellow because he did not kill himself rather than be enslaved.

Life in the Greek city-state was divided, therefore, into two realms, the private realm of the household, which its master ruled by force, and in which not only the business of rearing a family but also all the activities we call economic were carried on, and the public realm of politics in which the free citizen disclosed himself to his peers by speech and action and strove to win glory.

Miss Arendt is more reticent than, perhaps, she should be, about what actually went on in this public realm of the Greeks. My knowledge of Greek history is very limited, but the picture given by Thucydides is not, to my mind, very alluring. Miss Arendt may be right when she deplores Plato's attempt to eliminate the freedom of the public realm and turn politics into a form of craftsmanship, but the way in which the Greeks had used their freedom makes it understandable. They realized that the great political virtue was moderation and the great political vice *hubris*, but how their ideal man who, thanks to the labor of others, was freed from all natural necessity could escape the temptation to hubris, it is hard to imagine, for he was not a god but a mortal man leading something very like the life of a god. As Miss Arendt says:

> The price of absolute freedom from necessity is, in a sense, life itself, or rather the substitution of vicarious life for real life . . . for mortals the easy life of the gods would be a lifeless life.

To make a vicarious life real, to prevent it being meaningless and boring, the free Greek citizen had to seek to make it as extraordinary and daring as possible, and politics conducted thus are apt to end in disaster.

Miss Arendt's definition of political power, as distinct from violence or strength, is admirable, but I do not think the Greeks possessed it.

> Power is actualised only where word and deed have not parted company, where words are not empty and deeds not brutal, where words are not used to veil intentions but to disclose realities, and deeds are not used to violate and destroy, but to establish relations and create new realities.

If the Greeks made the mistake of attempting to split up the threefold nature of man, to assign his laboring body to one class of men, his working hands to another, and his active personality to a third, they were perfectly correct to value action so highly. While someone who neither labors nor works ceases to be human, it is in personal action, not in laboring to live or working to make a world, that a man becomes himself and gives meaning to his existence. A society dominated by the modes of thought proper to work, as was the mercantile society at the beginning of the nineteenth century, loses its *raison d'être.*

> While only fabrication with its instrumentality is capable of building a world, this same world becomes as worthless as the employed materials, a mere means to further ends, if the standards which governed its coming into being are permitted to rule after its establishment.

Our own modern technological society, whether it call itself capitalist or communist, is dominated by the modes of thought proper to labor; its members consider what ever they do primarily as a way to sustain their own lives and those of their families—the artist is virtually the only worker left—and their value to society is conceived in terms, not of what each produces but of his function in the collective productive process. So long as these standards prevail, the more successful our society becomes in achieving its goal—a mastery over natural necessity which will abolish the necessity for labor—the more meaningless it will get. Technology has already advanced to the point where it is possible to conceive of a society in which production has become automatic and the only necessity left to men is consumption. The land of Cockagne, so charming as a wish-dream, would be less charming in reality.

> The danger is that such a society, dazzled by the abundance of its growing fertility and caught in the smooth functioning of a never-ending process would no longer be able to recognise its own futility—the futility of a life which does not fix or realise itself in any permanent object which endures after its labor is past. . . . What we are confronted with is the prospect of a society of laborers without labor, that is, without the only activity left to them. Surely, nothing could be worse. . . . The spare time of the *animal laborans* is never spent in anything but consumption, and the more time left to him, the greedier and more craving his appetites.

The significance of the words *private* and *public* in the life of the modern nation state are almost the reverse of their significance in the Greek *polis.*

Politically, even in a democracy, we are divided, like the Greek household, into rulers and the ruled. The rulers, it is true, are not persons, but officials and the obedience of the ruled is secured less by naked violence than by the anonymous pressure of social conformity, but "the rule by nobody is not necessarily no rule: it may indeed, under certain circumstances, turn out to be one of the cruellest and most tyrannical versions."

Public Life, in the Greek sense, has been replaced by social life, that is to say, the private activity of earning one's bread is now carried on in public.

What a modern man thinks of as the realm where he is free to be himself and to disclose himself to others, is what he calls his private or personal life, that is to say, the nearest modern equivalent to the public realm of the Greeks is the intimate realm, and we have a noun, unknown to the Greeks, *the Public,* that curious body made up, as Kierkegaard said, of people at moments when they are not themselves.

The modern equivalent to the Greek man of action is the scientist who can say, like Werner Von Braun—"Basic research is when I am doing what I don't know what I'm doing," and the historical consequence of their deeds has been the alienation of man, not from himself, but from his world.

> What is new is not that things exist of which we cannot form an image . . . but that the material things we see and represent and against which we had measured immaterial things for which we can form no images should likewise be "unimaginable for however we think it is wrong; not perhaps quite as meaningless as a triangular circle, but much more so than a winged lion."
>
> What men now have in common is not the world but the structure of their minds, and this they cannot have in common, strictly speaking; their faculty of reasoning can only happen to be the same in everybody.

> At first sight it might seem logical to hand over the government of society to the scientists, but the only kind of action they understand is action into nature; with the human being they can only deal in so far as he is natural and impersonal.

> The reason why it may be wise to distrust the political judgment of scientists qua scientists is that they move in a world where speech has lost its power.

I hope that these remarks and quotations give a faint idea of the richness and fascination of *The Human Condition.* Let me end with one final epigram by Miss Arendt which we may, if we are unlucky, have cause to remember.

> It is far easier to act under conditions of tyranny than it is to think.

—September 1958

The Esthetic Society

Jacques Barzun

On George Sansom's *A History of Japan to 1334*

IT IS RECEIVED DOCTRINE that of the far eastern civilizations the one a westerner should grow fond of and admire is China's, not Japan's. For Japan would be nothing without China; the Japanese are but clever imitators who, just as they make cheaper and smaller toothbrushes and cameras than the west, once made a cheaper and smaller Buddhist and Confucian society than the great prototype, China.

By the accident of friendship, thirty years ago, I was introduced to Japanese art and literature by someone who knew them as a native and a student, so that ever since I have been among those condemned by the received doctrine—an admirer of Japanese culture, though a critical and unscholarly admirer, but one who could never work up much enthusiasm for the thought and artifacts of China.

Without being either militant or defensive about my deplorable upbringing in these matters, I was sustained by George Sansom's résumé of Japanese cultural history and by listening to some of his lectures at Columbia University a dozen years ago. Now that he has begun to publish the great history of Japan which he has been working on for many years, and of which the present volume takes us to the year 1334, I am confirmed in the suspicion that the received doctrine is but another of those tiresome snobberies with which narrow scholars try to fill a certain passional void. What should become doctrine is that there is no "ought" about cultural sympathies. The argument among diverse preferences can go on, but only about what is found here or there which attracts the student or observer.

What Sir George establishes about the first two great periods of his chosen span is that the Japanese, though they have "always been sensitive to new impressions . . . have never in their history—so long as they had freedom—surrendered the inmost stronghold of their own tradition." The influence of Confucian and Buddhist beliefs and of the Chinese language and literature unquestionably started the Japanese on the road to what is called civilization, that is, the complication of living arrangements and of consciousness about them. But great as this impetus was, it did not make of Japan a cultural colony of China. The Chinese administrative system, though imitated, did not really fit and take hold in Japan, and by the year 900—a bare 250 years after the reforms which brought in Chinese ways—Japan was once more itself, independent of its sources, and ready for a great artistic flowering, on the eve of political decay and a new start under feudalism.

The dates and the descriptive terms inevitably suggest parallels with western European history. Our author warns us how deceiving these may be, but hazards them himself from time to time. It is surely permissible to note how much more quickly than Europe Japan passed from barbarism to literacy, and how curious it is that Japanese feudalism should have come after, not before, a period of peace, high art, urban life, and would-be centralized monarchy. In reading this first of Sir George's three volumes, the student of western history has the impression of seeing a film backward and absurdly cut and condensed.

He sees, for instance, the Japanese receiving from China, through Korea, the results of bronze culture about 200 B.C.; then a mere seven and a half centuries later, Buddhism and the rise of a city culture; and within another five centuries the perfection of a unique society, which functioned and flourished on the principle of artistic taste—an esthetic society. In western Europe the span between the Bronze Age and (say) the Italian Renaissance is three times as long, and it embraces at least two intermediate civilizations, the Greek and the Roman; so that although Greece and the Eastern Mediterranean had reached a high point well before Japan emerged from barbarism, western Europe, which was to reawaken Japan in the middle of the nineteenth century, was culturally inchoate by the year 1000, when the Lady Murasaki was writing with the exquisiteness, almost the preciosity, and certainly the melancholy of a Decadent, her romance of Prince Genji.

It is undoubtedly this esthetic quality, which in Japan has endured for another millennium, that nowadays attracts so many Americans—the esthetic allied to ritual and confined to the small scale. For these are the opposite of our own dominant characteristics and, according to temperament, we find these features of Japanese civilization quaint, restful, delicate, judicious, humane. We tend to think of a culture the way we do of another's personality: as if it were wholly the result of deliberate choice, and as if its desirables were a net addition to whatever we prize in our own habits and circumstances. It is in truth the definition of Utopianism that we shall have in the future state all we value in ours *plus* all that the imagined rearrangement is designed to provide. And in the present love of the East, gratified among Americans by travel and reading and the indulgence of self-contempt, the main motive is Utopian.

To this, Japanese history is a good corrective. I say a corrective and not a refutation. Though they lose their quaintness as well as their miniature perfection, the Japanese remain after study one of the remarkable peoples of history. Their rapid, many-sided development is a magnificent and dramatic tale, which affords the westerner numerous occasions for curious or fruitful speculation, and—what is pertinent to our own malaise—good reasons for being a little more reconciled to our tradition than has lately been fashionable. In particular, Japanese history throws light on the workings of any esthetic society such as many westerners are now trying hard to substitute for the practical and political "materialistic" society they affect to despise.

The Heian world established at Kyoto in 794 was very small—perhaps five thousand people. It was dominated by the Fujiwara family, whose strength was based on wealth, intrigue, and the ability to provide daughters who could marry into the imperial family and thus provide a link with the traditional source of authority. It was in the name of the powerless Emperor that the Kampaku or regent ruled. What he ruled was the court, the heads of the provincial clans, and some Buddhist monks, for centralized government was at this period purely theoretical.

Moreover, the most and the best that political theory could provide was forms—ritual—the way a governor's report should be sealed and signed, not what it should tell the central authority about the state of the local rice fields. The very bases of Fujiwara power were, so to speak, accidental and unexplained, even after they had subsisted for centuries. The Japanese had government by habit, not by reason. At first sight, this seems excellent, or at any rate superior to the kind Europe knows, in which reason or argument is always threatening to topple authority. But one must ask what the habits were that maintained this relative stability for a few thousand men and women led by one clan among the rest.

The people at large, who are not heard from for centuries, were evidently passive under the rule of religion, native Shinto or Buddhist. Inured to poverty and slavery, they toiled on without visible aspirations and, except on the northern and western borders, without fear of violence and war. The local magnates strove only to make their lands tax-exempt, until the central government, lacking the means to carry on its limited business and to reward its favorites, passed into other hands; first, those of a new unlettered wealthy class, then those of military chieftains to whom impoverished freemen had "commended" themselves in feudal fashion.

Meanwhile, the cultivated aristocracy flourished and enjoyed itself, peaceably enough, in the usual occupations of aristocracies—gossip and intrigue, punctilio and precedence, self-adornment and society, verse, games, sports, and love-making. Because the Heian court life shows us the perfection of monarchial aristocracy, and shows it on a small scale, we perceive suddenly that the real objection to that life is not its injustice or even its frivolity, but its childishness. The connection between idleness and promiscuous love-making is obvious, but there may be an unsuspected connection between complete sexual freedom and the childishness which can be so solemn about games and etiquette. Children are natural ritualists and only gradually gain confidence in their power to vary the mode of encompassing their ends; they are slow to become "secular." And similarly, the art of a court tends to remain a means of local communication about the minutiae of formalized existence. Neither from Versailles nor from Kyoto should one expect the elements of what Goethe called world literature, though the (as it were) straitened circumstances of life at those courts can produce in art a sharpness of vision and of expression not elsewhere obtained: we reap *La Princesse de Clèves* and the *Tale of Genji*, the memoirs of Saint-Simon and the Pillow-book of Sei Shonagon.

It will not do, of course, to form an image of a society merely from its reflection in literature; there is always a bias in art, that of elegance, which is far more distorting than the bias of opinion in a historian. Yet as Sir George Sansom portrays it in its fullness, the Heian society was in fact governed neither by laws nor by a rule of conduct, but by a rule of taste. And taste means an avidity for things to taste. To this the Confucian critic of the period, Kiyotsura, attributes the growing poverty of the nation: "Each day brought a change in costume, each month a change in fashion. Bedrooms and nightdresses were more beautiful, banquets and dancing more frequent, than ever before. In this way half the entire revenue was expended. And so the treasury became empty and taxes were increased."

He might have added that dictators, even mild ones like the Fujiwara, maintain themselves by gifts and ostentation, which are costly. New Buddhist temples had to be built and adorned, to show one's taste and save one's soul; new lands had to be made into sho-en, that is, manors immune from taxes, to enlist support or stave off opposition. In short, taste, like intrigue, is voracious, and neither exactly strengthens the conscience of rulers; a government of artists and scholars such as Japan developed in its first golden age has nothing to recommend it *as a government*. The qualities for which we may admire it in retrospect, a little like the great age of Athens, are qualities that are irrelevant and perhaps antithetical to government as such—splendor, the refinement of manners, the ability to turn a phrase or cap a quotation, the building of useless temples to the detriment of agriculture, trade, and national safety—all things that are not the business of government. Beautiful in themselves, they spoil for the political eye the true esthetic of governing, as would garlands of roses around the chimney of a locomotive.

How the story "comes out" in Japanese history is something I leave to the more than competent hands of Sir George Sansom. In this first volume he manages to combine a predominantly topical treatment with a clear sense of chronology, and he neglects no aspect of life or its conditions. He is admirable on geography and climate, on the general and the personal aspects of politics, on economics and technology, on diplomacy and war. His knowledge of the cultural evolution is of course unrivalled, which may account for a somewhat clumsy explanation of the differences between Buddhism and Confucianism: he knows too much to make things clear to the newcomer. But after a few pages he regains his exemplary lucidity and never falters to the end.

Again, among his illuminating comparisons with familiar events of western history, he makes one extraordinary statement, which can only be classified in the *genus* blunder, and in these five hundred pages it is, I imagine, unique. Speaking of the promptness with which the Japanese threw off Chinese taste in literature, Sir George asserts that the literary use of the vernacular occurred much sooner than in Europe, in proof of which he says: "French verse began to contend with Latin in the time of Ronsard and the Pléiade, some of whom still wrote only in Greek or Latin. Even *Paradise Lost* might have been written in Latin and on the Continent Milton was known not as a master of English but as a Latin pamphleteer." The nature of a blunder is that its aberration is clear to the perpetrator as soon as it is brought to his attention: the Song of Roland, in the vernacular like many other poems of all genres, antedates Ronsard by four centuries. The Pléiade of Ronsard were *all* dedicated to the enrichment of the French tongue; the historian's error must be due to a confusion with the little Pléiad fifty years later, a group of *petits-maîtres* who made the most of their skill at writing Latin verse.

As for Milton, the point would seem to be rather that *Paradise Lost* was *not* written in Latin and that this was probably due to its coming a century after the birth of Shakespeare, when a good many dozens of English writers had molded the vernacular to their needs. There was also a rather famous translation of the Bible, fifty years before *Paradise Lost,* which may have kept Milton from making his epic as generally unintelligible as the despatches he wrote for Cromwell or the tracts he wrote against Salmasius.

But Sir George knows all this, and he never meant the opposite, except in his momentary zeal to make the important point of Japanese emancipation from Chinese models. What he tells us about this literary relation has implications worth pondering. The Japanese became civilized with the indispensable aid of the Chinese characters. The love of the Chinese classics and the faith in Chinese political science produced a class of Japanese scholars who acquired importance in their own government. But thanks to a general illiteracy and the exclusion of women from higher education, the native tongue retained its purity and strength. Soon it was found cumbrous to write the complex Chinese ideograms in order to spell Japanese, and the monosyllabic Chinese tongue seemed less and less congenial to the ear. A simplified syllabary was devised, permitting the Japanese to write the vernacular quickly and as quickly to abandon the use of Chinese for high art. The women led the way and it is notable that the two great masterpieces of the Heian period, *Genji* and the *Pillow-book,* are the work of women.

Add the fact that the nature of neither Chinese nor Japanese easily permitted the framing of precise abstractions, and you have the clue to many important differences between East and West. I have in mind the pictorialism of oriental thought, its absence of Intellect as we in the West understand it. The Japanese waka or short poem is not only, as Sir George says, limited to the expression of sentiment rather than fact, but it has neither means nor space to present a chain of ideas. It never moves from observation to conclusion; the observer merely hints a possible conclusion, usually the very generalized one of regret, sadness, futility, and the like. Anything like Wordsworth's famous Ode, or Shelley's, or Schiller's, lies outside the compass of the Japanese poet; and even the prose writer seems limited to imagism and analogical reasoning. This, at any rate, is what suggests itself to a sympathetic reader of the splendid anthology edited by T. W. DeBary and entitled *Sources of the Japanese Tradition.*

Whatever the expert judges may say on this point, it remains true that we in the West are not sufficiently grateful for the alphabet. Nor do we sufficiently take care of our extraordinarily flexible and precise prose. We wrongly suppose that it has always existed and is not an artifact to be kept in repair. We let the vocabulary be corrupted by the ignorant and the pretentious, and through laziness allow ourselves to be seduced into excesses of metaphor. And since the nineties we have gone wantonly imagist and Japanese, out of vague hostility to intellect and in disregard of our superior tongue. Perhaps the spectacle of the Japanese, struggling from the seventh century to the present with intractable means of self expression (alphabet reform is still a live issue in Tokyo) will awaken some westerners to the worth of the treasure in their grasp. In any event, the history of Japan as George Sansom spreads it out before us is an object of moral contemplation and a source of vicarious experience that will fully repay any thoughtful reader's attention. The author's prose is unassuming but manly and varied to suits its theme; the page is open and the type clear. Only the principal map, that of Japan, leaves something to be desired. Perhaps the publishers hope this will prompt you to go there and see for yourself.

—January 1959

"Apologies to the Iroquois"

W. H. AUDEN

On Edmund Wilson's *Apologies to the Iroquois*

MR. EDMUND WILSON is a specimen of that always rare and now almost extinct creature, the Intellectual Dandy. The generic name is paradoxical for, by definition, no dandy is like another; what they have in common is their unlikeness to anybody else. The Dandy is neither a conformist nor a rebel, for both these terms imply a concern for Public Opinion and the Dandy has none: on one occasion his views may coincide with those of the majority, on another with those of the minority, but in both cases the coincidence is accidental. The same is true of his interests. One of the ways in which an Intellectual Dandy can be recognized is by the unpredictability of his work; no knowledge of his previous books offers any clue as to what he will write next. Who, knowing Mr. Wilson as the author of *To the Finland Station, Classics and Commercials, Memoirs of Hecate County,* and a study of *The Dead Sea Scrolls,* could have predicted that he would become the author of *Apologies to the Iroquois?* By definition, a Dandy can have no followers: the only influence he can have on others is as an example of what it means to be oneself. It is impossible to imagine a "Wilson School" of writers.

A digression. Mr. Wilson is a bit of an anglophobe. Though, naturally, I do not share his feelings, I can understand them. It may take greater moral courage to become a Dandy in the United States than in England; nevertheless, I believe it is easier. British intellectual society is less boring, more intelligent and infinitely more charming than its American counterpart, which makes its collective influence much more dangerous to the individual—to resist seems rather piggy. Further, thanks to the physical size of this country, it is much easier here, if one wishes to be alone, to be left alone (in England, all one's intellectual relatives live within calling distance, and they keep dropping in).

Though the credit for making it financially possible for Mr. Wilson to write *Apologies to the Iroquois* belongs to *The New Yorker*—this magazine also printed Mr. Joseph Mitchell's 1949 study, *The Mohawks in High Steel,* which Mr. Wilson reprints as a prelude to his own—the conception and execution of the book are, clearly, the author's. For the word *apologies* in his title, Mr. Wilson has, I believe, two meanings in mind. First, he feels that he owes the Iroquois a personal apology for not having heard of their existence before June 1957, despite the fact that a house which had belonged to his family since the eighteenth century stood on the borders of their main reservation. To this personal apology, I am sure the Iroquois would reply: "We prefer White people who ignore us to those, like the tourists in New Mexico, who regard us as zoological curiosities to photograph and buy fake souvenirs from. As for those Whites who 'take us up' and deny their own race and culture because they hate themselves, we despise them and do not trust them. We welcome your interest because we can see that you are proud of being what you are, a Yankee from a long established Presbyterian stock."

Secondly, as a member of the white race, Mr. Wilson wishes to apologize for its behavior to the Indians from the time it first arrived on this continent down to the present day. What has been, and still is, unforgivable about us is not our criminal record, the brutalities and treacheries by which we stole their land—every invader in history has done likewise—but our cultural conceit, our conviction that any individual or society that does not share our cultural habits is morally and mentally deficient—it makes no difference if the habit in question is monogamy or a liking for ice cream.

The period of unabashed white exploitation of the Indian is over: what the Ogden Land Company could do in 1838 could not be done today.

> It was possible for the agents of the land company—resorting, if necessary, to liquor . . . to get the signature of some of the chiefs by bribery; others, who were ill, were induced to sign without knowing what they were signing; in other more difficult cases, the victim was made drunk in a tavern and engaged in conversation while, without his being aware of it, his hand was guided to make its mark. They also set up bogus chiefs. "The Company," according to Arthur Parker, "was reduced to the necessity of taking debauched Indians to Buffalo and penning them in an inn, where they were 'elected and declared chiefs' by company agents, and then for pay forced to sign the treaty." As a last resort, the agents forged signatures.

But the cultural conceit still remains, the feeling that an Indian ought to become a "good" American who loves private property, money, and gracious

living, American style. The Indians seem to have resisted "integration" remarkably well but not, alas, completely. According to Mr. Mitchell, the Mohawks, while they can reject our dependence upon running water and
plumbing, have become hopelessly addicted to the radio. I find it immensely
depressing that when unmechanized societies, whether Indians or Greek peasants, come into contact with ours, the one aspect of ours which none of them,
but *none*, can resist is that which, to me, is the most intolerable: its hatred of
silence—noise-makers have replaced liquor as our most potent agent of corruption.

In *Apologies to the Iroquois*, Mr. Wilson plays two roles. Part of the time
he is the *engagé* journalist, intent upon arousing public conscience against a
kind of tyranny which, today, threatens not only the Indians but every private
citizen, the tyranny of the Big Executive; the rest of the time he writes as a historian and anthropologist, the friendly but detached observer of the Iroquois
in a time of ferment and change.

The particular examples of executive tyranny to which he draws our attention are two: the Kinzua Dam Project, a Federal baby, and the Niagara Power
Project, a pet infant of Mr. Robert Moses. Both involve Indian reservations;
the first would flood four-fifths of a reservation belonging to the Senecas, the
second a quarter of one belonging to the Tuscaroras. Of the two, the Federal
project is the more disgraceful because, according to two of the best hydraulic
engineers in the country, there is a more efficient and cheaper way of controlling flood in the Allegheny basin, which is the ostensible purpose of the dam.
In fact, the Project

has merely served as a pretext for putting through at the public expense a
particularly costly contrivance intended to serve the interests of a group of
industrialists in Pittsburgh, who now appear as its principal advocates.
Though Pittsburgh itself is not seriously in danger from the flooding of the
upper Allegheny, certain Pittsburgh manufacturers have their reasons for
wanting the river diluted at the seasons when it is running low. The sul-
phurous drainage from the coal mines is from their point of view deleterious because it ruins their boilers by rusting them. . . . Mr. O'Neill, on behalf
of the Indians, contends that industrial pollution could be reduced by the
industrialists themselves at a cost of three or four hundred thousand dollars. (The dam will cost one hundred and fifty million.)

In resisting disappropriation, the Iroquois, ironically enough, are in a legally
stronger position than they would have been had they been Whites, for they
can appeal to two treaties made with them by the U.S. Government, the

Treaty of Fort Stanwix (1784) and the Pickering Treaty (1794). By the terms of these treaties, the Iroquois were granted their land in perpetuity and in common ownership; that is to say, none of the land could be bought from an Indian individually without the consent of his legal chief and the consent of the Federal Government. (As one might expect, the question of who is or was his *legal* chief is a lawyer's paradise.)

In the case of the Kinzua Dam, the future of the Senecas looks dark for, though President Eisenhower vetoed the Appropriation Bill last September, his veto was overridden both in the House and in the Senate.

In their battle with Mr. Moses over the Niagara Power Project, however, they have triumphed for, last February, the Federal Power Commission, by a 3–2 vote, decided in their favor, saying: "We regret that we have not been able to reach any other solution, but we cannot permit our personal views of what is desirable but must administer the laws as passed by Congress and as interpreted by the courts." This decision will delight everyone except Mr. Moses and those like him who know so much better than we do what is good for us. Indian or White, we can all recognize our common enemy by his tone of voice during negotiation:

> While we understand your reluctance to part with the land, we cannot delay longer. We are carrying out an urgent project of vital public importance under double mandate of State and Federal law, and in accordance with a Federal license. . . . It is high time for expeditious negotiation if you are in a mood to negotiate. The advantages to your Nation of prompt, friendly agreement on the generous terms the authority offers cannot be overstated. We hope you will decide to proceed in this spirit, but we must go ahead in any event;

and by his tantrums when his will is crossed:

> We have been jackassed from court to court and judge to judge, and are faced with the prospect of more litigation and further delays, postponement of permanent financing and perhaps stoppage of work. . . . How our democratic system can survive such stultifying domestic weakness, incompetence and ineptitude in the ruthless, world-wide competition with other systems of government more incisive and less tolerant of obstruction, is more than I can figure out.

Mr. Wilson's first encounter with the Iroquois was in June of 1957. Events have been moving so rapidly since then that, had he written his book in 1958, it would already, he says, be out of date.

The Iroquois is the name of a confederation of six Indian nations, the Mohawks, the Senecas, the Onondagas, the Oneidas, the Cayugas and the Tuscaroras. The first five of these formed their alliance in 1570; the Tuscaroras applied for membership after they had been driven out of South Carolina in 1722. It is possible that Benjamin Franklin was influenced by their political structure in framing the Constitution with its balance of Federal and States rights. Though no action can be taken without the unanimous consent of all six nations, the Onondagas rank first. The Senecas seem to be the most intelligent, the least hostile to Whites, and the most drunken. Each nation was divided into clans named after totem animals, and marriage within a clan was forbidden. The children of a marriage belonged to the wife's clan, and the wife's brother was responsible for them. Each clan had a clan mother who chose its chief. With the passage of time, however, other kinds of chiefs have appeared. Those Iroquois who lived in French Canada adopted the system of hereditary chiefs. Some of the Senecas formed a republic with a governing Council elected by universal manhood suffrage, and both the American and Canadian governments have tried to install elective chiefs who, in practice, seem to have been government stooges.

During the War of Independence most of the Iroquois sided with the British, but, after it was over, the American government forgave them, and their reservations lie in both Canada and the United States along or near the St. Lawrence. Of the eighteen million acres originally allotted to them in this country, only seventy-eight thousand remain: the rest were stolen from them during the nineteenth century.

Recent years have seen the birth of a nationalist movement among the Iroquois. From the point of view of the American and Canadian governments—at their most benevolent—the Indians have been regarded as wards, i.e., children who have not yet reached the age of consent. From their own point of view, the Iroquois regard themselves as an independent people who are not living in the United States but in their own country and, therefore, cannot be liable to any duties which the United States government may demand of its own citizens.

So long as they remained on their reservations and the demands made by the State were small, this difference of opinion caused little trouble. But today, it does. Thanks to their extraordinary sense of balance and fearlessness of high places, the Iroquois have found an important place for themselves in our technological society: as steel construction workers on bridges and skyscrapers, the Indians are superior to the Whites. These jobs are highly paid, and it is not unnatural, perhaps, that the government should question their claim to be exempt from income tax because, by the original treaties, they were exempted from property taxes. Again, it is only recently that military service has been made compulsory. In the First World War, the Iroquois made their own declaration of war on Germany; in the Second they did not and many of them went to jail rather than obey an authority which they did not recognize. (Though given the vote in 1924, very few of them exercise their right.) During the last few years their feeling of national identity has grown much more intense and has already led to violence in Canada. As in the case of most nationalist movements, it is difficult to tell how much popular support the politically active minority command. It is a little disquieting to learn that one of their leaders, Mad Bear, had a schoolteacher arrested for criticizing the notion of hereditary chiefs, on the ground that all criticism was treason.

Nor does one feel quite happy about certain eschatological aspects of the movement which prophesy the mutual destruction of America and Russia to be followed by the day of the Red Man. Such prophecies are always accompanied by the expectation of the advent of the Messiah, and messianic hopes are not a healthy symptom in political life.

Mr. Wilson makes no prophecies about the future of Iroquois nationalism nor passes judgment; he is only concerned that we should recognize its existence as an historical fact which can no more be ignored than Arab or African nationalism.

The religious beliefs of the Iroquois vary: most of the Mohawks, for example, are Roman Catholics; most of the Tuscaroras, Protestants. Recently there has been some spread, particularly among the more ardent nationalists, of a curious cult called the Handsome Lake Religion. Handsome Lake (1735–1815) was for much of his life a drunkard and a ne'er-do-well. In 1799 he fell ill, began to see visions and presently delivered himself of The Good Message. The ethical side of this was sensible though not very original: treat children with kindness, don't be malicious, don't boast, don't get drunk, be hospitable, etc. More interesting was his conviction that the Indian can only be destroyed if he tries to imitate the white man. Among his visions was one of Paradise, a place of absolute happiness and unlimited berries. No white man could ever enter it, though George Washington was permitted to live in a fort just outside the gates. One of the reasons given for the white men's exclusion was that they had been responsible for the death of Jesus, of which the Indians were innocent.

Some of Mr. Wilson's most fascinating pages are devoted to describing tribal dances he attended. I hope it is not mere denseness on my part, but I cannot discover from his account whether these dance-oratorios have become mere social customs or dramas which imply no religious belief in those who sing and dance them, or whether they are genuine rites, so that no Indian who is a Christian, for example, or a freethinker, could conscientiously take part in them.

But from Mr. Wilson's descriptions, there seems to be no doubt about their aesthetic beauty and emotional impact.

> The switch in the wall was turned off, and the ceremony proper began. The room with its Corn Flakes had vanished: you were at once in a different world. The single beat of a rattle is heard in the sudden blackness like the striking of a gigantic match, and it is answered by other such flashes that make rippings of sound as startling as a large-scale electric spark. The first of the two chief singers cries "Wee yoh!" and the second "Yoh wee!" and the first of them now sets the rhythm for the rattles, which is picked up by the rest of the company. In this section the tempo is uniform, and it reminds one of the rapid jogging that is heard by the passengers on an express train. . . . In the second section, the rhythms of the rattles are different. While the first and second singers are introducing the couplets, the rattles are going so fast that they seem to weave a kind of veil or screen—a scratching almost visible on the darkness—that hangs before the lyric voices; but when the chorus takes up the theme, this changes to a slow heavy beat that has something of the pound of a march. The shift is extremely effective. When it occurs, this accompaniment of the rattles—contrary to our convention—does not quite coincide with the song and the chorus but always overlaps a little. The big shimmer of the solo begins before the pound of the chorus has ended; in a moment, you are given notice, a fresh song will be springing up. . . . In this section the animals assemble . . . and presently these creatures begin to speak, as they are mentioned pair by pair in the couplets. They are mimicked by one or more singers—who have had their parts assigned them—as the arrival of each pair is announced.

Though, as I said at the beginning of this article, I cannot imagine a Wilson "school" of writers, I would recommend any young prose writer to go to school with Mr. Wilson's prose. Plain prose is the opposite of Pure poetry: in poetry, language calls attention to itself as an end; in prose, language is a self-effacing means. The test of good prose is that the reader does not notice it any more than a man looking through a window at the landscape outside notices the glass; if he does, it means that the window is dirty.

The most famous of all dandies, Beau Brummell, made inconspicuous dress the height of elegance; by the same standard, Mr. Wilson is, in my opinion, one of the most elegant prose writers alive.

—FEBRUARY 1960

Not All Are O.O.O.

Jacques Barzun

On Eric Partridge's *Origins*

As a man grows older it is likely that the new books to which he forms a permanent attachment are reference books. An encyclopedic reader such as Shaw observed this in himself and on this point, I know, my friends Auden and Trilling report the same experience as I. Hand over to one of us a new Dictionary, "Companion," or Guide, and our eyes first light up and then turn dreamy: we have seized the volume and are off, arm in arm with the guide or companion; the addictionary weakness prevails: we have dropped out of the conversation and fallen into the deep trance of following alphabetized definitions, row on row, the army of unalterable law.

This is not so crabbed and fossilized as it sounds. It does not mean that one is incapable of enthusiasm for a new novel or book of poems. What it means is that it has taken forty or fifty years to pursue and possess the great works of world literature, to discover the no less great works that by accident and perversity only a few recognize, and to pick out from the confetti of one's own times the few precious pieces that define not so much one's mind or taste as one's direction. What more is one offered? In spite of all generous illusions to the contrary, it is not true that a masterpiece in every genre is published every seven days. Only a weekly reviewer believes that, and even he believes it only on the seventh day. From which it follows that in privileged lives, free from reviewer's cramp, the intensity of response to new fiction, new poetry, new philosophies, new criticism, and new histories cannot help being tempered with the years. In compensation, the judgment grows stronger, buttressed as it is by the great piles of octavos incorporated into one's fabric. To have a library of 25,000 volumes under one's belt is a sobering cargo, even if most of them are mere bulk. The eye of the seasoned reader, without being lackluster, is generally hooded, and the mind, if it could be seen, would betray as regards the last sweet published thing a daunting serenity.

Why then does it glow youthfully again at sight of a new reference book? There are two reasons: good reference books are rare, great reference books very rare; and the substance of the good and great in this kind is far denser and richer than that of most other books. To a mind already stocked with ideas, impressions, and systems, the matter of a work of reference gives both an accrual of ballast and a pair of wings. For the contents of such a book are solid and true, yet their variety and arrangement incite to a cosmic freedom. The very letters designating each volume of an encyclopedia are an invitation to dream accurately, to thread associated notions and compel them to form a meaning: "MARY to MUS" says volume 15 of the *Britannica* which I see across the room; what can it be made to tell me without even opening it? Mary, the Virgin, the Queen of Scots, the daughter of Henry VIII; and then the odd notion the French have of calling a double boiler a *bain-marie:* from the sublime (or at least the mighty) to the ridiculous—the ridiculous *mus* or mouse of Horace's *Poetics,* born of the mountains' travail to make a critical point. And beyond it a smaller thing than the mouse, the imaginary musculus or little mouse, which by its appearance of running under the skin gives its name to muscle, with its mixed connotations of strength, of (musclebound) stupidity, and of criminal (muscling in) violence—the whole a joy-ride on three detached syllables.

Well before the end, the great miracle of language has struck one afresh: its fluidity and power, its progress by error and invention, by awkward tongues, bad ears, and punning minds, its untraceable meanders and profound rationality, its idiomatic traps producing laughter, and its fitness for making inexplicable beauty. All this sweeps over one like a flood and one knows suddenly that one does not want (at least right now) to think the arid thoughts of fictional beings in predicaments standardized by plausibility or momentarily refreshed by implausibility. One wants rather to draw on the wide memory of vicarious lives and dormant thoughts by following evocative words to their sources—any words, the words of a dictionary.

I will not linger to explain how bad an "approved" dictionary can be for the purpose, if one also has literary sensibilities. I only state as a generality that bad reference books on any subject are marked by spottiness and mechanical judgment, and I pass on to the pleasant task of showing by an example how the virtues of a great work in the genre give knowledge and delight without exhausting itself or the reader.

Some months ago, Mr. Eric Partridge, the author of many books on language, completed and published in London the work that had engaged his mind for some time, his long-awaited *Origins.* For years, at Christmas, he used to send his correspondents a thick folded card on which was handsomely printed an English word, its ascendants and descendants, with terse comments and illustrations of usage. The word, it may be said in passing, was never a sentimental reminder of the season. "Yule" was left to the headline writers, who write what everybody reads and no man speaks. Mr. Partridge had a more humane intention. He was putting together for our benefit his second lexicon, an Etymological Dictionary of Modern English. This, with his well-known *Dictionary of Slang,* is sure to turn the name Partridge into a superior common noun, like Webster, Fowler, and Johnson. As we now say: "In a fit of pique he threw the Webster at his little brother," so our posterity will be saying: "I flew to California with my Partridge on my knee."

The work is indeed indispensable to anyone who reads and writes habitually, and even to those who simply like to know a little more about the connections of the words they use than is picked up from casual dealings with prose. I know that among the demagogues of modern stylistics it is fashionable to decry etymology. Unless you are an expert, they are quite sure, you will only be led astray by a little learning of origins. Concentrate on reproducing the usages you hear and never mind the roots. You will be truer to your mother tongue if you play the game of follow-my-leader in all questions of taste. The *living* language, as they never tire of saying, is the unconsidered speech of Tom, Dick, and Harry. In this game, the leader is your neighbor and you are his.

But it is equally true that if you want to murder this indulgent mother tongue and permanently muddle yourself and your hearer, the shortest way is to reproduce without choice or judgment the usages you hear. Follow the broadcasters and newspapermen and you will be doing your bit for confusion by saying *mitigate against* and *forbid from,* using *flaunt* for *flout* and *fortuitous* for *fortunate,* and comforting yourself with the idea that only the depraved palate bothers to distinguish between *masterly* and *masterful, momently* and *momentarily.*

Well, no one can or wants to control your lips and tongue, much less your mind, and Mr. Partridge's book will not of itself tell you what to say or which words to prefer. Fowler was there, doing it before him. But suppose one impulse toward the light of clear reason, one little desire to deviate into sense, and Partridge can supply it with wisdom while giving its host enjoyment. For the author of "Partridge" has studied and grouped the principal words of the language that belong together through meaning, and he has traced their roots and links. These interrelations you might, if unaided, guess correctly, wrongly, or not at all. The chief law of their being is unexpectedness, which makes reading about them an adventure in a wild garden. Thanks to his brilliant scheme of etymological clusters, Mr. Partridge was able to treat some 10,000 words in the short compass of 950 quarto pages. Take one of these, page 336, as an example of this admirable and illuminative compression: we start with languid, languish, etc. and learn that the group comes from the Latin *languere,* which means to be or feel faint. From this we go to laches, lax, re-lax, laxative, and through Old French *relaissier* to release, lease, and laisser faire, then to relish and leash, to delay and relay, to lash, lack, slack, lag and laggard, to slake and slag.

On each of these we are given from one to ten lines showing the many languages traversed by the many forms of the one word; we are told how, for example, "*Lack* and *lag* together bring us to the adj *slack,* whence the n and v *slack* with extn *slacken,* and the abstract n *slackness* and the loose, informal trousers known as *slacks. Slack,* loose (physically, mentally, morally), ME *slak,* is OE *slaec,* akin to OS *slak,* OHG *schlack, slah,* ON *slakr,* a group akin to ON *lakr,* deficient, MD *lac,* deficiency. MIr *lacc,* feeble, (as in para 14)—cf also Gr *lagaros,* slack (of animal's flanks), hollow, s *lagar-,* r lag-."

To be sure it takes a little familiarity with the abbreviations to read this travelogue with fluency. But the very stumbles add to the pleasure, for they may take us to Eg (Egypt), or Port (ugal), and not always north to those damp root cellars ON (Old Norse) and OHG (Old High German). Rarely, thanks to the lexicographer's tireless hunt, are we met by the emphatic symbol of negation: o.o.o., which means "of obscure origin." On the contrary, if we consider that the passage from fanciful and impressionistic etymology to the present high probability of truth has occupied little more than a century and a half, the modern scholar's capacity to follow a clear path around a wide circuit and, as it were, corral a multitude of words and ideas is astonishingly great. Since the beginnings in the Romantic period, the noting of origins has of course been vigilant and close (*not* "meticulous"; see below). Thus for the avatars of a proper name like Tammany, we have all the needful facts and need not resort to o.o.o. "Tammany, corruption in municipal government, derives from *Tammany* Hall (orig. occupied by the *Tammany* Benevolent Society) occupied by a political club controlling the Democratic Party of New York City: from the wise and friendly chieftain *Tamanen* or *Tamanend* usu *Tammany,* lit. 'the affable,' who flourished c. 1700." From which we see also that the founding members of the club made a fitting choice among the many available Indian names: "the affable"—what could be better to denote a handshake of politicians?

It is less gratifying (*gratus,* received with favor, akin to Sanskrit *gurtas,* pleasing, dear), it is, I say, less gratifying to learn that the albatross, beloved of

Coleridge, Baudelaire, and us moderns who do not know what else to hang about our necks, has acquired his poetic name by a series of mistakes. Indifferently a pelican or frigate bird or cormorant, and with his resonant *b* restored to a *c*, he is nothing more than the Portuguese *alcatraz,* which (alas) means "bucket." The Arabic, Hebrew, Phoenician, and Greek roots alike boil down to *kad,* water jar, or as Mr. Partridge tersely concludes: "Basic idea— water carrier."

I have so far suggested two of the uses of *Origins*—as the starting point of an unending tour through the jungle of ideas and objects that man has named, and as an organizer of related sounds and senses. It has a third important use, as a discreet but firm counselor in the choice of written and spoken words. To any one who notices how the strong influence of the visual in modern life has adversely affected common speech, making it often a succession of vague images and ill-concealed metaphors, the search for origins becomes a recurrent duty. Intellectual honesty as well as the old-fashioned art of rhetoric both require that the dead figures buried in the most ordinary words be brought momentarily to life in order to see whether the linking of one image or abstraction with another is proper.

The common absurdity of saying, for instance, "a period of crisis" is more manifest if we know that period means a circular road, a rounded, completed portion of time or of discourse; and that crisis, which originally means sifting or judging, means by extension the decisive moment in an uncertain course of action, disease, or the like. To regard our century as an age made up of such turning points is ridiculously to flatter ourselves, and at the same time to hide an unlovely outcropping of self pity. For what the phrase "an age of crisis" really states is our sense of being miserable, more miserable (as we think) than any other age. If this is what we believe, let us say so and stand up for comparison and criticism. Meanwhile, down with muddled Greek; it only puts us in a class with the conceited technician of these days, artist or scientist, who continually coins pompous names for his work by assembling learned syllables misunderstood. *Origins,* I am glad to say, knows nothing of "automation," much less of Jean Tinguely's "meta-matic sculptures." More generally, the book omits scientific terms whose exact definition, if any, can be found elsewhere, and whose derivation is in any case no better than it should be.

But censoring the ridiculous in our speech by a larger awareness of root meanings has a positive side. When that awareness becomes habitual and semi-conscious it enhances the pleasure one takes in any good sentence. Someone wrote of Flaubert: "He was forced to listen there [at his country house] to much conversation that was not simply bourgeois and philistine, but was made still more narrow by provincialism. Traces of this aggravation are abundant in [*Bouvard*] etc." Now that the word "aggravation" has come to mean annoyance, there is pleasure in having the original sense of "worsening," "made heavier" strictly observed in the example just quoted. But to enjoy this doubling it must be perceived, and this takes practice. The writer who fairly steadily uses etymology to amplify or reinforce his intention is composing with chords instead of simple notes, and the listening ear needs training to receive more than the bare melody.

Here we find the reason for the purist's conclusive argument in his running debate with the partisan of market-place usage: the purist, provided he does not abdicate *his* judgment by turning fanatical, can always squeeze more meaning out of his and others' vocabulary than the ignorant or the heedless. It is in him a natural and praiseworthy selfishness to want to retain the full meaning of the richest words. He wants his money's worth of meaning, both to savor it and to make himself understood. If through the usual pedantry of the half-educated, "meticulous" comes to be used as a synonym for "careful," then the additional idea of "fear" in the carefulness is soon lost, and we have two words—one needlessly long and learned—for one commonplace idea. Uneconomic and suddenly ugly, meticulous becomes the plaything of the pretentious. What does *Origins* tell us about the meticulose, so that we may see whether the point is indeed lost or still recapturable? " . . . from metus, fear: o.o.o. but the root met- recalls that of L *metiri,* to measure, extn of IE me-: excessive measuring of, hence excessive thought about, a situation. . . ." Therefore, *not* "a meticulous scientist"—measuring is his proper business— but "my meticulous tailor," who measures me to excess for fear that I have impudently and secretly departed from his previous norms.

Though *Origins* will draw you in and lead you on in this manner through a mere 10,000 words, do not suppose you will soon come to the end of its stores. In the very nature of words and thought there lies a principle of infinite renewal. Aspects, relations, differences change while you think; you cannot remember them all with finality, for your mind takes you along the one line, however jagged, of your present purpose or dream. Not ten days ago I was reading the meaty article *Fail* and I recall the association *False.* But just now my eye catches again the beckoning sign: *Faucet,* see *Fail.* How do *fail* and *false* generate *faucet?* Did I skip or am I blind? A mystery—but I can always turn the page and follow the lexical imperative, which is: See . . .

—MAY 1960

Ultima Thule

Jacques Barzun

On Peter Freuchen's Book of the Eskimos

THERE IS A CLASS of books, high in favor today, to which I am the reverse of partial. I mean the books that say or suggest how far superior to ourselves are some primitive islanders, some remote peasantry, some head hunters exquisite in size and simplicity.

I dislike such books, not because of their reproachful thesis, but because of their peculiar falsity. That a man's vocation as missionary or anthropologist should draw his affections away from his own people and bring him to see all the merits of another, greatly different in manners and traditions, is understandable and often productive of wisdom. But equally often the choice of the career springs from disaffection to begin with, and the recital of the alien life becomes the indirect statement of a grievance. The writer turns every detail of his *vita nuova* into a symbol of perfection, like the stupid convert that he is, and we are asked to admire and relish what deserves contempt or disgust solely because it is associated with the touching and the lovable.

This attitude passes for liberal and misses the great point of true liberality of spirit, which is that humanity, though it hides behind infinite disguises, moves us whenever we rediscover it. Indeed, like children playing with their hands on their faces, we are most pleased when we see the sparkling eye between the concealing fingers. As regards the modern adulator of the primitive, one might say that his presentment has little or nothing to do with comparing cultures. Cultures remain to be judged on other grounds than their compatibility with sweet or shrewd or heroic individuals.

The force of this last principle, by the way, should govern our thoughts about cultural and racial conflicts at home. The individual as such deserves a respect which need not extend to his traditions, difficult as it may be to separate the two. The rights we accord him are, at any rate, based on the ability to see the man within the social shell; for we acquired this notion of rights from the eighteenth century, when the power of abstraction ruled the imagination of the best men. In that century as in ours, the love of the primitive rested upon travelers' tales of North America and the South Pacific. But the tales were not false in our peculiar, nagging modern way. They idealized in eagerness and wonder. It would not have seemed possible then to praise and demonstrate primitive superiority out of resentment or out of sullen preference for physical or moral sordidness.

Fortunately, not all our travelers are at the mercy of the self-exile's temperament and the present season brings us two books that transcend the class I describe. One is Lévi-Strauss's *Tristes Tropiques;* the other is *Peter Freuchen's Book of the Eskimos*. It is of the latter I want to speak, though briefly, lest I spoil something of its perfection by giving away in disconnected bits what should gradually disclose itself in its natural order. The perfection I could spoil is not, of course, the book's, but the reader's impression of it and pleasure in it.

Peter Freuchen was a Dane who first visited the Eskimos in 1906, established a trading post in Eskimo country and became administrator of the settlement that grew around it, married an Eskimo woman and had two children by her, lived and traveled, explored the North and wrote about it until his death in Alaska in 1957. His interest in the people whom he as it were adopted was practical as well as literary and scientific. Though he wrote a novel about his life, he was as much concerned about the Eskimos' access to fish, reindeer, medicine, rifles, and matches as he was about "the culture."

It is possibly this worldliness in actuality which makes the *Book of the Eskimos* so serene a romance between a European and an alien people. The author is perfectly at ease among the persons and symbols, the beliefs and the incidents that he deals with. He has shared the common life as a partner and an equal, not "studied" it as a scientific Peeping Tom nor sought to benefit it as the bearer of indispensable tidings.

The heart of the book is the description, simple and subtle all at once, of what draws us in any such book because we know we shall recognize ourselves in it: how do they eat, love, rear children, and deal with offenders? The rest is not negligible, but it is (as always) foreign words and picturesqueness— like those "flat cakes made of the native cereal, not unpleasant to the taste," which occurred in all the explorers' books of my childhood and gave me intenser pleasure than any meringue or éclair of common day.

What is remarkable about Freuchen's book is the way in which he unifies the admirably selected workaday detail with the atmosphere of love that pervades his observations. It is a remarkable feat of style for which he evidently deserves the full credit, since I can find no indication that the book, prefaced by his daughter, was translated. Let me give a short sample and be still:

> Fear of death is unknown to them, they know only love of life. The Eskimos are themselves unaware of the difficulty of their existence, they always enjoy life with an enviable intensity, and they believe themselves to be the happiest people on earth living in the most beautiful country there is. When an old man sees the young men go out hunting and cannot himself go along, he is sorry. When he has to ask other people for skins for his clothing, when he cannot ever again be the one to invite the neighbors to eat his game, life is of no value to him. Rheumatism and other ills may plague him, and he wants to die. This has been done in different ways in different tribes, but everywhere it is held that if a man feels himself to be a nuisance, his love for his kin, coupled with the sorrow of not being able to take part in the things which are worthwhile, impels him to die.

—AUGUST 1961

The Chemical Life

W. H. Auden

On David Ebin's *The Drug Experience*

A RAG-BAG OF A BOOK, but rightly so, for the subject is itself miscellaneous. Drugs have a literary interest because of the peculiar experiences undergone by those who take them. They are of anthropological interest because there are societies which make a sacred cult of them. Because of the deadly effect of some kinds of drug-addiction and the criminals who trade on this, they are a social-legal problem. Because of the analgesic and therapeutic effects of drugs, they are of interest to science, and, in the case of those drugs which appear to be physically harmless, there is the moral-religious question as to what effect indulgence may have on the character. Drugs, harmless or dangerous, ignore all social, professional, and cultural frontiers. Among the contributors to this anthology, for example, are naive, sophisticated, conservative, and avant-garde writers; jazz musicians, medical students, a Member of Parliament, an Oxford don, jailbirds and invalids, heroes and cowards. As to the judgment of the editor, I only regret one inclusion, Aleister Crowley's piece which seems to me a phony penny-novelette, and one omission, which perhaps was unobtainable, Robert Graves's fine poem to the Mushroom God. Whatever the editor's intention was in including it, I am grateful for the Symposium on LSD. It is one of the most extraordinary documents I ever read, or rather failed to read, in my life. The distinguished participants, if one met them in private life or even in their consulting rooms, would, no doubt, show themselves capable of human speech, but here, where they have to appear in public as psychologists, they do not talk badly because they do not talk at all; the noises they make are a sort of non-speech, null and void.

As everybody except the Narcotic Bureau now knows, there are two classes of drugs, the Junk Group which, because of the metabolic changes in the body which they effect, enslave those who take them, and the Hallucino-gen Group which are not habit-forming and, so far as is known at present, have no lasting physical aftereffects. Of the Junkies, the only one who has a good word to say for them is Cocteau, who was an addict of the least harm-ful of them, opium, and even he felt obliged to take a cure and to utter this warning: "Opium cannot bear impatient addicts, bunglers. It moves away, leaving them morphine, heroin, suicide and death."

As William Burroughs, in what is probably the best, as it is certainly the most terrifying, article on Junk in this volume, says: "There are no opium cults. Opium is profane and quantitative like money." Quite aside from the humiliations which a junk addict has to endure in order to procure his drug, and the agonizing withdrawal pains if he tries to give it up, the life of a seri-ous addict, as Mr. Burroughs describes it, is hardly appetizing.

> I lived in one room in the Native Quarter of Tangier. I had not taken a bath in a year nor changed my clothes or removed them except to stick a needle every hour in the fibrous gray wooden flesh of terminal addic-tion. I never cleaned or dusted the room. Empty ampule boxes and garbage piled to the ceiling. Light and water long since turned off for non-payment. I did absolutely nothing. I could look at the end of my shoe for eight hours. If a friend came to visit—and they rarely did since who or what was left to visit—I sat there not caring that he had entered my field of vision—a gray screen always blanker and fainter—and not caring when he walked out of it.

He recommends the apomorphine cure, but there seems to be insuffi-cient evidence as to whether apomorphine is a universal and permanent cure for addiction. One of the morphine-addict contributors, Barney Ross, seems to have broken the habit by heroic willpower, but all agree that very few who take a cure— those, for example, who are sent or vol-untarily go to Lexington—do not, sooner or later, relapse. Every junky agrees that society should take steps to reduce the opportunities for be-coming addicted, and they are unanimous in their belief that the attitude of the U.S. Narcotic Bureau, which regards drug-taking as a crime, in-creases the opportunities and encourages the illicit drug traffic. Nearly all the "pushers," those who are directly responsible for making new ad-dicts, are addicts themselves who push junk, not to make a living, but be-cause it is the only way in which they can get junk for themselves. Those who run the drug traffic and make fortunes are, of course, very wicked indeed. To quote Mr. Burroughs again:

Junk is the ultimate merchandise. The junk merchant does not sell his product to the consumer, he sells the consumer to the product. He does not improve and simplify his merchandise. He degrades and simplifies the client.

But moralizing is no use: unless and until the world finds a way to prevent the
manufacture of junk, anywhere on earth, except under strict supervision, the
junk merchant will exist so long as he can find clients. The only way to run
him out of business is to deprive him of clients, and the only country which,
so far, has taken a sensible step in this direction seems to be England. In England anybody who has become an addict can register himself as one. He in-
curs no penalty, his name is kept secret, and he is allowed a ration of drug
under minimal supervision. At the same time, the illegal importation and sale
of drugs is a criminal offense. In this way, it is hoped that when the present
generation of addicts has died off, the profits to be made from trafficking in
drugs will be insufficient to offset the risks it involves.

As for the way in which the police in the United States treat the drug taker,
even if the drug is as harmless as marihuana, no one can read Billie Holiday's
piece in this book without feelings of shock and shame.

Ever since Mr. Aldous Huxley published *The Doors of Perception in* 1954,
the hallucinogenic drugs, mescaline, LSD, the Mexican Mushroom, etc. have
become a topic for cocktail-party conversation, and hundreds of most respectable people have eagerly volunteered to be experimental subjects. Some
claim that their experiences under these drugs were indescribably beautiful,
some found them terrifying, some vaguely disagreeable, and some comic in a
silly way. But when one compares their various accounts, one begins to see
certain common denominators. Firstly, however extraordinary the experience
of an individual, it is not totally novel to him. As Baudelaire observed more
than a century ago:

> The dream will always retain the private tonality of the individual. The man
> wanted the dream, now the dream will govern the man; but this dream will
> certainly be the son of its father.

Secondly, a person under the influence of one of these drugs loses all interest
in other people; he has no desire to share his experience with others and becomes like Aristotle's apathetic God who "has no need of friends, neither, indeed, can he have any." Not only has he no desire to share his experience, he
cannot share it. Professor Zaehner, Mr. Ginsberg and Daniel Breslaw, more
educated and articulate people than the average, have taken drugs under experimental conditions in which everything they said was reported verbatim,

and all three of them talked drivel, strongly reminiscent of the drivel uttered by mediums in their trances.

One is inclined to suspect that habitual taking of this type of drug, even if it has no harmful physical effects, would lead to a selfish indifference towards the common world we live in and a withering of love and affection for others. Monsieur Cocteau complains that, without opium, "the world resembles those revolting films in which ministers unveil statues," and Mr. Ginsberg cries "I have to find a new world for the universe, I'm tired of the old one." Very true, no doubt: but better the old revolting world than a world, however beautiful, inhabited only by oneself. Some have claimed that their experiences under drugs were mystical visions of religious significance. Well, a tree must be judged by its fruits. In the case of the famous mystics, the effect of their visions, whether true or an illusion, was to increase their desire to do good works and make them capable of heroic deeds of charity. Has this effect been noted in any taker of mescaline or LSD?

As for the practical help which marihuana can be to jazz musicians, and it is widely believed that it can, Mr. Alexander King has this to say:

> The greatest jazz people are rarely addicts. The not-quite ace-performers, when they are off the stuff, will freely confess that junk has never helped their playing a bit. It can't make them play high; it just makes them *think* high.

No, on the whole, I think we had better stick to wine: it tastes nicer and it has even been known to improve the conversation.

P. S. IF ONLY I were rich, I would buy advertising space in the subway and fill it with these words by Billie Holiday: "I knew I'd really licked the drug-habit one morning when I couldn't stand television any more."

—JANUARY 1962

No Mean City

LIONEL TRILLING

On Jane Jacobs' *The Death and Life of Great American Cities*

THE DEATH AND LIFE OF GREAT AMERICAN CITIES is a book about the assumptions which control the thought of city planning. As such, it is a work of very considerable interest. America, whatever its dream of itself may be, whatever Edenic illusions haunt the fancy of its middle classes to draw them to the more or less reasonable facsimiles of country living, is ever increasingly an urban nation, and the questions of how our cities must be taught to grow or to reconstitute themselves must inevitably engage our lively attention.

But the interest of Jane Jacobs' big, gay, wonderfully readable book is not to be wholly defined by its avowed subject, large and immediate as that is. It is a polemical work which brings under intense criticism the leading accepted ideas of the most eminent city planners, yet its chief significance is not to be found in the objections it makes to the intellectual procedures of a particular profession, but rather in what it tells us, by implication, about the intellectual procedures of our whole culture, about the way we conduct ourselves in relation to ideas.

We all know it as a truism that modern civilization is characterized by its responsiveness to ideas. We have no difficulty in understanding what Hegel meant when he said that with the French Revolution the conscious mind was given a new decisive part to play in human affairs. Any one of us can exemplify the statement not only from politics and social organization but from our personal experience of business or domestic economy or child-rearing—we can all be readily aware how activities which were once habitual or directed by very simple rules, now require elaborate theory, even a "philosophy." Now and then we think with some wryness of the burden of thought and decision which the new dispensation has brought us, but on the whole, when we rise above the merely personal, we regard our modern intellectualized condition with satisfaction. We think it right that human existence should be directed by reason, and it has become part of our sense of life that the great trouble with our present social arrangements is that they do not permit good ideas to be acted on quickly and decisively enough. By good ideas we mean, of course, those which we regard as progressive, liberal, and humane, and we see it as the pathos of our condition that such ideas are resisted either by the conscious malevolence of special vested interests or by the mere brute inertia of society. It seldom occurs to us to take account of an inertia of a different kind, that which makes it virtually impossible to debate an idea on its merits, that which leads us to abandon intellectual effort in the face of experts who can muster against opposition not the convincing arguments but the social and moral attitudes which have the effect of suggesting that adverse views are impious.

A remarkable example of what I mean—it should have a permanent and conspicuous place in the history of the human intellect—is the establishment in this country of the so-called "Look and Say" method of teaching children to read. The enormous victory of that method is now in process of being reversed; the revolt against it has become general. But the long ascendancy of the idea has left behind it a devastation, several generations of perfectly intelligent people for whom reading is a difficult and painful activity, who are, indeed, something very like illiterate. The triumph of "Look and Say" is to be explained not by any argument which its proponents made for its efficiency— they were ready virtually to say that it was *not* efficient, and the better because it was not—but by the moral authority of certain concepts which were involved with it, such as the peculiar virtue supposed to inhere in "the whole" and the vicious unnaturalness attributed to "parts." On the basis of a misunderstood element of Gestalt psychology—which in itself has now but little academic standing—the reading theorists convinced the nation that children must learn to see words as "wholes" rather than as aggregates of letters. By mere force of assertion, that is, they succeeded in denying the advantages of the alphabet and the moral superiority of ideograms, and all on behalf of wholeness, integration, naturalness, immediacy, and the other words which have for us the charm of moral certitude. A large part of the teaching profession consolidated itself in a great vested interest in defense of this method, which it associated with the essence of the democratic ethos—there was a time when to invade educational circles with a question adverse to "Look and Say" was to subvert the very soul of the nation, to take the first step on the road to reaction.

Mrs. Jacobs does not refer to the phenomenal triumph of "Look and Say," but it is the thesis of her book that many of the ideas of the city planners are accepted not by reason of their true practicality but because of the moralizing aura which surrounds them. The first target of her attack is the idea that the big city is, by its nature, a bad place and inimical to the good life. Lewis

Mumford who, through all his admirable career, has waged war against the urban and whose influence upon city planners has been decisive, speaks of the great city as Nekropolis—the City of Death—and it can be said that this radically antagonistic characterization of the city is one of the most deeply ingrained and sanctified of modern beliefs. It is this moralizing hostility to the city, Mrs. Jacobs holds, which leads city planners to misconceive the nature of city life and, in their scheme for the correction of the manifestly bad conditions which cities do indeed develop, to devise new conditions which are or become in themselves deplorable.

The intention of Mrs. Jacobs' book may be described as that of substituting actualities for pieties, and she goes about her job with a vivacity and gusto which match her cogency. For me the book has perhaps a special force because more than once in the course of her polemic, Mrs. Jacobs directs us in her pleasant peremptory way to "consider the Morningside Heights area in New York City." I am the readier to obey her because I have lived in the "area" most of my life. And having duly considered it according to instructions, I can scarcely fail to agree with Mrs. Jacobs on all the essential points she makes. One of the planning pieties against which she makes a dead set is the antagonism to *the street,* which has induced the architects of housing projects to try to eliminate it by plazas and interior courts. But Mrs. Jacobs is right in defending the street as having at least two great advantages—it is interesting and it is safe. It is impossible to read Mrs. Jacobs' chapters on the street without feeling the better for living on one, without understanding why, for children above a certain age, it is a more secure place to play than parks or playgrounds, and all that Mrs. Jacobs says is confirmed by my own observation. Claremont Avenue, to be sure, is not any street, but it is not entirely unique, and the street life of its children, casual, natural, and spontaneous, and carried on from infancy through adolescence, is one of its advantages and charms. No doubt all this free, happy activity should in propriety be transferred to nearby Riverside Park, affirming another piety of the city planners who never weary of telling us about the value of open spaces, parks especially. But except on warm weekends in the daylight hours, Riverside Park is a wasteland which would require an outsize police force to make it safe for children or for mothers with infants. As for the handsome Morningside Park, only three blocks away, no one in his right mind has gone into it for the last thirty years or more.

If Mrs. Jacobs speaks of the Blight of Dullness which creeps into Quiet Residential Neighborhoods and destroys them, I do not have far to go to find examples, the more because of the special blight that develops around institutional buildings, and I have to consider that my own university, together with the Cathedral of St. John the Divine, whose Close and whose Canons are so pleasant, and St. Luke's Hospital, and Union Theological Seminary, and the Jewish Theological Seminary, and the Juilliard School, all dedicated to the spreading of light, have generated this dim grayness. Nor can I fail to see that the effort to counteract these sad conditions, which produced the housing projects at 125th Street, succeed only in creating bleakness of a different kind. And I cannot but give my strong approval to Mrs. Jacobs' idea that "developments" and "projects" are not the only means of solving housing problems, that every effort ought to be made to preserve and rehabilitate old buildings. My street is lined by old apartment houses—how old they are may be judged from the fact that almost every room has a vestigial painted-over bell-push: to ring for the maid! They are owned and very efficiently kept up by the University. They afford apartments which are spacious, quiet, and relatively cheap and they make a street that is distinctive and rather charming—there are few other streets in New York in which elaborate balconies are supported by Prix de Rome caryatids with calm faces and flowing robes. Of course the street was more attractive before Barnard College rudely backed on to it the flat, dull, featureless rear of its new library.

Mrs. Jacobs likes in a city what no one is supposed to like and what we all like well enough when we are freed to do so. She likes complexity and variety and denseness and strangeness and activity. "A city," she says, "cannot be a work of art," and she finds the root of the errors of city planning in the desire to impose on the city the canons of art. This is not, of course, to say that a city is without its own kind of order. But "to see complex systems of functional order as order, and not as chaos takes understanding." And Mrs. Jacobs goes on: "The leaves dropping from the trees in the autumn, the interior of an airplane engine, the entrails of a dissected rabbit, the city desk of a newspaper, all appear to be chaos if they are seen without comprehension. Once they are understood as systems of order, they actually *look* different." This, it need scarcely be said, is not Mrs. Jacobs' plea for *laissez aller.* She makes no such plea. She is far from taking a stand against city planning as such, only against such city planning as fails to understand the nature of what it seeks to improve. "There is" she says, "a quality even meaner than outright ugliness or disorder, and this meaner quality is the dishonest mask of pretended order, achieved by ignoring or suppressing the real order that is struggling to exist and be served." In directing our minds to the perception of the "real order" that a city may have, in freeing us from the cant that has grown up around all thought about the city, Mrs. Jacobs has done the culture a service which cannot be sufficiently praised.

—MARCH 1962

Novels and
Novelists

"Short Novels of Colette"

W. H. Auden

A review of the *Short Novels of Colette*

FOR YEARS I RESISTED every recommendation to read her. Her name conjured up for me the conventional anglo-saxon images of Paris as the city of the Naughty Spree—*La Vie Parisienne, Les Folies Bergères,* Mademoiselle Fifi, bedroom mirrors and bidets, lingerie and adultery, the sniggers of school boys and grubby old men. I was further suspicious because she was so often recommended to me for her prose style and it has generally been my experience that when a writer is praised for style it is because there is little else to praise.

I mention this because my prejudice seems to be common; all the five novels in this collection were published in the States between 1929 and 1936, unpropitious years maybe, without attracting much attention. Since I have now come to agree wholeheartedly with Mr. Glenway Wescott who, in his masterly introduction, declares without equivocation that Colette is the greatest living French fiction writer, I am convinced that others have only to read her work to experience the same conversion.

Her subject matter is exactly what one's hostile preconception imagined it to be. Her world has the same limited concerns as the naughty French farce: food, money, and l'amour; the same limited professions: one can be kept, one can have something to do with the stage, one can speculate on the Bourse, one can have independent means—and the same limited range of roles, more star parts for actresses than for actors, bit parts for servants and an occasional adolescent but none for small children. Yet out of this specialized, slightly shopsoiled stuff she has managed to create works of art the significance of which is profound, tragic and universal.

For Colette, as for any other writer, this alchemy was a process which took her time to learn. The publishers here wisely put the earliest novel of their collection last and the reader should follow their order. He should read the productions of her maturity, the two *Cheri* novels, *Duo* and *The Cat* before he reads *The Indulgent Husband,* if he is to get a proper measure of her growth. Technical skill she displayed from the very first, but the development in her imagination and moral insight is astounding.

The Indulgent Husband smells, at least to me, a little gamey, not because of its 'daring' theme but because Claudine, the heroine and narrator, instead of being honestly absorbed in her story, is too reader conscious; there are moments when, as it were, she turns in the midst of an embrace to wink at the audience and whisper, "Aren't I a naughty girl." For instance, her insight into her corrupt husband, Renand, is so penetrating that her decision to return to him at the end, or rather the reason she gives for it, is incredible and outrageous.

Yet there are glimpses in this book already of a great artist: when Claudine runs back to the Eden of her childhood, to her eccentric professor father and the countryside round Montigny, all giggles are hushed, and there are pages which are so beautiful one could cry.

So many roses! I'd like to say to the lush, "Take a rest, my dear, you have bloomed enough, worked enough, given lavishly of your strength and your perfume." The lush would never heed me. It wants to beat the record for rose as to both quantity and fragrance. It has endurance and speed, it gives every ounce that is in it.

When we come to *Cheri*, this pure awareness has enlarged and includes not only the world of innocence but also the worlds of sin and grief.

As in all tragedy, the final outcome is the result of an interaction between fate and free-will. Fate for Cheri is the world of high-class successful courtesans to which his mother and her friends belong. It is a world without fathers; the male exploits or is exploited but in either case his presence is temporary; he passes across the stage and exits, but the women remain. They leave or are left by their lovers but the bond between them is unbreakable—the unfriendly intimacy of kept women, the peevish affection of rivals stalking each others' first wrinkle or white hair, the comradeship of women with highly-developed characters, shrewd at gathering in the cash. Like every other world it has its own standards. Watch your figure. Guard your bank balance. Enjoy yourself when you can. Don't fall in love if you can help it but if you do never give yourself away. Love passes but good cuisine is a joy for ever. Never pity yourself. Fear nothing. As in a Greek tragedy, the decisive events have already oc-

curred when the story opens: Cheri has had his childhood, by turns adored
and forgotten, matured among blotchy maids and tall sardonic valets, his liai-
son with Léa has lasted six years, and, though neither he nor the others realize it, he is already doomed.

During their affair, both Léa and Cheri have imagined that they were bliss-
fully happy and not too involved with each other, but Colette indicates very
subtly that something was wrong. In a relationship between a boy of seventeen and a wise experienced woman of forty-three, there is only one level, the
physical, on which he can meet her as an equal. Cheri's fussing over the
household accounts is really a pathetic attempt to be the adult husband in
some sphere other than the bed. It is no use; the women treat it as a joke. His
only defense against the feeling of being the inferior is to retreat from consciousness into his senses; all his maturity, his sensitivity, his goodness is
buried in his body: his mind remains that of a spoilt child, just as greedy. He
is a splendid animal, but his animality is not natural; dogs and horses scent
this and he can never make friends with one. Only the vegetable and mineral
worlds are unafraid of him. Colette tells us how, when he was a soldier in the
trenches, "his fingers, black with mud and his own grime, were still able to
distinguish, by a single sure touch, medals and coins, to recognize by stem or
leaf plants the very names of which he did not know." Later, when he visits a
hospital with his wife, though consciously he is indifferent to the suffering of
the wounded, his senses know better than the doctors what could be done to
make them more comfortable.

For one brief moment when he sees that Léa is getting old and she, realis-
ing this, insists on a final break, he seems to be in the superior position, and
she the victim.

> Léa let the curtain fall. But she still had time to see that Cheri lifted his head
> toward the spring sky and the flowering chestnut trees and that in walking
> he filled his lungs with air like a man escaping from prison.

But in the terrible and magnificent scene in the second book when he
comes to see her again after a lapse of five years, we discover that it is she who
has escaped. He is still a young man haunted by her image, but she has grown
stout, simple and "merry, like an old man"; nature has delivered her. Once
again she is as she was in the beginning, the victor and he the vanquished. Re-
alising that their relative positions are now irrevocable, Cheri surrenders to
his obsession with its inevitable end.

Looking back to discover where and why the fatal error was made, one
can see that if the affair between Léa and Cheri had only lasted one year, the

tragedy would not have occurred. Cheri would probably then have developed, as his wife developed, into a shrewd tough acquisitive creature at home in his own world, a true son of his mother. But for Léa to have broken off the relationship in time, she would have had to be either as cold-hearted as her friends or gifted with supernatural charity; being neither, she followed the natural promptings of her heart and it is precisely her genuine love for Cheri that destroys him.

Had Edmée married another husband, she might have turned into a decent person, but whoever Cheri married, his marriage would have been bound to be a failure, for he was already incapable of loving anyone but Léa. Mr. Wescott hints, and I agree with him, that, after what has happened, the only escape for Cheri would have been the cloister.

In the little space left to me, rather than an inadequate discussion of *Duo* and *The Cat,* both of them masterpieces, I will conclude with two quotations to illustrate Colette's depth of psychological insight and the economy and felicity with which she can express it.

On Desmond, a night-club proprietor who has just discovered the joys of making money:

> He bathed in an enamelled zinc tub beside a fringe of water plants painted on the tiles, and the decrepit water-heater snored and wheezed like an old bull-dog. But the telephone shone like some cherished weapon in daily use.

On Copine, an old prostitute:

> She had bought a pipe for smoking opium, a lamp, a little jar of the drug, a silver snuff-box full of cocaine—a pack of fortune teller's cards, a case of poker chips and a pair of spectacles. She looked up with eyes like those of an indulgent grandmother who spends all her money on toys for the children.

Worlds apart as they may be in many respects, when I read such sentences, I am reminded of only one other novelist, Tolstoy.

—1951

Lorenzo the Magniloquent

JACQUES BARZUN

On *The Later D. H. Lawrence,* edited by W. Y. Tindall

LOVE HIM OR LOATHE him you are forced to admit that he possesses the first requisite of a novelist: he keeps you going. Yet it is easy to see in *The Later Lawrence* that this momentum is not imparted to the reader by the attraction of mere plot or story telling. You do not turn page after page of *St. Mawr*—an improbable and inconclusive tale of a woman and a horse—in order to find out what happens next. You are caught and pulled along by the intensity of the writer's concern with his subject, and sometimes by intensity, by passion in and for itself. Something vibrates unceasingly behind the page and you vibrate with it—or else hurl the book across the room. There is thus a perfect correspondence between Lawrence's work and his propaganda: he was committed to preaching not the prudent but the intense, and when he is not exhausted by it nor you by him, you are dragged a captive at his Pan-like heels.

This may sound like too strenuous a pleasure for a reading public sufficiently harrowed by life and its reflection in the daily papers, but there are, in Lawrence generally and particularly in this selection, both rewards and mitigations. To take the last first, the present volume contains the bulk of the writings—both essays and stories—that Lawrence produced within the last half dozen years of his life. By then, aged forty, he had learned to tune his individual note so that it was more alluring and no less magical than before. Works such as *Mornings in Mexico* and *The Man Who Died,* which we are given here, exert charm at once in the old meaning of a mysterious spell and in the weakened modern meaning of agreeableness. Similarly, essays such as the Autobiographical Sketch, Making Pictures, and the fantasia on the hymns Lawrence heard as a boy in his Welsh chapel disclose a humorous and well-schooled writer who suggests the tradition of Lamb and Gissing—if tradition it be to talk about oneself with eloquence muted to a chuckle.

These are the mitigations of the Lawrentian intensity. But as the editor of the volume, Mr. W. Y. Tindall, sagely observes, Lawrence is worth reading because he has something original to say and has found the way to say it. What was new with him was that he preached primitivism without flattering our egos or our senses. Rather, he launched his attack with the conscious animus of a mob orator. The reward of listening to him is not so much that he converts us to his views as that he accustoms us to his experience. Even when he wearies with his repetitious prose and revolts with his subject-matter or his inconsistencies, he is doing the work he has cut out for himself, of grinding down our well-bred prejudices and sticking our noses in the primordial mess of being. And when we look up again, we find that we are neither so genteel nor so frightened as before.

That Lawrence's message was needed in the supposedly sophisticated 1920's seems to be shown by the fact that his great fame followed the appearance of *Lady Chatterley's Lover.* But it is a question whether the lesson has been learned even now. The common impression is that Lawrence advocated sexual freedom, or perhaps license, to which he ascribed mystical qualities; that he was for instinct against reason, and therefore pitched into modern civilization like a hundred thousand other modern writers; and that he spoke of dark blood and snakes and the abominable at large like a relisher of riot.

The fact is that, as Norman Douglas pointed out, Lawrence was something of a Puritan. He was at any rate shocked and angered by what his blithe contemporaries made of sex and other bodily manifestations, and the reason he harped on these subjects in his novels and tales was that he was trying to convey his solemn yet direct intimations of a mystery. In the volume under review he gives one allegorical and one explicit illustration of this in, respectively, *The Woman Who Rode Away* and *Sun;* plus a didactic statement in the brilliant and characteristic essay, "Love Was Once a Little Boy." But Lawrence's awareness of the reproductive urge was ubiquitous. It underlies everything he ever wrote. It colors his opinions of art, society, religion, metaphysics, as well as causes him now and again to rant and scream at a world apparently blind to the obvious, or worse—anesthetic to feelings by definition simple and universal. Wild horses could not detach people from their artificial images of what life was like; or rather, only in *St. Mawr* did such a horse achieve such a result. And yet the single character on whom the vision of the life force has this salutary effect is left aimless after her divorce from "civilization."

Here we touch Lawrence's chief weakness as a creator, that is to say his lack of staying power in reasoning. He finds live truth while others only bandy words, and he goes on to find inspired phrases to transmit and preserve his truths, but after two or three steps in the direction he himself has shown, he flounders and backtracks and falls into cliché or easy colloquial evasion: "What do you make of that?"—"I give it up." Lawrence talks like the Sybil after giving the oracle.

Was it this same defect that kept him ignorant of his intellectual antecedents and parallels? It is hard to say, but the curious fact remains that if one wants the articulate counterpart of Lawrence's vision, one will find it in the contemporary writer who is superficially least like Lawrence—in Shaw. The religious feeling about the life force, the deliberate acceptance of *tragic* relativism, the repudiation of vulgar bourgeois society, the biological and evolutionary imagery, the high preference given to normal women, balanced by the interest taken in talkative men—all this links Shaw and Lawrence as inheritors of one doctrine dating roughly from the 1890's: read in *The Later Lawrence* the "Reflections on the Death of a Porcupine."

Though it is safe to say you will never forget the porcupine and the dog, will you remember Lawrence's earnest asseverations about Life with a capital L? Some will reply that Lawrence possessed the poetic powers that Shaw lacked and that doctrine makes no difference anyway. Let us read novels for fun and a diffuse kind of wisdom. Lawrence seems to say this himself in the superb piece of criticism on The Novel which follows the "Reflections." But he does not actually say it: what he says is that digressions and preachments at variance with the feelings embodied in a novel can be ignored. Certainly, when Lawrence preaches in his fiction there is no discrepancy between feeling and doctrine. None even when the talk is self-contradictory, for what we see before us is not a lecturer going through his routine but a passionate man quarreling, on behalf of his inner world, with the whole world outside. Without these groping harangues we could hardly have understood the bearing of the events, sensations and symbols set down in the novel for us to experience—to experience there and, once again, if we can, in life itself. Being civilized, we can do this only after we have understood. We yield, in other words, to the fact of Lawrence's originality by virtue of the rightness of his technique. So that if one failed to read Lawrence during his last, best decade, or if one's memory of him is now uncertain or mixed or resentful, one has awaiting him in this Lawrence Reader a world of fresh discoveries charged with elemental emotions. Lawrence is still a voice of our time and for our time.

—1952

A Triumph of the Comic View

Lionel Trilling

On Saul Bellow's *The Adventures of Augie March*

THERE HAVE BEEN FEW contemporary novels that I have looked forward to with so much eagerness and read with so much interest and pleasure as Saul Bellow's *The Adventures of Augie March*. Of Mr. Bellow's two earlier books, I didn't much like the first, *Dangling Man*. But the second, *The Victim*, seemed to me a work of extraordinary accomplishment. It was striking in its conception and it was marked by an originality of observation and a vivacity of moral insight that seemed to me unique in recent American fiction. *The Victim*, I suppose, was bound to make only a limited appeal, for it is the kind of novel in which the author develops a single controlling idea with skill and precision, calling upon his conscious intelligence to do a considerable part of the work of creation. Such novels need always to be defended, especially in America, where they are at a particular disadvantage. They have their own criteria of success and their own particular virtue when they are successful. But they are likely to have, as I think *The Victim* had, a certain enclosed and even claustral quality under which most readers become restive. And I dare-say I experienced something of this restiveness myself, despite my strong general admiration for the book, for although I took great pleasure in the wit with which Mr. Bellow managed the exposition of his informing idea, I nevertheless found myself more engaged by the author's looser, more spontaneous talents, by what might be called his old-fashioned gifts as a novelist, his ability to convey the sense of human actuality, energy, and variety. And I looked forward to the book in which he would assert these powers yet more boldly.

The Adventures of Augie March is that book, and it is very nearly as re-markable an achievement as I had hoped for. It is by no means free of "idea"—although the idea which controls it is not this time of a limiting kind, it is dominant in the novel to the point of constituting a thesis. But what needs to be spoken of first is not the idea, important as it is, but the beautiful success of what I have called Mr. Bellow's spontaneous talents, his old-fashioned novelistic gifts, which create a human reality at once massive and brilliant. The English nineteenth century perhaps made too much of the effect of personal reality, seeming to conceive of it as the very essence of the novel, and no doubt, in criticism at least, the preoccupation with it became a kind of sentimentality, so that it is understandable that some modern critics should in reaction have become indifferent or even hostile to the achieved illusion of reality, to the habit of talking of characters as if they had lives of their own rather than a literary existence as elements of a total poetic creation. Yet when we have taken account of the extravagances of esteem in which "reality" may be held, it still remains one of the great effects toward which literature directs itself. In *Augie March* the degree of reality is not constant—it is far more intense in the first three-quarters of the book than it is in the last quarter, but the larger part of this sizable work has a force and charm of actuality that are unmatched in American writing today and that make it, I think, not less than great.

The extent of Mr. Bellow's success in these pages may be judged from the familiarity of the matter upon which he exercises his talents. The life of the slums and the near-slums of Chicago or some other great city has established itself over the last thirty years as a canonical subject in our literature. It is a good subject; it has its own implicit richness; one can almost say that if a writer comes to it with honesty and painstakingness, he can scarcely fail to make something good of it. But no one has handled it as Mr. Bellow does, no one has presented it to us with so large, so poetic a responsiveness to fact.

If we look for the explanation of Mr. Bellow's peculiarly radiant quality of reality, we can find a clue in a phrase of the publisher's jacket blurb, which for once and for a wonder makes sense. It speaks of Mr. Bellow as being consciously in the comic tradition. What has the comic tradition to do with the created illusion of human reality? This, I think: that in its essence it affirms the importance, the real existence, of people who do not conform to the heroic tradition. It is amazing, when we stop to think of it, how the heroic tradition has dominated Western culture, and how the great comic writers, the masters of common reality—Shakespeare, Cervantes, Fielding, Dickens, Joyce—have been haunted by it, and have created the comic in its terms, have, that is, insisted on a reality that was not heroic by means of a comedy that is an inversion of the heroic. In the creation of a comic character the author seems to say to the reader, "You, of course, will scarcely believe in the actuality of what I am now showing you—you, dear reader, who have been so entirely reared in the heroic tradition, you who are in yourself an heroic personality. And yet, honored sir whose descent from the Cid is too well known to mention, such people really do exist. What is more, señor, they believe in their own reality quite as much as you do in yours—indeed, they go so far in their presumption as to raise questions about the reality of heroic personalities." Whereupon the comic person proceeds to expound the principles of his existence and its thickness and importance—that "exemplary role" that André Gide speaks of as "the supreme joy of a hero" is no less the supreme joy of the comic personality: the delights of the exemplary role are quite as available to Falstaff and Micawber as to Hamlet and Orestes.

The comic tradition retreated before the advances of social progressivism. In one of William Morris's Utopian romances in which everyone is well housed, well fed, well adjusted and beautiful and mannerly and serene, there is one man, a surly holdout against felicity, who sits in solitary dissatisfaction reading the novels of Dickens which no one reads any more, longing for the lost time when streets were dark, dirty, and dangerous, when people were odd, extravagant, and funny. Morris, although he sees to it that this subversive man is refuted and gently mocked, has paid through him his own tribute to the comic and has expressed his momentary uneasy sense that the impulse to an organized human perfection might mean a dimunition of human reality and interest.

Most American novelists who have dealt with people in less than comfortable or charming conditions of life have done so under the aspect of social criticism. And this is understandable and creditable, yet their books have always seemed to imply that if you are not Coningsby or Daniel Boone or Henry Adams, or some other character to whom distinction and freedom come naturally, you are really dead; or that, at the least, if you do not live in something like a Westchester suburb on something like a Westchester income, but of course without the foolish gentilities that an actual Westchester entails, you are not really a person at all but only an object of some actual person's— say a novelist's—sensitivity and pity. You live out your life but you do not live. But Mr. Bellow, with his comic vision, believes that people who live in "conditions" really do live. With no impulse whatever to obscure sordidness with a beglamorizing haze, he also has no impulse to let his own sensitivity take first place, that sensitivity which, if allowed to refine itself far enough in awareness of "conditions," may issue in a revulsion from the human condition itself. Mr. Bellow accepts the bad or depressed environment in the way that it is accepted by most of the people who inhabit it—they accept themselves in it. Which is not to say that they do not estimate accurately everything about it, and perhaps hate it; but they do not suppose it is their death—it is their life: their "conditions" are charged with, conditioned by, their passions, their enterprises, even, if you will, their despairs, which accord with their own vital and personal principles. In the hierarchy of existence which D. H. Lawrence expounded, they might not be as high as they wish—who is?—but they have what Lawrence would call their own flamey being. Mr. Bellow's Grandma Lausch, his Einhorns, his Coblins, his Kleins, are not the "little people" of the lachrymose progressive journalism of the late Thirties—largeness of stature is more easily available to them than it ever was to any editorial writer for *PM*. They are not to be comprehended by their conditions, which in any case they are often able to overcome, for Mr. Bellow is far removed from the "proletarian" myth which used to dominate our social vision and his awareness of the American social mobility is an element of his power to create personal reality.

In this creation the language of *Augie March* plays a decisive part. It is, we are asked to believe, the language of Augie himself—that is, of a young man of unusual intelligence, perception, and feeling, who has gone to college only a little but who has read very widely and is committed to ideas, yet who refuses to think of himself as an "intellectual" or a writer, and who maintains, for reasons of his own, much of the intonation and idiom of casual speech. We have, then, a prose which is articulate to the last degree, very fluent and rapid, yet thick with metaphor and epithet, simple in any one of its rhetorical elements, complex in its combination of elements. It is contrived so as to say everything about the characters, to demonstrate their specifically intellectual vitality without any condescension; and as it glances easily—sometimes with an extravagant, an enforced, a slightly false ease—at historical personages and large cultural examples, the characters are brought, so to speak, into the full light of civilization and their reality is by that much still more enhanced.

It is the "idea" of Mr. Bellow's book, it is the formulated belief of its protagonist Augie, that to see people as I have tried to suggest that Mr. Bellow does see them is the test of righteousness of life, and that whatever fixes life and specializes and limits a person to a function, whether it be that of a social class, a profession, a theory, or a principle, endangers the wholeness of the self which makes possible the relation to and the perception of one's fellow men. As this informing idea emerges, we become aware of the genre of the novel with which *Augie March* has a perhaps conscious affinity. It has, of course, a clear connection with the picaresque novel in the sense that it is a series of more or less loosely connected adventures; also in the sense that its protagonist is, although virtuous, now and then literally a *picaro*, a thief, and that, like any Gil Blas, he has a natural aptitude for bypassing respectability. And it has, too, its connection with the *Bildungsroman,* for it is a novel of growth and education which has more than one similarity to *Wilhelm Meister.* But it is best thought of as the inversion and negation of the kind of nineteenth-century novel of which *The Red and the Black* may be taken as the prototype, in which the hero, rising from poor or provincial beginnings, directs his heroic ambitious will upon the world of power and glory. For Augie makes it the great point of his life to reject the power and the glory—at first unconsciously, then with growing awareness of what he is doing, he refuses the "heroic" in favor of what he believes the heroic destroys, a complete humanity. It is in this formulated rejection of the heroic will that *Augie March* is most specifically and essentially comic.

Augie is as well equipped for the power and glory as any Julian Sorel, for he is handsome, intelligent, charming, teachable, and he has, too, something of that charismatic quality of Julian's which draws people to help him. His origins are even lowlier than Julian's, for he is one of the three sons of an ignorant, humble woman and of a father who had early deserted the family. As Julian had the Napoleonic major to form his ideas of the great world, Augie has the redoubtable Grandma Lausch, who lodges with the March family and tries to instruct it in the world's ways as she had learned them in her wealthy days in Odessa. Like Julian, Augie is lifted suddenly out of his humble environment and given the chance to move in a society of at least some exclusiveness and elegance—a well-to-do Evanston couple are so pleased by his social possibilities that they offer to adopt him. His elder brother Simon, who moves toward power and glory with a Balzacian directness, arranges a wealthy marriage. And Julian's Mathilde de la Môle, the aristocratic girl who dreams of great deeds and can love only a man ready to die for a cause, has her counterpart in Augie's Thea, for whom life must always be at the stretch of adventure, for whom love is a preparation for action. But Augie begins with the knowledge with which Julian ends his life—that the fruits of the will are ashes in the mouth. He resists every effort to recruit him to any form of establishment, eminence, or power. Julian learns that the black coat of the Church and the red coat of the Army are equally strait; Augie never submits to wearing any cloth at all, or not for long. His emblematic beast is that eagle which Thea trains to hunt the giant iguanas of Mexico, which accepts its training, and then, at the great moment of test, refuses the heroic role with the calmest comic indifference—to all appearance a perfect Hotspur of a bird, he flaps away from the conflict with a Falstaffian imperviousness to what is required of one of his breed, noble and armed.

Augie is not a young Falstaff, except as he does not consent to be a Hotspur. If he refuses the heroic status, he is not in the least the poltroon, living for himself and the main chance. He is brave, he has large powers of love and loyalty. When he does begin to fantasy a way of life for himself, it involves a rural home in which he shall care for his blind mother and his mentally defective brother George, and give refuge to orphan children; or it has to do with the raising of bees. He simply will not accept any direction from the fierce superego; he will not be, to use David Riesman's terminology, an "inner-directed" man, he will be nothing less than "autonomous." He makes use of the comic negation of the heroic to bring himself into the tradition of American personalism. I speak of this as an American tradition because, although it has become an element of French existential thought, it has been most notably defined by Melville, Emerson, Whitman, Thoreau, Mark Twain, E. E. Cummings, Sherwood Anderson at his best, and even—Heaven help it!—by William Saroyan and Henry Miller. A person, as Mr. Bellow defines him, has a fate rather than a function, and powers of enjoyment and of love rather than of achievement.

After the climax of the eagle, the nature of *Augie March* changes. The climactic event brings the idea to full consciousness, the book moves into a relative abstractness, and discourse dominates event. The efforts to recruit Augie to some fixed principle or plan of life are now repeated as intellectual farce or burlesque, in the episodes of the eccentric millionaire who wants Augie's collaboration on a great work which shall define the nature of man, and of the mad scientist in the lifeboat who has synthesized protoplasm and wants Augie to join him in further biochemical triumphs. The tension of the story lessens; the new characters are less passionate and less passionately seen, and the narrative moves meditatively and at the easy gait of the idyll as Augie finds that it is possible to practice the virtues he has admired: "Why, I am a sort of Columbus of those near-at-hand and believe you can come to them in this immediate *terra incognita* that spreads out in every gaze. I may well be a flop at this line of endeavor. Columbus thought he was a flop, probably, when they sent him back in chains. Which didn't prove there was no America." With these words the book comes to its conclusion.

It is possible, I suppose, for a reader to protest his disappointment at this development of the novel, but to do so is, I think, to deny the book the freedom which its genre should bestow. For all its human richness, it is a novel of specific moral, intellectual intention—that intention being, as it happens, the demonstration of how to achieve and celebrate human richness—and it must be allowed discourse; it is a novel of education and it must be allowed the resolution and relaxation that comes with the sense of something learned. And its relaxed quality is in accord with the idea of the book, which is, as it were, the negation of drama, of the heroic will that makes for the intensities of drama. As for the idea itself, the reader's temperament will decide for him how far he can put himself in accord with it, but his intelligence cannot fail to respond to its importance. Which is, I suppose, my way of saying that, admiring Mr. Bellow's book as heartily as I do, I resist its propaganda, holding an opinion the direct opposite of Mr. Bellow's, that without function it is very difficult to be a person and have a fate.

—September 1953

A Review of the Alternate

W. H. AUDEN

On J. R. R. Tolkien's *The Fellowship of the Ring*

SEVENTEEN YEARS AGO there appeared, without any fanfare, a book called "The Hobbit" which, in my opinion, is one of the best children's stories of this century. In "The Fellowship of the Ring," which is the first volume of a trilogy, J. R. R. Tolkien continues the imaginative history of the imaginary world to which he introduced us in his earlier book but in a manner suited to adults, to those, that is, between the ages of 12 and 70. For anyone who likes the genre to which it belongs, the Heroic Quest, I cannot imagine a more wonderful reading experience. All Quests are concerned with some numinous Object: the Waters of Life, the Grail, buried treasure, etc.; normally this is a good Object which it is the Hero's task to find or to rescue from the Enemy, but the Ring of Mr. Tolkien's story was made by the Enemy and is so dangerous that even the good cannot use it without being corrupted.

The Enemy believed that it had been lost forever, but he has just discovered that it has come providentially into the hands of the Hero and is devoting all his demonic powers to its recovery, which would give him the lordship of the world. The only way to make sure of his defeat is to destroy the Ring, but this can only be done in one way and in one place which lies in the heart of the Enemy's country; the task of the Hero, therefore, is to get the Ring to the place of its unmaking without getting caught.

The hero, Frodo Baggins, belongs to a race of beings called hobbits, who may be only three feet high, have hairy feet and prefer to live in underground houses, but in their thinking and sensibility resemble very closely those arcadian rustics who inhabit so many British detective stories. I think some readers may find the opening chapter a little shy-making, but they must not let themselves be put off, for, once the story gets moving, this initial archness disappears.

For over a thousand years the hobbits have been living a peaceful existence in a fertile district called the Shire, incurious about the world outside. Actually, the latter is rather sinister; towns have fallen into ruins, roads into disrepair, fertile fields have returned to wilderness, wild beasts and evil beings on the prowl, and travel is difficult and dangerous. In addition to the Hobbits, there are Elves who are wise and good, Dwarves who are skillful and good on the whole, and Men, some warriors, some wizards, who are good or bad. The present incarnation of the Enemy is Sauron, Lord of Barad-Dur, the Dark Tower in the Land of Mordor. Assisting him are Orcs, wolves and other horrid creatures and, of course, such men as his power attracts or overawes. Landscape, climate and atmosphere are northern, reminiscent of the Icelandic sagas.

The first thing that one asks of an adventure story is that the adventure should be various and exciting; in this respect Mr. Tolkien's invention is unflagging, and, on the primitive level of wanting to know what happens next, "The Fellowship of the Ring" is at least as good as "The Thirty-Nine Steps." Of any imaginary world the reader demands that it seem real, and the standard of realism demanded today is much stricter than in the time, say, of Malory. Mr. Tolkien is fortunate in possessing an amazing gift for naming and a wonderfully exact eye for description; by the time one has finished his book one knows the histories of Hobbits, Elves, Dwarves and the landscape they inhabit as well as one knows one's own childhood.

Lastly, if one is to take a tale of this kind seriously, one must feel that, however superficially unlike the world we live in its characters and events may be, it nevertheless holds up the mirror to the only nature we know, our own; in this, too, Mr. Tolkien has succeeded superbly, and what happened in the year of the Shire 1418 in the Third Age of Middle Earth is not only fascinating in A. D. 1954 but also a warning and an inspiration. No fiction I have read in the last five years has given me more joy than "The Fellowship of the Ring."

—MARCH 1955

Proust's Way

JACQUES BARZUN

On Marcel Proust's *Jean Santeuil*, translated by Gerard Hopkins

THOUGH ONE NEED NOT be a Proustian to take a lively and sustained interest in the abundant pages of *Jean Santeuil*, it helps to be emancipated from the conventions of the novel, even the very loose conventions of the modern novel. *Jean Santeuil* is fiction without story, and the reader who looks in it for plot, or even for rounded incident, will do what Dr. Johnson predicted of the man who should go to *Clarissa Harlowe* with the same exclusive purpose: he will hang himself.

As probably everyone knows by now, *Jean Santeuil* never existed in legible form until M. Bernard de Fallois, a leading Proust scholar, unexpectedly found a mass of discarded sheets and notebooks in Proust's spidery hand, and conceived the idea of putting them in some order inferred from their contents. Proust himself seems to have abandoned the work some time around the turn of the century. He abandoned, that is, this particular set of drafts and sketches, for we can now see in them through M. de Fallois's reconstruction the faint outlines and parts of the substance of the other, the great though unfinished masterpiece that Proust began to publish in 1913.

Here and abroad vehement protests have been made to the publication of the rejected *Santeuil* materials in a form that cannot help being conjectural and misleading. That eminent and judicious scholar, Mrs. Mina Curtiss, has written that the "concoction" is "of value only to the confirmed Proustian" and might well alienate from the real novel the person who has never read it. The notes and sheets, she thinks, should have been presented purely as notes, themselves fully annotated for the enlightenment of students of literature.

As one who is anything but a "confirmed Proustian," and whose well-disposed ignorance puts him almost in the category of those Mrs. Curtiss is trembling for, I may be permitted, if not to rebut her conclusion, at least to show its complementary opposite.

First comes the simple fact of experience: one can read *Jean Santeuil* from page one to page seven forty-four without flagging. All one need do, as I said, is to relax the customary expectation that events or ideas will be strictly followed up. The question of propriety in compiling a "novel" from the notes then becomes one of choosing between an occasional confusion or disappointment and the more arduous effort of imagination that would be needed to synthesise fragments, dragging with them a retinue of footnotes. I can conceive the value and the interest of the dates, conjectures, and parallels which would cling to each germ of *Swann* in *Santeuil*. But it is this other, scholarly presentation, surely, which would address the "confirmed Proustian" and which might well put the layman off the "real novel." By way of comparison, who but a Flaubertiste delights in the first version and scenarios of *Madame Bovary*? Who but a Jamesian can read the *Notebooks,* for all their solicitous editing? Heaven knows, I am not against the *study* of literature; but I rejoice when I am led, as by M. de Fallois's completely hidden scholarship, to find a piece of literature, new or old, accessible in the open air. Notice that it is the confirmed Proustians who have shuddered at the mild imposture. They feel cheated though not deceived, and I should be the first to say that they are entitled to their notes in a future edition. Meanwhile, if my experience is in any way typical, the non-specialist reader of *Remembrance* who takes up *Santeuil* as it stands will happily, steadily enjoy "floating double, *Swann* and shadow."

The image suggests that the time has come to ask what it is in the made-up book that, in Henry James's phrase, supplies the "current to draw one on and on." This forward movement is the test of fiction, no matter what the genre— epic, novel, or drama. To be drawn on and on means that we have been made to dream. The author has hypnotized us and we believe. The sensation is so unmistakable that when we encounter a work of history or philosophy which transports us by high art, we say that "it reads like a novel," meaning: it seems a world apart in which we have somehow been lured to live.

The great point of *Jean Santeuil* is that we live there easily, confidently, despite the rugged terrain. It is a recognizable dwelling-place despite the broken floors and the holes in the ceiling. Which implies that neither form nor the development of character but something else is the secret of the novelist's power. We ought to have known this from reading Petronius, Cervantes, and *Gulliver.* We have been misled by the weight of differing examples, as well as by our pretentious vocabulary of criticism—the pride of calling for architectonic virtues and the like. Proust or anybody else is a novelist from the moment he begins to produce his characteristic substance. Substance is not exactly style, though it is related to it. Rather it is a completely idiosyncratic product, a secretion of the organ of inner vision, which turns out to be unlike any other. We use a truer image than we suppose when we say that a man "spins a yarn." The reality comes out of him, not out of an intelligible comparison of words with things. All the qualities of a tale seem to belong to it without any act of will or choice on the part of the teller. And the importance of his uniqueness is not that it reflects his merit, but that it insures his credibility. Even the real must be strange before we can believe it, and mere accuracy of description will not do. That is why intelligence, "insight," and technical skill are not enough. The novelist needs, not virtues, but powers. We see this very clearly today when we follow the productions of some of our non-fiction novelists such as Mr. C. P. Snow and Mr. Arthur Koestler. Their works are "interesting," full of observation and talent and even wisdom, but as far as fictional faith goes, we are left to make the effort by ourselves. On the witness stand, after reading one of their highly-charged essays on the contemporary scene, one would have to hold up one's right hand and say "I don't believe a word of it."

Jean Santeuil, per contra, is the ocular proof that Proust was a born fictioner. Everything he touches turns to substance. Here is a piece of it:

> When they returned for lunch his uncle said to his mother, "We've been having a look at the camellia: it is really superb!" And to Ménard (the gardener), he never tired of saying, "Ménard, that is really a superb tree!"— "Yes," said Jean's mother, "it's very lovely."—"Oh, it's a beautiful tree, a superb tree," replied Jean's uncle. "But you shouldn't go and see it now, it's lost a good half of its blossoms," he added with the modesty and also the self-satisfaction becoming the owner of the tree, and with the fussiness of those who are more knowledgeable about one thing or another than prone merely to love; who require that the Beethoven symphonies be played by famous orchestras, and who think it not worth while to see Sarah Bernhardt in a given part.

The trademark is unmistakable. Even if we have never read a line of *Swann,* we know that this is a voice distinct from all others. It has the supreme self-assurance that makes us want to know what it has to say about anything. As soon as it starts to speak it generates the current to draw us on and on. Compared with this power, Proust's notions of Time and Remembrance, his use of cake crumbs or musical phrases as agents and symbols of continuity, are of secondary importance and interest. What is primary is the novelist's innate conviction that the entire real world tends one way, whereas we all see it incoherently. He is obsessed with the desire to show it as it is, and the result is that we end by seeing it as he does. We carry away for our own uses the sense of the new color he has imparted to the whole, and say of an experienced fact (as of a literary imitation): "This is Proustian, this is Dickensian, this is pure Balzac, this is Hardyesque." James must have had this kind of homogeneity in mind when, in writing about Balzac, he remarked that great novelists create a single aura of time or season for all their works—a bright morning or a late afternoon or a perpetual autumn.

Jean Santeuil ostensibly takes up many things, among them the Panama scandal, and the Dreyfus Affair; the hero's early childhood and his time of military service; the snobbery of the aristocracy and its imitation by the bourgeoisie. But looking back on the multitude of portraits and events, one is struck by the thought that the mind through which we see them all is that of an ailing child. I use the words at once neutrally and metaphorically, in just the way that James spoke of a uniformity of season throughout a man's works. The character of Jean Santeuil is established by a long account of his infantile relation to his mother, which is at once autobiography and high art. And we know that this was written well before Proust himself took to his cork-lined room and the ways of an invalid. Yet his style already has the garrulity of the man who lives largely within himself, who lives, indeed, on his memories, and whose loneliness engenders a curiosity always verging on pruriency—like a child's.

I repeat that I am trying to describe, with no intention of diminishing, Proust's achievement. My terms, in fact, denote only the extreme point of development in the fundamental attitudes of the novel as a genre. The novel is a modern bourgeois diversion which satisfies two or three rather low motives— curiosity (how the other half lives and works, the truth of the gossip about intimacies and private thoughts); snobbery (what the really best people will do and feel); and pedantry ("this actually happened and to prove it I'll choke you with details"). These three motives are at their most acute in the child, and his normal mixture of self-regard with wonderment is a characteristic of the invalid. It is consequently not strange that Proust's circumstances and method should have produced, thanks to his genius, the culminating masterpiece of a genre.

The reader who understands how Santeuil's character was formed by a typically French upbringing at work on a nervous temperament will also understand why the grown man's life of sociable idleness and hothouse affections perfectly satisfied him. And obviously, it is through such a man's eyes that we can best see the panorama Proust had to show. Two passages only will seem out of keeping—that in which young Santeuil has a purely physical affair with a lusty serving girl—unbelievable on all counts; and that in which he berates a politician in defense of his own father—unbelievable in language and authority. The improbability does not arise from the few hints of homosexuality scattered in the book; it comes from our conviction that Santeuil participates in life rather than lives it. Not a passive observer, he brings to people and events chiefly his excitable heart, high intelligence, and charming manners. He is thus a good deal more than James's emasculated, tale-bearing agents who listen at keyholes. But he shares with them the profound sense that being is preferable to doing; the sense out of which comes the technical importance of "the point of view," and which defines an epoch. For novelists can be divided into those that know and those that find out. And down to Flaubert, the majority are omniscient without half prying. The only thing they know nothing of is the sanctity of the point of view.

Just because in *Santeuil* the author's skill does not cut us off so completely from comparisons as it does in his later work, we can better judge his position in the history of art. He himself indicates it by his explicit references to Balzac and Stendhal. These two writers haunt him; he loves them and argues with them and wishes they had never existed. The nearer Realists and Naturalists are no bother to him. Proust retains from their practice the heavy ballast of household detail. But Balzac already has Proust's theme of the invasion of the old aristocracy (Côté Guermantes) by the top layer of the bourgeoisie (Côté Swann), and he handles it almost like an old story, with a casual brevity fit to crush a latecomer with envy:

> The Duc d'Hérouville, polite to everyone like the genuine nobleman that he was, gave the Comte de la Palférine that particular kind of greeting which, without marking any esteem or intimacy, proclaims to everybody else "We are of the same species, the same race, we are equals!" This greeting, this *shibboleth* of the aristocracy, was created to inspire despair among the talented members of the upper bourgeoisie.

Half a dozen lines: Proust takes as many pages in the section "Portrait of a Friend" to show us birth and politeness in the makeup of Bertrand de Réveillon, and a hundred more elsewhere to show—since the peculiar virtue is inherited—how Bertrand's mother and father say "How do ye do" and act in other trivial particulars. And then there is in *Santeuil* a chapter on Balzac himself, possibly for the comfort it gave Proust to write two revealing remarks: "Balzac was a snob as well"; and "All the same, our lives are not wholly separated from our works. All the scenes I have narrated here, I have lived through. How can they be of less value in real life than in a book?"

At this stage, it would have comforted Proust to read Mr. Harry Levin's memorable essay of 1950 on Proust and Balzac, in which justice is admirably done to both: a task did remain after Balzac had done his; the task of organizing *nuance* in a large mosaic—the task of the nineties. For periods, like books, have their destinies, and De Quincey enunciated a general truth when he said: "Finding themselves forestalled as regards the grander passions, they [the creative energies] will be likely to settle upon the feebler elements of manners." This marks a decline only in energy not in art, and the loss in ruggedness is made up for in delicacy. So completely, in fact, that many in our own period of post-delicacy are ready to deny art to the rugged pioneers.

Proust had no illusions on that point. We must, he said, "reread the masters with more simplicity. We shall be astonished to see how living they still are, how near to us, yielding a thousand examples of success in the very attempts where we ourselves have failed." The second master that Proust read with simplicity was Stendhal. Proust disputes his theory in the section "On Love," but cannot help agreeing with him about "crystallization," love's power to create the thing it desires, while "our instinctive life continues to unfold in a part of ourselves of which consciousness knows nothing." When Jean Santeuil is falling in love with Charlotte, the first inkling of it is the thought "How pleasant it would be to kiss her." Opening Stendhal's *On Love,* we find in Chapter Two: "Here is what goes on in consciousness: (1) Admiration (2) One says to oneself: 'How pleasant to kiss her, to be kissed, etc. (3) Hope."

But there is more than doctrinal agreement between the two novelists. On the one hand, Santeuil's jealousy (like Swann's later) is the full working out of what Stendhal only sketched; on the other, Proust's linking of thought to thought—and especially of present fact to artistic recollection—is visibly influenced by Stendhal. No other writer between their two lifespans had used this kind of freedom to unite art and autobiography. If Stendhal's *Life of Henry Brulard* now reads like a telegraphic version of Proust, it is only because the man of the nineties is more didactic than his predecessor.

Proust's work is indeed one long explanation of a mystery never stated. And this takes us back to the question of substance, whose effect we cannot account for though we know its features. A Proustian thought proceeds by a series of appositions, continually modified by doubts and quiet surprises. There is, so to speak, a Romantic piling up of examples, each altered by the subjective nuance of Impressionism, while also the drama of Romantic antithesis is replaced by a Symbolist simile out of context. For instance, Jean as a child is afraid of the dark and thinks about the nightly lighting of lights. "Very soon his big lamp would come, spreading a warm radiance, flooding his heart and his table with its powerful kindliness, laying a sweetness all about him. But when the actual moment of going to bed arrived, the comfort he had found in activity and light was taken from him. No longer could he put off the saying of good nights, in other words, the leaving of the whole world for a whole night: he must give up all hope of talking to his mother if he felt miserable, of climbing on to her knee if he felt too lonely: even the wretched candle must be put out and he lie there, without moving, so that sleep might come while he lay there, abandoned, silent motionless, and blind. . . ."

The associated ideas go on for a page more, tied together with "in this way," "or rather," "as such." Sometimes, despite the unflagging appositeness of the next comparison, the reader wearies of discoveries and reminders. He feels he is being talked to like a retarded child. He would give anything to arrest the massaging of his eardrums by that quiet relentless voice. He almost sees the invalid in bed, remembrancing all things past without fear or favor, uttering them in the unmodulated tones of a ten-year-old. It is rare to find in Proust the abrupt turns so usual to Stendhal, but they occur: "If anyone ventured to speak a word, she cast a reproachful look at the offender, following the silent rebuke with a smile intended to soften this mark of her disapproval, like a dancer playing the part of a lieutenant."

One might expect that the dialogue would provide a contrast with the steadily poetic or philosophic imaginings of the narrator. But Proust's dialogue is uniformly and, no doubt, purposely trivial. It is not even seasoned with colloquialisms in quotation marks, as in the later Henry James; it remains lifelike in being platitudinous. In all of *Jean Santeuil* there is not one quotable spoken "mot." Indeed, this banality at times affects the commentary, as when we read: "The woods no longer garnished with the sun's brilliant dyes had lost all their poetry"; or: "Much that for us is fraught with happiness or misery remains almost unnoticed by the rest of the world."

We then remember that we are reading, illegitimately, unrevised writing. But apart from this we would still reach the conclusion that criticism has no business discussing Proust's mind. He is not a thinker, of any sort, even about esthetics. He himself saw more truly when he insisted on the primacy in his work of sense impressions and involuntary memory. *Santeuil* is the diary of a sensualist who reflects. The letter Proust wrote to a friend in 1912, shortly before the publication of *Swann's Way*, and in which he expounds the famous principle of the crumb in the teacup, rightly asserts the superficiality of conscious thought for his purposes. Again, in another fragment, he deprecates "the noting down of things, accurately enough as they seem to the mind, but without that intoxication which is the only sign of the truly remarkable." It is thus absurd to find in the outward meaning of Proust's fictional remarks any notable truths. To take one example, he made use of music, rather than said anything valuable about it. No one could carry on as he did about "a little phrase" from a sonata if music were really a language he possessed like a native. More important, his social theme was but the servant of his pre-existing substance, and as such his panorama of pettiness and decadence is not to be measured against any more deliberate social critique, like that of Flaubert or Zola. Proust's world is actually minuscule, and the "disintegration of the aristocracy" that goes on there was nothing new in 1900. Two interpretations are then open to us: either the decadence is that of an insignificant social group or it is emblematic of life as a whole. If the former is true, we have no historical picture of a modern decline and fall; if the latter, then the picture is true of all times and places.

Proust's limitations as a thinker do not of course impugn the depth of his perceptions, about which he was miraculously articulate; and he had no need of more than this to produce a fresh embodiment of an ancient mood, the mood of the melancholy gazer at transiency. In this he is often sublime. But here too he seems to me to owe more than has been suspected to his older contemporary and fellow impressionist, Pierre Loti. A passage such as this from *Jean Santeuil* reminds one of Loti not solely by its images of travel but by its cadences: "It is as though we were chained prisoners in the ship of some conqueror, or rather one of those travellers whom we see in passing, on a night journey, overcome with sleep and without the strength to open their eyes to take one last look, in the moments that remain, at what they will never see again. For the separate periods of our heart's life are like islands which will be swallowed up in the ocean once the traveller has taken leave of them; and of which, though they may leave fond memories with him, he never more will come upon a trace."

The question of style raises that of the present translation and its original. *Jean Santeuil* contains much of loose and lumpy writing, as we should expect in discarded notebooks. At best, Proust's way of piling up images, coral-like, does not lend itself to immediate clarity, much less to balance, which was in any case no virtue with his Symbolist generation. This explains why he had to pay in order to get his first volumes published. Bernard Grasset (who died only the other day) was not quite up-to-date enough in 1912 to take a chance on stuff so strangely put together. The new writers were Gide and Giraudoux, and we know how Gide, acting for the *Nouvelle Revue Française,* was put off by the "bizarreries" of *Swann's Way* and rejected it. Gide's apology two years later gives us a measure of how original Proust's substance was:

I thought of you, I must confess, as . . . a snob, a man of the world, and a dilettante—the worst possible thing for our review. And your offer to help us finance the book—a gesture which I can understand so well today and which I should have found charming then if I had only interpreted it *correctly*—only served, alas, to plunge me deeper into error. The only portion of your manuscript I had to go by, I opened absent-mindedly, and as ill-luck would have it, my attention fell at once into the cup of camomile tea on page 62; then stumbled over the sentence on page 64 (the only one that I do not even now clearly understand . . .) where there is talk of a pediment with some vertebrae showing through.

The far worse blemishes of *Jean Santeuil* confronted its experienced translator, Mr. Gerard Hopkins, with the uncomfortable dilemma of literalness versus improvement. Literalness is no solution, for as too few readers recognize, there is no such thing as giving an exact equivalent of confused thought. As for improvement, it always amounts to interpreting, to saying without much warrant: "This is what he would have done if he had revised." Mr. Hopkins was so beset by these opposing perplexities that although he gives us a wonderfully readable and largely Proustian text, he sometimes goes too far in tidying up and occasionally misses the sense altogether. In principle the former is worse. Proust repeats words like the obsessed creature that he was and should be allowed to remain. Why introduce elegant variation in epithets when we have to leave his proper names as they are, almost all beginning with S? But what is more distressing than Proust's banging on one note and the translator's muffling of the sound, is the fatally easy transliteration that misleads. The reader will wonder what those "wooden horses" are in the Champs Elysées, until he is told that they are a merry-go-round, just as "lusters" are better known as chandeliers. "Egotism" will fall oddly in many places where "selfishness" would be clear, and the peculiar force of "Old Man Hugo" (the poet) will be lost if "Old Man" is diminished into "Daddy."

There is more, but none of this—and it is the mystery of art—dents our awareness that what we are absorbing (with camomile tea and vertebrae thrown in) is the induplicable stuff of fiction.

—April 1956

Dostoevsky in Siberia

W. H. AUDEN

On Fyodor Dostoevsky's *The House of the Dead*

THE HOUSE OF THE DEAD is not Dostoevsky's greatest work but it is, perhaps, his least irritating. The slavophil and west-hating Dostoevsky has not yet appeared and there is very little of the Creeping Jesus. What is disturbing and, in the end, unpleasant about the novels is Dostoevsky's inability, despite all the talk about Love, to create a single character whom the reader can *like*. As D. H. Lawrence said of them:—"All the people are *fallen angels*—even the dirtiest scrubs. This I cannot stomach. People are not fallen angels, they are merely people. But Dostoevsky used them all as theological or religious units. . . ." Dostoevsky may have made up some of the incidents in *The House of the Dead,* but it does not read like fiction; it reads like straight factual reportage upon life in a Siberian convict prison of which we know Dostoevsky had personal experience. One does not feel that the facts have been tailored to suit a particular kind of imagination but that any man in Dostoevsky's position would have had the same experiences, though he might not be able to express them.

The memoirs purport to be written by a member of the minor gentry, Alexander Petrovich Goryanchikov, who had murdered his wife in a fit of jealousy and then given himself up. Having been released from prison he remains in the small Siberian town and lives by giving lessons to children whom he loves; adults he hates and avoids.

It is interesting that Dostoevsky should have made his *alter ego* not a political offender like himself but a murderer who, one presumes from his giving himself up, must have repented of his act and wished to atone for it. A political offender cannot be guilty in his own eyes for it is his own conscience, or so he must think, that has made him commit his offence, and he must wish that every one else should do likewise. Dostoevsky himself must have been doubly estranged from the majority of his fellow prisoners, first, like Goryanchikov, because he was gentry and they were peasants, and, secondly, because in his eyes they were criminals and he was not. On the other hand, Goryanchikov has his special kind of isolation. Though he never, thank goodness, refers to his own crime, he is presented as the one prisoner who, in contrast to the rest, recognizes that he has committed a crime which deserves punishment.

> I never once saw among these men the slightest sign of remorse, the least gnawing of conscience, and that the majority of them believed themselves to have done nothing wrong. . . . I heard tales of the most terrible, the most unnatural actions, the most monstrous murders, told with absolutely irrepressible, childishly merry laughter.

One is never allowed to forget—and in this lies the greatness and terror of the book—that prisons, with all their senseless horrors, are populated mostly by horrid people. Even if we could eliminate from criminal law all notion of retribution, the necessity to segregate the criminal would remain, and criminals, however humanely treated, are unlikely to reform in each other's company.

Here are some of Dostoevsky's observations about his fellow inmates:

> Generally speaking, the whole tribe with the exception of a few unquenchably cheerful souls, who for that reason enjoyed universal contempt, was sullen, envious, terribly conceited, boastful, touchy, and preoccupied in the highest degree with forms . . . they were all vitally concerned about one thing: what sort of figure they cut. . . . All the prisoners robbed one another shamelessly. . . . As for informing in general, it commonly flourishes in prison. The informer is not subjected to any infamy; nobody so much as thinks of being indignant with him. He is not shunned, his friendship is acceptable, and anybody who tried to demonstrate the full vileness of informing would be quite incomprehensible. . . .
>
> After dinner we learned that the fugitives had been captured in such-and-such a village seventy versts away. It is difficult to convey the impression produced on the prisoners by this news. At first they all seemed to fly into a temper, then gloom overwhelmed them. Later an inclination to jeer showed itself. They began to laugh, no longer at the pursuers but at the recaptured men; at first it was only a few who laughed, but afterwards almost everybody except a few strong and serious characters. . . . In a word, Kukilov and A were now just as much decried, and even decried with pleasure,

as they had before been extolled. It was as if they had somehow done every-body an injury.

Such disagreeable characteristics may be aggravated by life in prison, but the prisoners already possessed them when they came.

Dostoevsky was the first novelist to make a serious study of the criminal personality, and our present knowledge has not advanced very far beyond the point to which his insights brought us.

He shows us that what distinguishes the typical criminal from the average man whose criminal wishes are not realized in action is that the former's conception of himself is fantastic; quite literally he does not know who he is. The average man can distinguish between wishes which he knows are fantastic and his real desires which are possible to fulfill because they are grounded in his actual nature; the criminal cannot. Thus, while all men desire to be valued by others, the "normal" man recognizes that if this desire is to be gratified he must do or make something valuable, and that what he himself can do depends upon his capacities and his circumstances; the criminal, on the other hand, does not want to be valued for this or that concrete reason, he simply wants to be important and, since this desire is without relation to anything concrete, he desires to be infinitely important, and other people, except in so far as they minister to this, have no reality for him.

> There exists, for example, and in very large numbers, the following type of murderer. This man lives quietly and meekly. His lot is bitter but he endures it. Let us suppose that he is a peasant farmer, a house-serf, a tradesman or a soldier. Suddenly something snaps inside him: he can stand it no longer and sticks a knife into his enemy and persecutor. Now begins the strange part: the man runs temporarily amock. His first killing was of his enemy, his persecutor; that was criminal but understandable; there was a motive; but afterwards he kills not enemies but chance passers-by, kills for amusement, because of a harsh word or look, for a string of beads, or simply: "Get out of the way and don't let me catch you; I'm coming!"

The fact that the first murder was not enough is evidence that what seemed to be its motive, a concrete revenge, was not its real motive.

OVER AGAINST THE FANTASTIC existence of the criminal, however, stands something equally fantastic, the Penal System, based on the impossible notion of impersonal retribution or punishment. The replacement of the blood-feud by the Law of the State is no doubt an advance in civilization, but if it is made, then the notion that the criminal should be punished must be abandoned because punishment cannot be inflicted by the State but only by individuals acting on its behalf. A man who kills another in a blood-feud may be cruel but he remains human; he has a personal motive for his action and he accepts it as his own. The Public Executioner who tortures and kills, not for any personal grievance but because torturing and killing are his legal "mystery" is a monster.

> Although the flogging may give him satisfaction, he hardly ever feels any personal hatred for his victim. The skill of his hand, his knowledge of his art, the desire to impress his fellows and the public, all stimulate his vanity. . . . It is strange that all the many executioners I have come across have been fairly highly developed people with common sense, intelligence, and unusual vanity or even pride . . . before the beginning of the punishment the executioner is in a state of great exaltation, conscious of his strength and knowing himself to be supreme; at that moment he is an actor; his audience is filled with wonder and dismay and it is certainly not without some pleasure that he cries out to his victim, before the first stroke, the familiar and ominous words: "Hold tight, I'm going to flay you!"

Of the other prison officials whom Dostoevsky describes, some, like Lieutenant Zherebyatnikov, were simple sadists; some, like the major Commandant, tyrannical because afraid; and some, like the house surgeon, kind and good. How a man will behave towards others is determined partly by his character and partly by his occupation. Generally these are related. The one who chooses a profession the function of which is the relief of suffering is likely to be someone who, consciously at least, does not desire to inflict it, and the habit of relieving suffering will develop his compassion. Vice versa it is impossible to conceive of a kind-hearted man choosing the profession of executioner, or even a job in which he would exercise absolute power over others. But it has been made only too clear in recent years that occupational habit is a stronger force in most cases than character. Put an averagely decent man, who would never have chosen the job for himself, in charge of a concentration camp and he will presently come to enjoy cruelty.

In Utopia there would be no executions because nobody would consent to be the executioner: in the world we know, we can only abolish the death penalty by law and deprive the would-be executioner of his fun. We cannot do very much, for, so long as there are criminals and lunatics whom for our safety we must deprive of their freedom, dreadful things will always occur, however "advanced" our methods of treatment: a psychologist can be as cruel as a warder.

Many books have been written about prison life since *The House of the Dead,* some about worse prisons, some about better, but they have found little to add to Dostoevsky's account and nothing to contradict. The best and the worst prison are more like each other than they resemble any sane and civil community.

—NOVEMBER 1956

The Story and the Novel

LIONEL TRILLING

On Isak Dinesen's *Last Tales* and James Agee's *A Death in the Family*

PUT THE TWO BOOKS side by side, Isak Dinesen's *Last Tales* and James Agee's *A Death in the Family*: it might well be thought that no other two works of fiction written in the same age could be so different from each other. Nor is theirs an indifferent difference but a fierce antagonism of incongruousness, as if the author of each had known exactly what the author of the other was doing and had set out to controvert it by doing the opposite. If one were to take a length of the brocaded red velvet which must inevitably curtain the windows of the room in which Isak Dinesen's Cardinal Salviati sits in high compassionate worldliness, and were to lay beside it a length of the wash-faded denim whose moral and aesthetic value James Agee once expounded, the two fabrics would seem no more reconcilable than the two books.

But perhaps the suspicion will already have arisen that I make so much of the difference only with a view to saying, at some point further along, that it is after all not what it seems; that if we look again with an enlightened eye, the two books will be understood to have something, even a great deal, in common; that, as a matter of fact, between the two authors there is a spiritual affinity of the closest kind. The suspicion is well founded. This is indeed the (rather fatigued) critical tactic I meant to use. But before I come to my *peripeteia,* in which it will be made plain that the Danish countess and the Tennessean who looked much as Daniel Boone would have looked if he had gone to Harvard are really brother and sister, separated in infancy by some hard but significant fate—before I reach this startling but unavoidable disclosure, I should like, for the sake of the drama, to maintain a little while longer our sense of the difference between them.

In her *Last Tales*—the title makes an ostentation of stoicism which seems to me pleasing—Isak Dinesen continues the genre and the manner of her *Seven Gothic Tales* (1934) and her *Winter's Tales* (1942). As to the manner, it is intentionally mannered. When I first encountered it, the conscious affectation of the prose irritated me. Now I find it interesting and attractive, and this is not only because its extravagance in the first volume was chastened in the second and even more in the third. It is a prose that is about as *managed* as prose can be; it uses all the devices of contemporary rhetoric that are available to a prose that can still be thought of as modern. Yet its tone is colloquial— the tales are always *told* rather than written, and this is true even when there is no fictional narrator and the author writes in her own pseudonymous person. The diction is scarcely less elaborate than the rhetoric. It is choice, elegant, not abashed by its occasional ornateness.

It is manifest that the prose of the *Tales* is seen by the author as a costume in which, to use an old phrase, she "clothes her thought." The costume is an archaic one—it is meant to be emblematic of an old and vanished aristocracy, worldly, formal, curious, credulous, and having the wisdom of credulity, in general the wisdom ascribed to all vanished races.

It isn't easy for all readers to come to terms with this manner, although many do so with no difficulty. Of those who do find it hard, some will object that they are being invited into a social arcanum which they have no hankering for—the manner is thought to be merely a display of snobbery. Others will make the more complicated objection that the manner is false, because true aristocracy doesn't need to be at such pains to mark its existence.

The second objection is based on the modern belief that there ought not to be any concern with the outward and visible signs of inward and spiritual states, and that if any such signs are consciously shown, they will necessarily be false. This is an unexamined belief, and to maintain it is to deny the possibility of all good prose, which, even in its simplest forms, is the expression of a personal ideal of some sort. Anyone who has ever taught Freshman English is aware that—knowledge of rhetoric apart—the difference between a good writer and a bad one is the belief that there is some important connection between one's notion of one's self and one's mode of expression. When we consider more developed prose, we see that style ought to command respect not only because it is interesting in itself but because it is intellectually useful. For instance, and to stay with the aristocratic manner, how much of the power of Tocqueville's mind derives from the style of his prose, which, modelled on that of Tacitus, is meant to be the utterance appropriate to a nobleman who has been dispossessed of his old privileges and yet keeps the disinterestedness of his Aristotelean "magnanimity," or, as one translator, Philip Wheelwright, renders the Greek word, his "aristocratic pride." So too does the manner of

Isak Dinesen's prose undertake to embody personal qualities of no small intellectual value. And not only are these qualities characteristic of the narrator of the tales (or her fictional surrogates)—they are presumed to be characteristic of the audience as well.

And this leads to the answer to the objection that we are invited to share a class prestige which is not proper or becoming to us. Actually the manner has no very serious social purpose: it has to do chiefly with establishing the possibility of our belief. The archaic formality, if once we accept it, suggests that we must in courtesy practice a certain credulity, that we have committed ourselves not to ask vulgar modern questions. And I think that we are the readier to yield to the condition that the prose implies because it is charged with feminine *chic,* with a happy and graceful exhibitionism, with a fairly frank avowal of role: it intimates that its behavior is in some part ambiguous and flirtatious, that it aims to beglamour and to induce belief for this particular occasion only.

Which leads to the matter of the genre. This is defined in an elaborate apologia for her tales which the author puts into the mouth of one of her characters, the Cardinal Salviati. On this occasion she calls them stories, rather than tales. Perhaps she wishes for the moment to bring to mind the overtones the word has from childhood—adults sometimes do speak of tales, although even they really use the word only in the plural and chiefly in the titles of books; children never do. "Tell me a story," is what they say, and we would be justifiably alarmed if they asked for a tale. And at least it used to be true that polite children said, "You're a big story-teller," when they meant a big liar. Isak Dinesen's stories are all lies. Their matter is magic and witchcraft, infants exchanged at birth, brothers and sisters who marry unknown to each other, beautiful giantesses, undying passions—suchlike nonsense. These lies are told with an air that leads us to believe that they are involved with truth of a kind not available to minds that submit to strict veracity. This does not—it is a relief to note—relate them to myths, of which everybody tired a few years ago. They are quite simply, or complicatedly, stories.

The truth that is claimed for them is not a truth of generalization, not even the generalization that life is compounded of improbabilities and marvels. It is a truth of perception and evaluation. This is the point of the apologia with which "The Cardinal's First Tale" concludes. The story begins with the lady in black asking Cardinal Craviati who he is. The Cardinal remarks that she is the first of his penitents to ask that question. All the problems that had ever been put to him, he says, have been "but so many variants of one single cry of the heart, of one question: 'Who am I?'"; yet no one has ever asked him who *he* is. The lady in black is not to be deflected from her purpose. With bland courtesy the Cardinal says that he will tell her a story, and does so. Its incidents need not concern us; it is enough to know that it is sufficiently strange and that it is really about the Cardinal himself. When the story is done, the lady in black says, "Your Eminence in answer to a question has been telling me a story, in which my friend and teacher is the hero. I see the hero of the story very clearly, as if luminous even, and on a higher plane. But my teacher and adviser—and my friend—is further away than before. He no more looks to me quite human, and alas, I am not sure that I am not afraid of him." To this the Cardinal replies that such is the effect of the story—of the true story—upon character. He goes on to speak of the rise of the novel, the new art form, which has precisely the opposite effect upon character. "This new art and literature," he says, "—for the sake of the individual characters in the story, and in order to keep close to them and not be afraid—will be ready to sacrifice the story itself." He praises the novel as "a noble art, a great, earnest and ambitious human product." "But," he continues, "it is a human product. The divine art is the story. In the beginning was the story." As to that, it may be so, although it doesn't seem to be a discussable proposition. But there is considerable substance to the Cardinal's remark that "where the story is, the characters will gather," and to his statement that the character, which is to say, the hero, is made by the story, that when the "new literature shall reign supreme, you will have no more heroes," which is to say, no more characters.

The Cardinal's compatriot, Professor Mario Praz, recently published a massive attack on the Victorian novel, denouncing it root and branch for having denied the idea of heroism. But the essence of the novel is exactly this, the denial of the idea of heroism, not necessarily out of antagonism, although sometimes for that reason, but in the interest of some other preoccupation. The denial of heroism goes along with the denial of the value of the story as such. It seems but a childish thing. Far more justifiable, far more *mature,* seems the interest in character and in the circumstances that make—that account for—character. Yet by a paradox, the less concerned with story we have become and the more concerned we are with characters and with understanding them, the less we have been able to perceive and conceive character. It is where story asserts itself, where the novel most frankly allies itself with what Henry James called "romance," that character is most memorable. Julian Sorel is clear to our minds because he is the youngest son of a woodcutter. Gatsby has the status of a legendary person for much the same reason, and Leatherstocking and Captain Ahab are what they are for reasons that are analogous. Like the remembered heroes of the famous old stories, they are known to us not through their traits but through their fates—it is less true to say of them that their characters are their fates than that their fates are their characters.

* * *

IT COULDN'T BE a farther cry from Isak Dinesen's tendentious notion of the story to James Agee's novel. *A Death in the Family* has but one large event— the young father of a family, driving into the country to visit his own father, who is thought to be dying, is killed when his car gets out of control because of a mechanical defect. The Cardinal, when he contrasts the nature of the story with that of the novel, makes it a characteristic virtue of the story that "it does not slacken its speed to occupy itself with the mien and bearing of its characters, but goes on." *A Death in the Family* may be said to do nothing but occupy itself with the mien and bearing of its characters. It does so with a minuteness of observation which is common enough in modern literature; those who know Agee's writing, especially the once slighted, now famous *Let Us Now Praise Famous Men,* and those who were personally acquainted with Agee and remember the contortion of his face and body in the effort to get, or to suggest the importance of getting, the precise nuance of meaning, it is not surprising that he should practice so well the brilliant modern art of description in which the poetic and the scientific impulse to accuracy seem to meet. Just what Charlie Chaplin did, just what each expression on his face signified, just how a boy of six responded to the comedy, just what the boy felt when he was out with his father, just how the father speaks to the boy, just how he arranges his shirt-tails in his trousers, just how he cuts his pancakes, just how he compliments his wife for their quality and for having got up so early in the morning to make them—it is with innumerable details of this kind that the novel preoccupies itself, using the trifling details of the routine of life as a base from which it reaches upward to take note of the details of shock, of the slow realization of the sense of loss, of the gradual invasion of grief.

Here indeed is the antithesis to the story, here is what the Cardinal sees as the characteristic work of the novel, the presentation of individuals in intimate knowledge, "so close to the reader that he will feel a bodily warmth flowing from them."

And yet the further I read in *A Death in the Family* the more it seems to me to have an affinity of tone and of evaluation with *Last Tales.* When I try to account for this, I do indeed take note of the fact that there are similarities to be found in the prose of the one work and of the other. Agee of course does not try for the aristocratic overtones of Isak Dinesen, but it must not be thought that because his theme is homely his prose is homespun. On the contrary, it has its own formality, even its own courtliness, and certainly its own elegance and elaborateness. But the explanation of the curious consonance of this novel of American family life with the *Tales,* in which love is almost always an intrigue, or a witticism, or a healthy and vivacious naughtiness, must be explained on some other ground than that of prose.

In a long and excellent piece on Agee which appeared in *The New Yorker* some weeks ago, Dwight MacDonald remarked on Agee's being distinguished among modern writers by his eager response to goodness. " . . . Agee believed in and—what is rarer—was interested in good and evil," Mr. MacDonald said. "Lots of writers are fascinated by evil and write copiously about it, but they are bored by virtue; this not only limits their scope but prevents a satisfactory account of evil, which can no more be comprehended apart from good than light can be comprehended apart from darkness. Jay Follet is a good husband and father, Mary is a good wife and mother, and their goodness is expressed in concrete action, as is the evil in the boys who humiliate their son. . . . The theme [of *A Death in the Family*] is the confrontation of love, which I take to be life carried to its highest possible reach, and death, as the negation of life and yet a necessary part of it."

Agee's interest in virtue was indeed one of the most interesting things about him. But it really isn't quite true of him that he was interested in good and evil. Good was the whole of his preoccupation. He could exemplify goodness to its last detail. Evil was relatively an abstraction for him. (Mr. MacDonald can adduce as the only example of evil in *A Death in the Family* the episode in which the boys humiliate little Rufus, tempted to do so by his defenselessness and his genteel manner. The boys are rather horribly subtle in the amusement they contrive from their victim's innocence, but they are not quite evil. And indeed I felt that Rufus's excessive innocence was as much to blame as their depravity.) And certainly Agee could not understand what E. M. Forster calls good-and-evil. It is an admirable thing to say that the theme of Agee's novel is the "confrontation of love"—love being indeed for us nowadays a thing to be "confronted," like danger. But what Agee did not confront was ambivalence, the coexistence of tender with hostile feelings. It was not merely an unconscious refusal on Agee's part—I remember that in one of the last conversations I had with him he attacked the idea of ambivalence with great intensity, calling it one of Freud's "obscenities."

This did not wholly surprise me. I had had from the first the very greatest admiration for *Let Us Now Praise Famous Men*. The one reservation I had expressed in my review of it was that, in writing about the sharecroppers in a passion of sympathy which was the more impressive because of the virtually savage resistance it offered to the temptation of pity, Agee had not been able to represent them as anything but good. They made for him the population of an idyll; their pastoral virtue was not to be qualified. That they might have some measure of the ugliness of spirit that undoubtedly marks the people who would read the book written about them seems to have been for Agee an intolerable idea.

And it is intolerable to him that anyone in his novel should give evidence of the fallen human condition. Jay Follet is, as Mr. MacDonald says, a good husband and father, Mary Follet is a good wife and mother. Nothing interrupts the flow of their tenderness and consideration for each other. But two human wills, however gentle and enlightened, inevitably limit and control each other; two personalities will inevitably reach points of divergence, and the more they expect of and give each other, the greater will be the grievance at disappointment. The situation of the child must inevitably generate ambivalence, which is the natural outcome of even the most fortunate dependence, yet little Rufus Follet seems quite unable to be angry at his parents.

It seems to me that this inability to confront ambivalence constitutes a deficiency in Agee's moral vision. But it must also be said that it has, in *A Death in the Family,* a positive effect of which we must take very respectful note. It is not merely that, as Mr. MacDonald suggests, the exclusive preoccupation with goodness has the effect of being a relief from the predominant preoccupation with evil and the inability to imagine virtue. The negation of ambivalence gives the novel the legendary quality that constitutes the charm of Isak Dinesen's *Tales.* That we know how Jay Follet puts on his trousers or cuts his pancakes, or just how much whiskey Mary Follet drinks to sustain her against shock, does not prevent the characters from appearing "luminous" and "on a higher plane." (They are not, however, as the Cardinal says the characters in a story are, frightening.) And the quality of transcendence which I remark is the result of Agee's refusal to confront ambivalence. If it deprives the characters of a degree of circumstantial actuality, it endows them with a kind of abstract reality that is perfectly analogous in its charm to the quality of the people in Isak Dinesen's *Tales.*

Isak Dinesen's *Out of Africa* is in many respects similar to Agee's *Let Us Now Praise Famous Men.* Both books are records of actual experience written in the first person. Both are written out of a passion of love for what is observed, whether it be Agee's delight in the faces, manners, and household gear of the share-croppers, or Isak Dinesen's admiration of her English friends, natives, and animals. In both books the love precludes the perception of anything that might qualify or complicate the beauty of the loved objects—it is as if both writers, the one so consciously European, the other so consciously American, were setting their faces against the modern world with its habit of asking adverse questions and were determined to make it plain to all that grace and innocence did really walk the earth.

So there is my *peripeteia* all complete, just as I said it would be.

—January 1958

An Investigation of Modern Love

Lionel Trilling

On Lawrence Durrell's "Alexandria Quartet"

Justine and *Balthazar*

ONE OF MY college teachers said that the day comes to all men when they no longer delight in reading novels. The words fell heavy on my sophomore heart—here was yet another instance of that prognostication of the passing of joy that one's elders, and literature and philosophy, were always making. For years after that dark prophecy was uttered, I read fiction under its shadow, testing myself to see if it were coming true. There was no sign of change for a considerable time; my appetite for novels seemed scarcely to fail of its adolescent fury, which could not be really satisfied except by a collected edition of a novelist but which could find at least a momentary happiness in almost anything in covers that had a beginning, a middle, and an end.

But then the moment did come. I found that it was possible not to finish a novel once begun. I had never been indiscriminate in my judgment of novels, only in my reading of them. That is, it very seldom happened that the obvious badness of a novel was an argument against my reading it. But now it began to be. And as time passed, it was not merely manifest inferiority that prevented my pleasure. I found that even undeniably gifted new novels were likely to produce in me a curious depression. This is the only word I can think of to suggest the drooping of spirits, the devastation of hope, that I more and more frequently experienced. For not only had the day gone by when it seemed that almost any new novel could tell me something new about life,

"An Investigation of Modern Love," as it appears here, is a composite of the two pieces that Trilling wrote about Lawrence Durrell's "Alexandria Quartet."

but the day had come when virtually any new novel told me what I could not really believe to be true: my depression was the natural response to half-truth and mere plausibility. Did life—bad as it was—really move to the half-alive rhythm which sounded in the prose of most novels? Were people—unsatisfactory as I was finding them to be—really as dull and as concerned with dull things as most novels represented them?

One thing saved me from believing that the years had had their way with me and that the prophecy had come true. My teacher had seemed to be talking about all novels but it was only new novels that I feared to read. If I went back to certain old novels—and they did not have to be *very* old: it could be *Ulysses* as well as *The Red and the Black,* or *The Sun Also Rises* as well as *Little Dorrit*—the responses of my earliest youth seemed to be still in force. Perhaps I did not read with the same wild avidity, but I experienced no depression, no despair. Indeed, the world seemed all new again, and again I was receiving fresh information about it.

I am far from the first to put an especial emphasis on the informative function of the novel, to say that the novel must be novel, that it must bring us the *nouvelles,* the news. It is the literary genre that tells us about new circumstances of life and about new emotions, or new combinations of old emotions, or new occasions for emotions. It thus has a peculiar role as a *naturalizing* agent in culture; it has the effect of bringing into the circle of accepted things what at first seems strange, impossible, unacceptable. And it is from its carrying out of this function that it derives its literary qualities. For when the strange, the impossible, the unacceptable have come to seem matters of fact, the things taken for granted by generations of readers, what remains to enthrall us is the novelist's obsessed belief in the newness of what he is telling us, his passionate certitude that he has remarked something of importance for the first time.

Something in contemporary life makes that obsessed belief and that passionate certitude hard for the novelist to come by. But that, though hard, it is still possible is suggested by the instance of Lawrence Durrell. I shan't undertake to rate Mr. Durrell as a novelist, to try to say, after having said that he is very good, just how good he is. I am aware of aspects of his work that I am not quite easy with, haven't yet come to terms with. But Mr. Durrell is the first contemporary novelist in a long time to lead me to believe that he is telling me something new, to convince me that he is truly interested in what he is writing about, and to capture my imagination.

Justine and *Balthazar* are the first two of a series of four novels upon which Mr. Durrell is at work. The third is *Mountolive,* published earlier this year. The fourth is still to appear. The setting of the first three novels, and I should suppose of the fourth too, is Alexandria some two decades ago. Of *Balthazar* Mr. Durrell says that its "central topic . . . is an investigation of modern love," and this applies as well to *Justine*. (*Mountolive* develops certain political intrigues which are adumbrated in the first two books, but it does not abate the concern with love of the earlier volumes.)

Mr. Durrell's ability to make no bones about his novels having a "central topic" and the simplicity with which he identifies this "topic" as an "investigation" suggest that he shares something of my view that the function of the novel is to discover and inform. And if the subject of his investigation is indeed to be described as "modern love," as he says it is, then he is certainly telling us about something new and strange. No one who has formed an idea of love from contemporary American and British fiction is likely to take for granted what Mr. Durrell is writing about; no one is going to find it easy to believe that what he is investigating is really modern love. For none of Mr. Durrell's lovers has the slightest interest in *maturity* or in *adult behavior* or in *mutuality of interest* or in *building a life together* or any of the other characteristics of a *healthy relationship* which we suppose modern love to be. Tenderness plays some part in the feelings of some of the lovers, and on several occasions it is highly praised; the lovers do not expect from each other *emotional support* or *confirmation* or a *sense of security:* they may want things still more difficult to get or give, but none of them, in order to obtain these things, enters into one of those therapeutic alliances which, under the name of marriage, passes with us for the connection of love.

Yet it is indeed love that absorbs them. Certainly it is not sex as we know it from our novels. No one raises the question of sexual gratification as such, or as a problem; nor does any woman say, "I never knew it could be like that," nor any man, "It was good for me too." There are many episodes of sexual encounter, but no descriptions of the sexual act for, as it were, their own sake; the author seems to assume that his readers can supply the details. And although the two loved women of the novel, the gentle Melissa and the proud and fierce Justine, are said to be beautiful and often have occasion to be naked, we are given no inventory of their intimate charms; by their lovers, as by the reader, they are known in no dichotomy of body and spirit, and their breasts and rumps and thighs are not, so to say, detachable.

The behavior of the lovers is not controlled by respectable propriety; they use their bodies freely and are not physically faithful to each other. Yet ideas of an ultimate fidelity have great force with them, or with some of them, and their involvements with each other are nothing if not personal, having to do with their deepest sense of themselves. To such an extent, indeed, that they are all injured and some of them are destroyed by their obsessive commitments of themselves. "I realized then the truth about all love:" says the narrator, "that it is an absolute which takes all or forfeits all. The other feelings, compassion, tenderness, and so on exist only on the periphery and belong to the constructs of society and habit. But she herself—austere and merciless Aphrodite—is a pagan. It is not our brains and instincts which she picks—but our very bones." And later he speaks of the "austere mindless primitive face of Aphrodite."

But this surely is not the love-goddess known to the moderns who inhabit Westchester and Fairfield Counties and Hampstead and St. John's Wood, or to the novelists who chronicle their no doubt useful lives.

If the love that Mr. Durrell describes is indeed to be called modern, it is so by reason of its affinity to love as Proust represents it. That is to say, it is obsessive, corrosive, desperate, highly psychologized. These adjectives do seem to propose a distinctively modern condition, but not the modern condition of love between the sexes. And indeed Proust in his representation of love is much closer to the classic drama of the 17th century than to any literary work of our own time. The same can be said of Mr. Durrell. His Justine is in the direct line of Racine's Phèdre. Her husband Nessim, in the grandeur of his worldly power and the chivalric delicacy of his conduct, is a character with whom Corneille would have been quite at ease. The interplay between passion and duty and the high moralizing of passion are the habits of the French classic stage. All the characters of the two novels, no matter what their position in life, no matter what sordidness of circumstance they may accept to further the fulfillment of their love, maintain in their conduct some element of moral heroism. The emotion of friendship is held in high regard and there is a kind of general agreement among all the characters to accord each other a grave respect. The elaborate psychologizing in which the two novels abound never has for its purpose the belittling of the person upon whom it is directed. Neither the lust, nor the pride, nor the curiosity, nor the emptiness that may instigate love, nor the pain or devastation that may result from it, are made a reason for contempt.

The affinity of the two novels with the French classic drama is confirmed by the setting of the story, although *setting* is a word which carries too much implication of the static to suggest how active is its part in the story. The modernity of Mr. Durrell's Alexandria is bound up with its antiquity of three thousand years. Almost all the characters, both the English and the Egyptian, are of the most extreme sophistication, but their modern subtlety of morality and psychology exists in a world as primitive and as barbarous, as cruel and as dangerous, as the ancient world which imagined the stories or lived out the histories from which the French classic drama drew its themes.

In a Note prefacing *Balthazar* Mr. Durrell speaks of his novelistic method in this way:

> Modern literature offers us no Unities, so I have turned to science and am trying to complete a four-decker novel whose form is based on the relativity proposition.
>
> Three sides of space and one of time constitute the soupmix recipe of a continuum. The four novels follow this pattern.
>
> The three first parts, however, are to be deployed spatially . . . and are not linked in a serial form. They interlap, interweave, in a purely spatial relation. Time is stayed. The fourth part alone will represent time. . . .
>
> The subject-object relation is so important to relativity that I have tried to turn the novel through both subjective and objective modes. The third part, *Mountolive*, is a straight naturalistic novel in which the narrator of *Justine* and *Balthazar* becomes an object, i.e., a character.
>
> This is not Proustian or Joycean method—for they illustrate Bergsonian "Duration" in my opinion, not "Space-Time."

This is rather more forbidding than it need be, and rather too much like those profound statements of their intentions that even excellent painters have taken to writing for their catalogues. The method of *Justine* and *Balthazar* may be described much more simply. The narrator is an English schoolteacher and unsuccessful novelist (we do not know his name, Darley, until it is mentioned toward the end of *Balthazar*); he is the lover of Melissa, a cabaret dancer, and also of Justine, the brilliant, haunted wife of Nessim Hosnani, a Coptic banker of enormous wealth and great sensitivity. The narrator's observation of events is supplemented by that of Arnauti, Justine's first husband, who has published a novel about their marriage and her neurosis, and by that of Pursewarden, an English novelist of some distinction. Three novelists in a novel is no doubt much of a muchness, but it is rather fun than otherwise. The narrator also has available to him the diaries of Justine and of Nessim, not to mention the special knowledge of the physician Balthazar and of the saintly painter Clea. The purpose of this plethora of historians is not to play the quasi-philosophical game (very dull it is) of contrasting and opposing points of view, and, so far as I can see, not to serve whatever scientific-aesthetic purpose Mr. Durrell announces in the Note I have quoted from, but to suggest the difficulty of ever knowing (especially in love affairs) what has actually happened and what people's motives really are; the understanding that prevails at one moment is replaced or modified by the understanding that comes with new information, and the true explanation of an event virtually never comes at the time of its occurrence. This does indeed have an aesthetic effect in that it proposes a new kind of verisimilitude and, by instructing the reader that he must be careful to accept no statement at its face value, involves him in the story in an especially active way. It is not true, as Mr. Durrell seems to suggest in his Note, that his first two novels do not move through time. Their movement through time is certainly not simple, but neither is it so complex or unorthodox that we do not readily perceive the climaxes and resolutions of a story which is in the highest degree dramatic and weighty.

—AUGUST 1959

Mountolive and *Clea*

WHEN I WROTE about Lawrence Durrell's *Justine* and *Balthazar* last summer, I said of the author that he was "the first contemporary novelist in a long time to lead me to believe that he was telling me something new, to convince me that he was truly interested in what he was writing about, and to capture my imagination." This was meant as high praise and I did not modify it much by what I said thereafter. But I did put up a signal to let it be known that I might want to make some reservations at a later time—I said that I was aware of aspects of Mr. Durrell's work that I was not easy with and had not yet come to terms with. That statement was more definite than it should have been; actually I was not "aware" of any "aspects"; all I really meant was that there was something about Mr. Durrell's novels that troubled me, although I did not know what it was.

Now that I have read the third and fourth of what Mr. Durrell calls "The Alexandria Quartet," *Mountolive* published earlier this year and the recent *Clea*, I think I know what disquieted me. It is that all the novels, and the Quartet as a whole, stand in a peculiar negative relation to the will.

Having identified the disturbing element, I must admit that I cannot put it forward as an aesthetic fault. Who would undertake to say that the faculty of the will should be manifest in any given novel to this or that extent, or that it must be judged to have one or another degree of importance in human life? Yet the history of the novel shows it to be the genre which is characterized by its preoccupation with the will, and we naturally respond with some surprise or uneasiness when the traditional tendency does not show itself, or is reversed. The great essential subject of the novel would seem to be the individual who is in some way disadvantaged by circumstance and who is determined to overcome his disadvantage and to achieve freedom or fulfillment. And then, apart from the behavior that seems to us to be the novel's natural concern, there is the temperament of the novelists themselves. Of all literary artists they are the most overt in their commitment to the will. They are the most ambitious personally; they seek most to impose themselves, and to demonstrate their power in the range of their production and in the authority of their moral judgment. A *Lives of the Novelists* which would begin with Richardson and end with Lawrence, Proust, Joyce and Mann would give us a collection of the most imperious wills of modern times.

Perhaps it was the sense of this intensity of will and the intuition that it could grow no greater, that led people about a decade ago to talk about the novel as being "dead." In effect they were saying that they could not conceive how anyone could go beyond the modern masters in their determination to engage and surround and fascinate and dominate the souls of their readers. And if one could not, how was one to be a novelist at all, except in a way that didn't matter?

We can almost suppose that Mr. Durrell confronted this question explicitly, and hit upon the answer that the only possible way was by inverting the tendency of the novel, by chucking out the will. We can fancy that at this crucial point in his career he read *The Man Who Died* and found in Lawrence's story of resurrection a parable of the possible rebirth of the novel—the world to be thought of not as a field upon which the battle for salvation is fought but simply as the offer of life. Or we can imagine that he read Schopenhauer's *The World as Will and Representation* and said: "The World-as-Will is about played out—we are tired of the moral will and the social will and the disguised religious will; the novel is tired of all these wills. Let us now try the World-as-Representation, the world seen quietly, as an object, and if not without desire, then at least without fierce, ultimate, abstract desire. This German philosopher tells us that the purpose of art is not to arouse but to compose the soul. Perhaps he is right; let us try."

The will, of course, cannot be dismissed out of hand, and the artist cannot (alas?) do without it. At the end of Mr. Durrell's Quartet the novelist Darley, who clearly bears some close surrogate relation to the author, having long failed to write in a way that pleases himself or anybody, is at last able to know that he has achieved salvation, that he is at the great moment of "an artist coming of age"—as bold as that, quite as if we had reached the end of *Sons and Lovers* or *A Portrait of the Artist as a Young Man,* or any of the scores of lesser *Bildungsromane* of the 1920's. No, the will is not easily got rid of, neither in the novelist nor in his characters. One of the chief dramatic elements of the Quartet—it is fully disclosed in *Mountolive*—is the great Coptic political intrigue in which Nessim Hosnani is involved; in a remarkable love scene, Nessim, who has failed to win Justine in marriage, does at last overcome her resistance and draws her into a passionate involvement with him by telling her of the plot and making her party to it; she is captivated by his display of will.

Yet the very will itself becomes an element of the World-as-Representation. The actual political meaning of the plot has no great weight with Justine; for her the real value of the enterprise lies in its danger—the threat of death makes love and sexuality the more intense. And it may be said in general of the acts of the will in the Quartet that they are drained of their literalness, of their directness and force, that they are performed *as if* they were real, the actors being conscious of the *as if*. Ideals of loyalty and responsibility suffuse the Quartet, and have reference not only to persons but to nations—it is striking, indeed, how important the idea of the nation is in the novels, and how much feeling the characters direct to entities as large as Egypt, England, France, and Greece. Leila Hosnani, the mother of Nessim and Narouz, loves the young David Mountolive not only because he is charming, but because he is English, and he loves her because she is for him the soul of Egypt. Even the outrageous novelist, Ludwig Pursewarden, who has conducted a lifelong war against English culture, is committed to his nation, and even his friend, Pombal, of the French foreign service, falls in love with defeated France at the same moment, and in much the same way, that, after a career of sexual athleticism, he for the first time falls in love with a woman.

But even the idea of the nation is absorbed into the general *as if,* and succumbs to the prevailing unreality of the objects of the will—was any English ambassador ever so little concerned with the actualities of diplomacy, with the facts of power and intrigue, as Mountolive? As any reader of the Quartet is likely to conceive of the will, it is a peculiarly European faculty, which has found its modern expression in Protestantism, Romanticism, and the ideals of the middle class in its classic period—it is highly moralized, giving the greatest possible value to individuality as far as it can be thought of as one's own, seeing the world as the great stage which has been readied for the significant behavior of the hero: all our notions of tragedy depend upon our conception of the will. But the tragic European will simply cannot function in the Quartet, if only because the locality in which its action takes place does not submit to being made into the great stage of the world. Alexandria, so far from being a stage, is itself the protagonist of the action, a being far more complex and interesting than any of its inhabitants, having its own way and its own rights, its own life and its own secret will to which the life and the will of the individual are subordinate.

The intensity of the personal existence of the city derives in large part from its history, and history is a felt presence in the Quartet, conceived of as a tendency of happening in which human will may indeed assert itself, although to little avail. Mark Antony is virtually one of the dramatis personae of the novels; in *Clea*, Darley and Clea make love on the tiny island which Clea believes to be the one to which Antony fled after Cleopatra had brought about his ruin by her panic at Actium; the music under the earth that was heard when the voice called "the gods desert Antony" still reverberates in the city, and not only because it is the subject of one of the most famous poems of Cavafy, the Alexandrian poet who is made to figure in the Quartet as the city's soul become articulate.

What we of Europe and America call the past is part of Alexandria's actual present—ancient ways and the ancient peoples are before our eyes, and scenes that would seem bizarre and perfervid in the pages of *The Golden Bough* are of common occurrence, such scenes, for example, as the days-long mourning for Narouz Hosnani with which *Mountolive* ends, or, earlier in the same novel, the cutting-up of the still-living camels for the feast, or the religious festivals with their circumcision and prostitution booths and their possessed holy men. The ancient modes of thought are still in force—the existence of occult powers is taken for granted; scrying, second sight, palmistry, necromancy are matters of received fact with people of cultivation as well as with the primitive masses; this is the "mysterious East" of Western legend, with its belief in Kismet, or in guessed-at wills before which the will of man is of small account. And death or disablement or disfigurement can strike suddenly either at the behest of an occult or of some more powerful or beforehanded human will than one's own.

In this ancient circumstance the nature of the human personality is different from what we of Europe and America expect it to be. It is not, as I have implied, that the human virtues that we know have no existence and no appeal. Loyalty, devotion, tenderness, concern for the welfare of others are, indeed, displayed in a notable way by all the characters of the Quartet. "Moral" is a word that would be beyond their powers of utterance, perhaps beyond Mr. Durrell's, yet their lives are touched by considerations of goodness at every point; what is lacking is the binding force of the will which keeps steady the objects of their desire, and creates the idea of permanence and intention. This accounts for the ease and grace of their existence, for their never being torn between two possible ways of behavior, for their never displaying the harshness of moral judgment of each other. Two things only are of undoubted value in the Quartet and both are beyond the reach of the moral will. They are love and art—love which must follow its own laws and is not to be constrained; art which submits to no rule or purpose, existing for itself. The love that is represented in the Quartet is never linked to moral sanctions of any kind. The art that is imagined is without that moral urgency which is the hallmark of modern art; perhaps its paradigm is the scene in which Justine, searching for her kidnapped little daughter in a brothel, holds enchanted the swarm of child-prostitutes with an ancient romance; and the four words which, we are told, "presage . . . the old story of an artist coming of age" are "Once upon a time. . . ."

And indeed the aesthetic of the Quartet can best be understood by reference to the author's desire to recapture in the novel whatever charm lies in those four words, all that they imply of pleasure rather than will. It is to this end, for example, that Darley has been created to serve as the narrator of all the novels except *Mountolive*. Darley is himself a character among others and he is not held in especial esteem by his friends and lovers; he never knows everything that might be known and he is the victim of a most elaborate deception practiced upon him by Justine and Nessim. Yet he does what he can, he tells what he knows. The devices that Mr. Durrell permits him to use to gather information are transparent and not always credible—the novels of other men, diaries, letters of infinite length, monologuists who are nearly as untiring as Conrad's Marlow; there are even two friends who, when he wants to evoke the image of the transvestite police-officer Scobie, are such perfect mimics that they can "do" Scobie for pages on end. It is as if Mr. Durrell were telling us that he has no intention of setting up as the novelist, of sitting enthroned like the Logos itself, in the fashion of Proust or Joyce or Mann or Lawrence. I include Lawrence because of his novels which are in the control of strict, impenetrable, universal logic; but the Lawrence of many of the shorter stories was manifestly trying to shed the weight and solemnity of his role of Genius-novelist, to speak in the voice of human intercourse, not in the voice of Art; and for that reason perhaps, among others, he is one of the literary heroes of the Quartet. Lawrence had his own express quarrel with the will and he sought a prose in which the rhetoric of the will was not dominant.

And this, I take it, is the prose that Mr. Durrell is trying for. I am not always of a single mind about it, but I know that it is doing a very useful thing—it is helping to save the language of the novel from Joyce. For the fact is that after reading Joyce it is very hard to take the prose of most novelists: Joyce makes it seem slack, vulgar, overfamiliar. Indeed, if one reads Joyce with admiration, one conspires with him in his feeling that the presence of a reader is an impertinence, that to use language for purposes of communication is disgusting, a practice of the lowborn. Thus far had the creative will gone in pride, and the only way a novelist might again find a language was to do what Mr. Durrell has done, to take the posture of the man who begins "Once upon a time . . . ," to announce, that is, that he is going to tell a story—really *tell* it as against representing it—and that it is he who is telling it, and that he, or his simulacrum-surrogate, can only speak in his own way, as a person, sometimes high, sometimes low, sometimes businesslike, sometimes moved by wonder.

That last is important. My impression of most contemporary novels that come my way is that they say to me, "Let me give you for your file yet another instance of what you know so well, thus reassuring you of your high degree of sympathy with human frustration at no cost whatever. I will also tell you what, of course, you quite understand, how very bad The Culture is, and how it is to blame for the way people are when it isn't their own fault." Mr. Durrell's novels are much more naive, they say, "Let me tell you something interesting. Once upon a time . . ." Some of the things he tells I listen to with one or another degree of incredulity. I don't believe in homunculi made in a bottle by Cabalists. The camels sitting quiet while they are dismembered I can scarcely credit, but why should Mr. Durrell lie about a thing like that? The prophecy and second sight and scrying are amusing to suspend disbelief in, and if I am truthful I have to confess that I was once set back on my heels by what someone read in my palm. The story of the physician Amaril and the beautiful girl with no nose (she is eventually provided with one) is implausible, but I like Isak Dinesen. It is at least apparently true that the holy men do pierce and burn themselves without harm or pain. Maybe this is all storyteller's nonsense, the usual mystery of the East, but it consorts with my sense of the way people ought to be, in a novel at any rate—that is to say, objects of wonder. And it is in the element of wonder that Mr. Durrell's characters move, like Clea and Darley in one of their several underwater scenes, flaming with phosphorus. I find it possible to suppose that if they were to be taken "in themselves," as we say, that would not be so very interesting, but in their ambience of Alexandria and of wonder they exist with a quite splendid intensity of life. I make an exception of the great Pursewarden at whose wit and wisdom and charm everyone marvels—I find him a self-conscious bore, and in nothing is he so disappointing as in Darley's discovery that his bitterness is really tenderness. Mr. Durrell can do much better than that, and does, in the fierce, fluctuating passions of Nessim and Justine, in the Esau-like figure of Narouz, in the beautiful, brilliant and ruined Leila, in the canonized clown Scobie, in the general, curious vivacity of the Quartet.

—April 1960

The Magician from Mississippi

W. H. AUDEN

On William Faulkner's *The Mansion*

I THINK I CAN RECOGNIZE three species of novel: the Prose Poem, the Feigned History, and what, for lack of a better term, I must call the Fairy Tale. Most novels are, of course, hybrids but, as in the case of plants and animals, one set of characteristics is usually dominant and the others recessive, so that the classification may still be useful.

By the Prose Poem I mean a novel in which, as in Poetry, Form and Content are inseparable: it would be impossible to translate into another tongue without loss, and impossible to imagine it a page longer or shorter. Examples that occur to me are Virginia Woolf's *The Waves,* Joyce's *Ulysses* and, I think, the later fiction of Henry James. (What equivalent in a foreign tongue could there be for those extraordinary sentences of his?)

By the Feigned History I mean a piece of fiction which attempts to give the reader the illusion that he is reading about real historical characters in a real historical society *as seen from the inside.* (I will try and explain what I mean by this in a moment.) An obvious example is *Anna Karenina.* A great many novelists try to write feigned histories and very few succeed, for any feigned history is a failure unless it convinces an intelligent and sensitive reader that it provides him with a deeper insight into human beings and their history than he could obtain from observing himself and his friends and reading historical documents.

Faulkner's novels—like those of Scott, Dickens, Ronald Firbank, and Ivy Compton-Burnett—are, to me, examples of the Fairy Tale.

The Fairy Tale is unabashedly fiction; it presents us with a world of beings and events more extraordinary, more surprising than the world in which we live, and at the same time less problematic, less obscure. What in the historical world is internal and known by introspection and intuition is, in the fairy tale, externalized and made manifest to the senses. Thus the fairy tale tends to represent the conflict between good and evil impulses which goes on inside all of us as an external battle between good and bad beings; it tends to isolate the various passions, for love, for power, for understanding, etc., which compete for the attention of our hearts and minds, and embody them one by one in monomaniac beings, whose physical appearance, behavior and conversation are caricatures in the sense that they reveal the life within immediately and exactly; there are no psycho-somatic contradictions.

In real life we encounter, of course, extraordinary and grotesque individuals and events, but the true Feigned Historian, like Tolstoi, makes little or no use of them. To ourselves, we each feel unique, but none of us feels himself to be extraordinary, and the better we know someone (that is to say, the more we see him, like ourselves, from the inside), the less significance we attach to any external oddities he may possess. Our friends seem to us "normal" like the characters in Tolstoi; it is the stranger we meet for a moment in a railroad train or a cafeteria who seems to have come out of Dickens or Faulkner.

An author is not a God who can create a world out of nothing; any imaginary world he creates, however fantastic, is fashioned out of experiences taken from the real historical world and is the creation of a certain person born in a certain time and place and living in a certain culture. In reading a fairy tale, therefore, a problem arises which does not arise when reading a feigned history, that of distinguishing, so to speak, between the "real" stones and the "dream" architecture. Yoknapatawpha County is one world for a Southerner, another for a Yankee, and yet another for a European. By birth and upbringing, for instance, I am a native of the fairy tale world of Barchester County. In Barchester we had no Negroes, so when I visit Yoknapatawpha where they are common, they are a fantastic element, as dwarves or elves would be. In Barchester we had our feuds—the Archdeacon and the Cathedral Organist were not on speaking terms for years; the Squire and the Vicar of Horninglow kept exchanging abusive letters—but, aside from the chastisement of children, physical violence was unknown. In *The Mansion*, which is one of Faulkner's gentlest novels, I find reference to three murders, two attempted murders, two suicides, two beatings-up, and one tarring-and-feathering. I accept these as a dreamer accepts odd events in a dream; but, just as sometimes something happens in a dream which is so extraordinary that the dreamer cries—"Wake up! You must be dreaming!"—there is one feature of Yoknapatawpha which completely bewilders me, namely, the social status of Baptists. Sure enough, we had Baptists in Barchester, but they delivered things at the back door and one never met them. Occasionally some unstable relative might become a Catholic "pervert" or a British Israelite or a free-thinker; this was deplorable but to be accepted as one of those misfortunes which occur in every family. But the notion of anyone who "mattered" socially becoming a Baptist would have been unthinkable.

However, after discounting all that may only seem strange to me, but to a Southerner is real and natural, I still have no doubt as to the kind of novelist Faulkner essentially is. For example, in real life one can certainly come across, in various places and at different times, persons who strike one as being totally devoid of human affection and caring only for money or power. One might invent a word-label for such people, so that one could say to a friend: "O, I met a perfect Snopes this morning." But only in a fairy tale could the word-label become a family name; only there could such a set of monsters as Flem, Wesley, Byron, Clarence, Vergil, Montgomery Ward, and Orestes not only all be blood relatives but also collected in the same small town of Frenchman's Bend. Again, in real life, we are frequently aware of a struggle between what reason or conscience tells us we ought to do and what some passion would try to make us do: we may have behaved like Gavin Stevens yesterday but that is no guarantee that we shall not behave like Flem Snopes tomorrow. It is only in a fairy tale that persons are good or bad by nature, that it should be as impossible to imagine Gavin Stevens committing a base act as to imagine Flem doing a decent one.

In real life we make two kinds of decision, the strategic or practical, and the personal. My nature and circumstances "give" me a certain goal as desirable and, in my efforts to attain it, I have frequently to decide whether this course of action or that would be the best; the course I take may turn out to be right or wrong but neither I nor others will wonder why I took it. But occasionally I make a decision which is not based upon any calculation of its future consequences (which may turn out to be grave) but upon my immediate conviction that, whatever the consequences, I must do this, or refrain from doing it, *now.* However well I know myself, I cannot explain completely why I take this kind of decision, and to others it will always be mysterious. The personal decision is one of the main concerns of the Feigned Historian; a great one, like Tolstoi, succeeds in making the reader understand his characters better than they could ever understand themselves. In the pure fairy tale novel, there are no personal decisions, only strategic ones. The characters may be extraordinary and do extraordinary things, the accidents of chance may be extraordinary, but, given their characters and their situations, there is nothing mysterious about why they act in the way they do. In *The Mansion,* I find several examples of a personal decision and in each case I find Faulkner's attempt to explain the mystery unconvincing. For example, the future lives of many people would have been very different if Eula Varner had married Hoake Mc-Carron, by whom she was pregnant with Linda, instead of Flem Snopes. Why didn't she? This is the explanation Faulkner puts into Ratliff's mouth:

> It was Eula herself that done it. . . . That simple natural phenomenon that maybe didn't expect to meet another phenomenon, even a natural one, but at least expected or maybe jest hoped for something at least tough enough to crash back without losing a arm or a leg the first time they struck. . . . I ain't talking about love. Natural phenomenons ain't got no more concept of love than they have of the alarm and uncertainty and impotence you got to be capable of to know what waiting means. When she said to herself, and likely she did: "The next one of them creek-bridge episodes might destroy him completely," it wasn't that McCarron boy's comfort she had in mind.

Again, in 1923, when Mink's prison sentence is nearly up, Flem, who knows Mink means to kill him, is prepared to play a complicated and very dirty trick so as to keep Mink in prison for another twenty years, but refuses to have him bumped off which, as Montgomery Ward points out, would be the obvious way to ensure Flem's safety. All the explanation Faulkner gives us is this:

> So there's something that even a Snopes won't do. No, that's wrong; Uncle Mink never seemed to have any trouble reconciling Jack Houston up in front of that shotgun when the cheese begun to bind. Maybe what I mean is, every Snopes has one thing he won't do to you—provided you can find out what it is before he has ruined and wrecked you.

I cannot help feeling that what is presented as the personal decisions of Eula and Flem is really the strategic decisions of their author; that is to say, they have to act as they do for the sake of his story, just as, out of the many kinds of injury which Linda might have suffered in the Spanish Civil War, only deafness would make possible the extraordinary platonic love scenes between her and Gavin which Faulkner wished to write.

> "But you can . . . me," she said. That's right. She used the explicit word, speaking the hard brutal gutteral in the quacking duck's voice. That had been our problem as soon as we undertook the voice lessons: the tone, to soften the voice which she herself couldn't hear. "It's exactly backward," she told me. "When you say I'm whispering, it feels like thunder inside my head. But when I say it this way, I can't even feel it." And this time it would

be almost a shout. Which is the way it was now, since she probably believed she had lowered her voice, I standing there while what seemed to me reverberations of thunder died away.

A scene like this, and there are dozens of others, comic and pitiable, as good, makes me grateful for the limitations in Faulkner but for which they would not have got written.

The Mansion is a collection of tales, major and minor. The two major tales concern Mink and Linda. The first covers only a few days in 1946, between a Thursday morning when Mink is released from Parchman Penitentiary and the following Tuesday evening when he fulfills his vow of 1908 to shoot Flem. The second covers ten years of Linda's life, between her marriage to the sculptor Barton Kohl in 1936 and her participation in the murder of her official father, for she, too, though no one else knew this, had vowed vengeance upon Flem since her mother's suicide in (I think) 1928. In addition there are a number of subsidiary comic tales, the tale of Montgomery Ward Snopes and Reba Rivers, the Memphis Madam, the tale of Meadowfill, Orestes Snopes and the Hog, the tale of the political rise and fall of Clarence Snopes the Unspeakable. I shall not spoil a reader's pleasure by giving away what happens in any of these stories, but, no doubt, he will be glad to hear that Virtue is victorious, Vice gets its deserts, and Justice is finally done.

Judged by the standards of the Prose Poem, a novel like *The Mansion* is formless: as regards the tales of Mink and Linda, there is nothing inevitable about the order in which the incidents are related, or even about their number—the stories could have been told in greater detail or in less; as regards the subsidiary tales, there is no compelling reason why just *this* tale should be told and not another one. But the Jamesian formal standard is irrelevant to novels of this genre. Faulkner is not concerned with constructing a perfect verbal object, but with keeping us enchanted, with making us laugh, cry, gape, shudder, hold our breath. Form here is a sort of conjuring trick; it is right if we are kept so fascinated that we never ask how it is done. The story of Mink is a fast-moving "thriller" of action; by frequently breaking off at an exciting moment to tell the story of Linda, which is slow-moving and more concerned with feelings than acts, Faulkner excites in the reader the maximum amount of suspense, and he heightens the pathos and grimness of both their histories by relieving us at the point where sadness might become monotonous, and our attention about to wander, with scenes of farcical comedy.

Faulkner is no thinker—his occasional reflections on politics or the race question do not illuminate their subjects; he is no poet—his purple passages are embarrassingly bad; he is not even, in my opinion, a profound psychologist, but he is a very great magician who can make twenty years in Yoknapatawpha seem to the reader like twenty minutes and make him want to stay there forever. Furthermore, he employs white magic, that is to say, his charms have a moral purpose: he would teach and, I believe, succeeds in teaching us both to love the Good and to realize the price which must be paid for that love.

—January 1960

Fifty Years of "The Wind in the Willows"

LIONEL TRILLING

On Kenneth Grahame's *The Wind in the Willows*

IT IS NOW FIFTY YEARS since Kenneth Grahame's *The Wind in the Willows* was first published, and Charles Scribner's Sons has marked the semi-centennial anniversary by bringing out a new edition of the work that has become one of the best loved and most habit-forming of children's classics. It is an appropriate and pleasant volume, the page tall and nicely proportioned, the type-face strong and simple, and to the happy, modest little black-and-white drawings which he made for the 1933 edition, Ernest H. Shepard has added eight attractive full-page color illustrations. My own first experience of the book involves the Arthur Rackham illustrations, and for Rackham I have a particular admiration, but perhaps for the contemporary taste his idiom is a little difficult, and it might even be said that, charming as his plates for the book are, they lack gaiety, they are touched by something like gloom. But Mr. Shepard, although not so subtle in his picturing of the Wild Wood and the adjacent terrain, is considerably jollier and funnier and brighter. Melancholy plays its part in *The Wind in the Willows*, but so does jollity and funniness and brightness, and on the whole it is better if the reader discovers the melancholy through the jollity, funniness, and brightness rather than the other way around.

The Wind in the Willows is not one of the sacred books of my childhood, but it might have been—it was just that no one gave it to me or read it to me—and I am sorry that it is not. I had better explain what I mean by my category. The books that belong to it are sacred not merely because they have been first known in childhood, but because they have a certain aesthetic quality which makes its greatest effect in childhood and is remembered in maturity with pious gratitude. Modern literary criticism would be quite at a loss if it were to try to deal—but it doesn't—with this quality. There is no way for me to explain in public why I think *The Jungle Book* is a very great work, no way to enforce my belief that the first hundred pages of *David Copperfield* and the first half of *Treasure Island* are transcendently beautiful. For my pains, I am sure, I should be thought only whimsical or perverse or ironic. But I shall at least try to isolate the quality that leads me to think of these books as "sacred." It is a serenity which manifests itself in the prose style of the work, and within this serenity there is fear and sadness. What the child responds to is the reality that he finds in the representation of fear and sadness in an ambience that prevents them from being terror and grief. This reality has for the child a magical and liberating power—it tells him that literature has something to do with life as he knows it; that someone else, the author, has known life as he has known it (his parents always insist that life is never sad or fearful—aren't *they* there?); that he is a real person with emotions and a fate. A book that can do this and at the same time suggest that not everything is to be feared, that sadness need not prevail forever—such a book is surely to be thought of as having had a sacred part in our lives.

All the sacred books of childhood were written in, or close to, the 19th century. They cannot possibly be written now because no one is permitted to believe that fear or sadness should be presented to a child's consciousness. Adults nowadays like to read about troubled children; it reminds them both of how put upon and how delicately understanding they are and also of how nasty Society is. But it is plain that a culture that cherishes *The Catcher in the Rye* can't understand and doesn't deserve Mowgli or David or Jim Hawkins, or even Peter Rabbit. Kenneth Grahame—in real life he was Secretary of the Bank of England—came not a moment too soon; already he is a little touched by self-consciousness. But he did get under the wire of time, and by a generous and happy margin.

Grahame's two earlier books, *The Golden Age* and *Dream Days,* are about children but not for children. *The Wind in the Willows* is for children but not about children. It is about animals. They are not *ferae naturae,* they have all domesticated themselves in a peculiarly English way, each living the comfortable bachelor existence that best suits his peculiar oddity. Mole, Rat (water variety and anything but morally and physically repulsive), and Badger are very much of the time at which they were conceived, when a prevailing and attractive ideal was the abiding loyalty of a group of men friends living in blessed singleness (see, for a prime example, Dick Heldar, Torpenhow, and the Nilghai of *The Light That Failed*). Badger is stolid, isolate, and a rock of strength; Mole is rather on the hypersensitive, even weak, side, and he and the sturdy Rat are touched by immortal longings. Their devotion to each other is of the most delicate and enduring kind, and all three are committed to protecting Toad from his own sad deficiencies of character (and perhaps upbringing). While all the animals live in homes which, although cozily furnished, may well be called natural habitats, Toad is rich and lives in an actual and all-too-elaborate house, a manor house or something, which he has named nothing less grandiloquent than Toad Hall. The sad fact is that Toad is vulgar, and his vulgarity shows itself by his preferring Automobiles to Anything Else In Life.

The importance of the motorcar in the story—this is only a few years after John Tanner and Enry Straker made their run—will suggest the relation of the animals to the world. They are not alienated—it is within their competence to drive not only automobiles but horses, they have communal relations with human creatures, they use money, they are subject to the laws of the land; they have large and elaborate emotions, and even quasi-religious experiences. Yet they know themselves to be animals and respect themselves as such, gentleman animals, middle-middle-class animals, decent, loyal, brave, home-loving, Southward-yearning, passion-eschewing animals of the true English breed, animal hearts of oak. We shall not look upon their like again.

Recently, on the flap of the dust-jacket of a children's book, I came on what I thought to be a misprint: at the bottom, in small type, it said, "140 up." But it was explained to me that this was not an error but a new way of designating the age of the children the book was intended for; the consumers had expressed resentment over being given books appropriate to their ages, and of course a child who was "up" didn't want to read a book intended for the age he was up from, and so this rather sneaky and quite ineffectual method of disguising the designation had been invented. I cannot say whether *The Wind in the Willows* is for children of 70 or 80 or 100. It is very much a matter of chance. With certain elaborate passages omitted and some turns of speech altered, I have seen it enthrall a listener of 50. There will be readers of 120 who will find it too young, and readers of 150 who will find it too old. Among the young the response to it will be found to be a matter of temperament and taste, not of age level—Cheers! But any reader over 250 will find pleasure in it, especially if he can find some good—or at least acquiescent—young reason for reading it aloud.

—JUNE 1960

A Disturbing Novelist

W. H. AUDEN

On Muriel Spark's *A Muriel Spark Trio*

IT IS ALL TOO EASY for a reviewer to confuse his job with that of a literary
critic. A reviewer must remember that his audience has not read the book
which he is discussing; a critic starts with the assumption that his audience is
fairly familiar with the work or author he is reexamining. A critic says, as it
were, "This work has certain virtues or defects or technical devices which, so
far as I am aware, no reader has perceived except myself. Here they are. Look
at the text again and see for yourself if I am right or wrong." The principal
duty of a reviewer, on the other hand, is not judging or explaining, but describing. What he ought to say is, "I have just read a book sent me by its publishers. Let me tell you the kind of book it is, so that you can decide if it
sounds like the kind of book you would like to read."

Some kinds of book are easier to describe than others. A reviewer can give
a fairly just notion of a book concerned with ideas by outlining its general argument and, if he will only give enough quotations, one can tell immediately
whether a new lyric poet is one's cup of tea, but describing prose fiction is
much more difficult. One of the great pleasures in reading fiction is that of suspense and surprise—What is going to happen next? What new character is going to appear? What secret is about to be revealed? Consequently, if a reviewer
describes the plot or the characters too fully, he spoils half the prospective
reader's fun; yet, without doing so, how is he to give a fair idea of the novel?

One can read Miss Spark's novels, as one reads most fiction, as feigned histories. Her characters, that is to say, their speech and social milieu, do not belong to some private imaginary world but to twentieth century England; one
could meet their like at dinner or on a bus. But presently, particularly if one
has read several of them, one becomes aware of another dimension than the
simply historical. The principal concern of the writer of feigned histories is the

exploration in depth of individual human characters; since he cannot do this without, as we say, "getting inside" them, his novels are usually confined to the same kind of social milieu, the one to which, by birth or circumstances, he himself belongs, for only there can he feel sure of his insights. But the milieu of each of Miss Spark's novels is different from the others and no reader could conceivably guess the setting of the next. *The Comforters* deals with the upper middle class, *The Ballad of Peckham Rye* with the new post-war lower middle and working classes, *Memento Mori* returns to the upper-middle but all the characters are over seventy, and in her latest novel, *The Prime of Miss Jean Brodie,* all but Miss Brodie herself are pre-adolescent girls. Moreover, Miss Spark deliberately refrains from analyzing her characters in depth; on finishing one of her books, one is left with a set of question marks—her characters have become more and not less mysterious from what we have learned about them. In some of her novels, too, events occur for which it is difficult to find a rational explanation. A man writes a letter to a girl and tears it up, yet it appears verbatim in the novel she is writing; a woman becomes invisible when she falls asleep in the back of a car; mysterious phone calls which the police cannot trace remind a number of aged people that they will soon die.

The reader begins to feel that Miss Spark's characters, plot and background have a parabolic significance beyond their historical reality; each has something and something different obliquely to say about the human condition, irrespective of time and place and, as in all parables, what is obliquely meant is, and must be, different for every reader. To me, for example, *The Comforters* is a parable about Imagination and Experience; we cannot ever know either what is "real" or what is "pure imagination." Is it a novel about a world in which and about which a girl is writing a novel, or is it that world as transformed by her into her novel? *Memento Mori* seems to be concerned with showing how Pride is the mortal sin from which all the other six are derived. Gluttony, lust, anger, envy, avarice seem "natural" in the able-bodied, mentally active and ambitious; that is to say, the concrete temptations of pleasure and worldly satisfaction seem sufficient explanation for indulging in them. In showing us a group of persons who are senile in body and mind who continue to commit these sins long after committing them can bring any pleasure or happiness, Miss Spark seems to be saying that in all such sins there is an ego factor of willfulness and defiance to which considerations of pleasure or happiness or prudence are irrelevant. *The Ballad of Peckham Rye*, as I read it, is about the vulnerability of the inarticulate and semi-educated to manipulation by clear-headed evil; its villain Dougal Douglas is not a politician but, like Hitler, he is a mesmerist who makes those about him behave in a way they would never have thought of for themselves.

Dougal Douglas is only one example of a kind of character who turns up in most of her novels, someone who, judged by the moral norms of society, is thoroughly bad and, in a parabolic sense, is also a human instrument of the Devil whose name is Legion. In *The Comforters,* the Devil acts through a pious "church cat," Mrs. Hogg; in *Memento Mori* through a blackmailing housekeeper, Mrs. Pettigrew. With their help he is able to cause a good deal of harm and suffering but, in each case, his power for evil is limited by the particularity of the human being he uses; each of them is a specialised tool, highly effective for certain purposes but useless for all others. Moreover, he can never succeed in making his human instruments sympathetic and lovable even to their victims. In the end everyone gets bored with them and their master has, so to speak, to fire them; Mrs. Hogg gets drowned, Douglas ends up writing "cock-eyed books," Mrs. Pettigrew retires with her ill-gotten gains to a South Kensington hotel.

I must confess that I opened my first novel by Miss Spark with some misgivings, having heard that she was a Catholic convert. Converts who write novels are apt to become overexcited by the discovery that there is a difference between sin and unethical conduct; they tend to make their Catholic characters, practising or lapsed, behave worse and suffer more than Protestants or unbelievers and, in particular, to take a ghoulish delight in the plight of Catholic lovers who, for one reason or another, must either part or be debarred from the altar. But Miss Spark, I am happy to say, shows none of this theological romanticism. In *The Comforters,* Laurence Manders, a lapsed Catholic has been living with Caroline Rose, presumably a lapsed Protestant. She, however, has recently been converted to Catholicism and, consequently, has had to give up cohabiting with him. But Miss Spark carefully avoids making this situation melodramatic. Both accept the situation with good humor—if one is a Catholic, one has to put up with the Church's rules—continue to be good friends, and see each other without hysterical scenes. It is clear to the reader that they are made for each other. One supposes that Laurence had not married her earlier because he was uncertain of his feelings; afterwards it is Caroline who hesitates because she feels that, so long as Laurence remains a lapsed Catholic, complete mutual understanding will be impossible. At the end of the novel, their future is uncertain, but one feels that, probably, Laurence will return to the Faith and all end happily.

As I said at the beginning of this piece, it is not for a reviewer to make detailed critical judgements. I will merely say that I find Miss Spark's novels beautifully executed—she seems to know exactly what she is doing—funny, moving and like nobody else's.

—MAY 1962

James Baldwin

Lionel Trilling

On James Baldwin's *Another Country*

THERE IS PROBABLY NO literary career in America today that matches James Baldwin's in the degree of interest it commands. The reason for this is as deplorable as it is obvious. For it is not alone his talents, although these are indeed notable, but his talents in conjunction with his social circumstances that have put Mr. Baldwin into the unique position he holds in our cultural life. He is at the moment the only American Negro with a considerable body of respected work to his credit. And with the exception of Ralph Ellison, who has been silent for too long, he is the only Negro who has taken his place in the literary and intellectual *avant garde*—when he speaks to the general public about the life of his ethnic group, he is not confined to the wholesome simplicities of American libertarian thought, but ranges over the subtleties, complexities, and perversities of the modern ideology, and includes in his purview not only the particular anomaly of the Negroes in their disadvantaged situation, but the whole moral life of the nation.

Mr. Baldwin would surely be the first of us to wish that his uniqueness were not an element of his literary existence, that there might be standing with him other Negroes as articulate as he, and as fully heard. But things are as they are—Mr. Baldwin does stand in a striking isolation, and, as a consequence, what he writes must sound with an especial significance, and there will inevitably be a more than usual concern with the way he conducts his literary and intellectual life, with his powers of growth, with the changes and developments of his attitudes and opinions.

The position, it need scarcely be said, is an almost insupportably difficult one. How, in the extravagant publicness in which Mr. Baldwin lives, is he to find the inwardness which we take to be the condition of truth in the writer?

How is he to make sure that he remains a person and a writer and does not become merely a figure and a representative?

Some such question would seem to have been present to Mr. Baldwin's mind from the very beginning of his career. His first novel, *Go Tell It on the Mountain,* was autobiographical, and this story of a family emigrated from the South to Harlem certainly had its due sense of a public issue in its due awareness of the bitterness of Negro life. Yet what made the book notable in its time was its bold assertion that it existed as a literary entity, as something more than a "social document." No reader could fail to be aware that Mr. Baldwin was determined not to fall into the stereotype of the Negro novelist which then prevailed. It was as if, by his concern with style, by his commitment to delicacy of perception, he insisted that his novel was not validated by its subject—to which every ordinarily moral reader was required to respond because it adumbrated a great national injustice—but by the writer's particular treatment of his subject. In making this insistence Mr. Baldwin laid claim not merely to some decent minimum of social rationality, but to all the possible fullness of life, to whatever in art and culture was vivacious, beautiful, and interesting. He was explicit about that claim in his well-known essay, "Everybody's Protest Novel," in which he declared his independence of the settled expectations which readers and critics had of the Negro writer. It was a remarkable statement, made the more dramatic by its comparison of Richard Wright with Harriet Beecher Stowe, for Bigger Thomas, Mr. Baldwin said, was really only the other side of Uncle Tom, falling as far short of human actuality in his raping, murdering rage as Uncle Tom fell short in his pious humility. Mr. Baldwin's point was that to see man under the aspect of "protest" was to see him in a merely institutional way, in a way that did not represent him in his variety and complexity and thus not in his full humanity: in effect, the protest novel affirmed the very qualities of society that it undertook to denounce. Only a mode of art which was subtle and complex and untrammelled by social theory could truly propose the idea of freedom by exhibiting the true nature of man.

This belief was implemented by Mr. Baldwin's second novel. *Giovanni's Room* abjured the advantage that any novel about Negroes almost inevitably has, that of bringing the news about a condition of human existence which is certain to involve the reader in the powerful emotions of guilt and indignation, and perhaps also in a covert and complicated envy. Set in Paris, and telling a story of homosexual love, *Giovanni's Room* dealt only with white people. It was manifestly the work of a very good and very serious writer, but it was not a really interesting novel. I am loath to believe what some people said and what perhaps Mr. Baldwin himself came to believe, that it was relatively a failure because its author had "denied" his "essential experience." The extent or nature of its failure was no different from that of any gifted novel which is primarily committed to observation and sensibility, which is not written out of some strong, even if hidden, intention of the will. But perhaps the failure in Mr. Baldwin's particular case seemed the more salient because there was so readily available to him a subject which required to be dealt with by many human faculties, but most especially by that of the will.

It was, I feel sure, all to the good that Mr. Baldwin took for a time the stand he did take. It was all to the good that he insisted upon his right and his duty to be first of all an artist, that, like Henry James's Hyacinth Robinson, he laid his claim to the full heritage of the culture into which he was born and gloried in its possibilities. It should be said at once that, unlike James's young proletarian revolutionary, Mr. Baldwin never did come to feel that his claim to full artistic freedom lessened his attachment to the social cause to which circumstance almost inevitably committed him—he was never led by his sense of a personal fate to become indifferent to the actualities of the Negro situation. Yet the emphasis did fall on the personal fate, and this, as I say, was all to the good. It was of the greatest value to his development that he withdrew for some years from the American scene to Europe, and that he should have written a novel which made no reference to Negroes. His new novel, *Another Country,* may be read as a very large modification of the earlier position, but there can be no doubt that it derives much of its force from Mr. Baldwin's refusal to be limited by the special exigencies of the Negro writer's life, by his having moved out into the larger and more various world.

Yet there also can be no doubt that the power of *Another Country* derives equally, and perhaps more than that, from another source. In recent years, Mr. Baldwin, who never, as I have said, was anything but committed to the Negro cause, has become responsive to the growing Negro intransigence and considerably more willing than formerly to conceive of himself as a Negro writer, or, at any rate, as a writer who speaks out of his identification with his ethnic group, which is, of course, also a social and cultural group. As such, he has become an increasingly public figure. I have heard it said in criticism of him that he has become an all too public figure; indeed, in the pages of this magazine, the reviewer of *Nobody Knows My Name,* Mr. Baldwin's latest collection of essays, chided him for an excessively ready acceptance of "his new role as 'a famous Negro writer'," which presumably would be deleterious to his creative gifts. This is not my sense of the matter. In the face of all our pieties about the artist's privacy, I think that the new public role has done Mr. Baldwin great good as a novelist.

I do not take *Another Country* to be a *fine* novel. It is not a novel controlled by delicacy of perception. But I do take it to be a powerful novel, a *telling* novel. If I compare it with another novel of equally intense contemporaneity and of similar theme, Philip Roth's *Letting Go,* it seems to me that, although Mr. Roth's novel is the more virtuose and accomplished of the two, *Another Country* has an actuality of existence which *Letting Go* does not approach. Both novels deal with the difficulty, or the impossibility, in this country and at this time, of people having satisfying and significant relations with each other. And if I try to say why Mr. Roth's novel, for all its fullness of detail and frequent brilliance of representation, is merely depressing in its extended exposition of its sad subject and, for all its bulk, eventually not *there,* while Mr. Baldwin's novel, despite its faults, is invigorating and substantial, I should make the explanation in terms of Mr. Roth's having written chiefly out of sensibility and observation, and with some almost programmatic negation of will, while Mr. Baldwin has in this instance affirmed the primacy of the will, his affirmation arising out of his angry awareness of the Negro situation. *Another Country* is not a "protest novel"—it differs from that genre of the Thirties and Forties in the respect that anger at social injustice is but one element of the lives of certain of the characters. But it is an element that is definitive of their being, and Mr. Baldwin not only condones it, but celebrates it and makes it the presiding passion of his story.

I would not wish to palliate the faults of *Another Country.* No one of his natural delicacy of mind and ear should write as badly as Mr. Baldwin sometimes does in this book. " . . . The wind nibbled delightedly at him through his summer slacks." No, the wind did not, and nothing is gained by saying it did. "Newsstands, like small black blocks on a board, hold down corners of the pavements and policemen and taxi drivers and others, harder to place, stomped their feet before them and exchanged such words as they knew with the muffled vendor inside." This is as factitious as it is awkward. The time has long gone by when it was possible to say that "a hotel's enormous neon name challenged the starless sky," or that a subway train rushed "into the blackness with a phallic abandon," and what impulse of literary regression could have led a writer, in any year after 1910, to say of a woman that she wore "all her beauty as a great queen wears her robes"? It does not show respect for either love or language to say that the memory of the beloved's eyes "afford" the lover "his only frame of reference." Mr. Baldwin does indeed sometimes achieve a prose manner that is unexceptionable and even admirable, but it is always being threatened either by violent cliché or such flatness as marks the narrative of some of the social scenes: "Cass appeared in a high-necked, old-fashioned burgundy-colored dress, and with her hair up. Richard put on a sport shirt and a more respectable-looking sweater, and Ida vanished to put on her face. The people began to arrive."

Yet it does not matter, just as it does not matter in Balzac, just as it usually does not matter in Dreiser. The novel as a genre does not depend on fineness and delicacy of art, and there are even occasions when it is the better for doing without fineness and delicacy of art. I take *Another Country* to be such an occasion.

Another Country is about love, which is to say that it is about hate, rage, violence, and despair. The crucial figure of the story is Rufus Scott, a brilliant jazz drummer. He is loved by a perfect Griselda of a Southern poor-white girl, to whom he is bound and upon whom he inflicts extreme physical and emotional abuse, eventually driving her past distraction to insanity. Rufus is not, as we say, a naturally cruel person. It is in large part out of remorse for his treatment of Leona that he commits suicide. So far is he from being evil that he is celebrated throughout the novel as an especially beautiful and precious person. His parents cherish him, his sister adores him, and almost all the characters in the book direct toward him a sweetness and affectionateness of regard which they speak of as love. And Rufus is represented as being preeminently worthy of love because he is so capable of joy.

Why has Rufus become inaccessible to love, why has his own power of love turned to hatred, so that every erotic act must be violent and destructive, so that his very seed presents itself to his mind as "venom"? The formulated answer comes quickly; we all know it quite as well as Mr. Baldwin does. Rufus is a Negro, and American white society has robbed him of his self-respect. That is why his joy has turned to gall, why his love has turned to cruelty.

The fate of Rufus Scott is to be understood in terms that are no different from those in which we were asked to understand the fate of Bigger Thomas. Not much has changed since *Native Son* appeared in 1940. Where Bigger vented his rage in a single act of sexual violence, Rufus destroys his victim slowly and, as it were, with her consent, but the symbolic meaning of the behavior of each is the same. And yet there is a difference to be noted, for where Richard Wright conceived of Bigger as standing wholly outside white society, Mr. Baldwin represents Rufus as being sufficiently related to white society to serve as the limiting case of *Another Country*. His is the extreme fate, but almost all the other characters, black or white, suffer some corruption, perversion, or frustration of their erotic lives. Ida, Rufus's beautiful and talented sister, checks and bridles her own power of love in the interest of mastering the social order that had destroyed her brother—hating the white world, she moves toward a denial of herself on the tide of her contempt and revulsion. Her white lover, Vivaldo Moore, an undistinguished but warm-hearted young man, is unable to achieve the sense of identity which will permit him to be a novelist (or anything) and lives in a perpetual torture of sexual jealousy. His friend and former teacher, Richard Silenski, having at last achieved success with a mediocre book, becomes, or is discovered always to have been, a mediocre person, unable to maintain his once happy relation with his admirable wife Cass, who, having lived for love, is almost destroyed by the deprivation.

When the ruin is represented as being so widespread, we are ready to hear that a bad society has brought it about. The burden of *Another Country* is that our society corrupts and distorts the human spirit, poisons the roots of life and the well-springs of love. And although Mr. Baldwin is too intelligent to believe that American society is unique in this respect, he yet represents it as mitigating the spiritual devastation by far fewer creature comforts than another society might give—the New York by which Mr. Baldwin exemplifies American life is wholly without grace or charm, is nothing but sordid and ugly, a veritable City of Dreadful Night.

From its doom only one person would seem to be saved. Eric Jones, an actor of considerable talent, is a young Southerner of good family. His homosexual tendencies, manifested in his boyhood, had made life in a Southern town impossible; in the freer atmosphere of New York and Paris, he has been able to "accept" his homosexuality. He alone exists with a degree of dignity and direction—he is in possession of himself, of *a* self, as none of his friends is. How he achieved this fortunate condition is not made clear; presumably it has a connection both with his homosexuality itself and the moral straightforwardness and balance with which he confronted it. One aspect of his selfhood is that he does not permit himself to fall prey to what Freud called "the overvaluation of love." It may be said that for Eric love is an emotion, but not, in the sense in which Spinoza used the word, a *passion*. His relation to Yves, the French youth he loves, is as constant and orderly, as controlled by the intelligence as if it had been imagined by Jane Austen. And by reason of his clearly defined selfhood, he has the power, when he engages in an affair with the deserted Cass and in a single erotic encounter with the confused and troubled Vivaldo, of giving these people some sense of the actuality of their own beings.

But Eric is an exception in the general ruin of lives. It is an old tale now, the story of generous aspirations baffled and perverted by society. It might be said that Mr. Baldwin tells us nothing that we did not know from Dos Passos's *USA,* and before that from Flaubert's *Sentimental Education* and Balzac's *Père Goriot.* But we cannot doubt that we will hear it again, and often, for it is the classic and typical story of the modern world, and it cannot possibly fail to be of moment if it is told, as Mr. Baldwin does tell it, with passion.

—SEPTEMBER 1962

"Lord of the Flies"

Lionel Trilling

On William Golding's *Lord of the Flies*

ONE OF THE MOST STRIKING literary phenomena of recent years is the success of William Golding's novel, *Lord of the Flies*. Published in this country in 1955, it received but an indifferent critical press and no "promotion" at all. Yet over the intervening years it has found its way to many thousands of readers, of whom a great many are quite young. First, apparently, in the colleges, then in the secondary schools, it seems to have captivated the imagination of a whole generation.

In this special appeal which *Lord of the Flies* has made to young readers there are two circumstances which are of particular interest. One is the literary quality of the novel. Given our usual low estimate of the literary taste and training of American youth, it must be a matter for considerable surprise that Mr. Golding's book should have made its way so smashingly with our students. For although it cannot be called a "difficult" book, it is close-textured and highly wrought; the narrative is straightforward but the prose is not always so, it comes at its object from unexpected angles; the ideas that are adumbrated are not abstruse but they are certainly not obvious, and altogether the book requires a degree of close attention, quite considerably more than we might expect young readers to give of their own free will.

The second circumstance that is worth remarking is that the last book that charmed the young to the same extent as *Lord of the Flies* was *The Catcher in the Rye,* and it is hard to imagine two novels more unlike each other in moral import. If we wish to be solemn about it, we may say that the enthusiasm for Mr. Golding's novel, following upon the enthusiasm for Mr. Salinger's, amounts to something like a mutation in culture.

It always seemed very easy to understand why *The Catcher in the Rye* appealed so intensely to the young. And, of course, by no means only to the young—in England even more than in this country it is regarded with a passion of admiration by quite serious and intelligent adults, and it is often referred to by reviewers as one of the best and most significant novels of our day. One has the impression that among those who do admire it—I am not one of them—it has achieved the status of a holy book, that it is almost as rude and unfeeling to question its merit in the presence of one of its devotees as it is to mock the religious attachments of some gentle, inoffensive person. Adverse remarks about it are met with a hurt, unargumentative silence; something tender and precious has been affronted—something no less tender and precious than self-pity, or the certitude of innocence. The enchanting theme of the book is that (as they say in *The Wind in the Willows*) *no blame attaches.* It doesn't, that is, attach to any Nice Individual, although plenty of it attaches very firmly to parents, to teachers, to institutions, to The Culture, to Society. We came innocent into the world, and some of us (each of us knows Who) maintain our innocence into first youth, some even beyond that; but in the degree that we are free of guilt and guile, we are done in by our fellow creatures from whom the innocence has departed, or, sometimes, by internal forces which are themselves an expression of our natural sweetness.

The modern world dislikes Original Sin and got rid of it long ago, before it ever thought to eradicate typhoid and tuberculosis. It was inevitable that a work which affirmed the innocence and superiority of the accused as feelingly and engagingly as does *The Catcher in the Rye* would establish itself in the affections of the world and especially in the hearts of the young, who, of course, are more accused than anyone else.

But now comes *Lord of the Flies* about which everyone says, and they are not mistaken, that its subject amounts to an affirmation of, exactly, Original Sin. A young person who reads it may perhaps exempt himself from the general burden by identifying with the decent and defeated Ralph, but the book gives him no license—as *The Catcher in the Rye* does in so plenary a way—to exempt his generation from the imputation of guilt. In a group of English boys marooned on a tropical island in an episode of a future war, the bad impulses of some of them and the weakness or cowardice of others are inherent and cannot be said to manifest themselves at the behest of a bad social environment. And yet, in the face of this uncomfortable doctrine, *Lord of the Flies* has had the success I have described.

It is, I suppose, a formal flaw in Mr. Golding's fictional device that the boys are, after all, not wholly "natural" creatures starting from moral scratch, for some of them are as old as twelve and all have been reared and schooled by elders whose deficiencies are made clear by their being engaged in a suicidal war. Yet Mr. Golding is able to override this inescapable circumstance and persuade us that the boys are not finally under the control of previous social habit or convention. (I can't help thinking though, that I should not have credited this quite so readily of American boys, who would not, I believe, have been so quick to forget their social and moral pasts.) We see their behavior as, first, the expression of native personal temperament and individual endowment. One of the boys, Ralph, is naturally a leader and organizer; another, Piggy, naturally sees things in their consequences; yet another, Jack, is naturally courageous, charismatic, and dominating; Simon is naturally a visionary; Roger is naturally cruel and crafty. And in addition to their individual traits, they are moved by impersonal, even anti-personal, impulses. The dark irrational mind of the tribe, which is unlike the mind of any one of them, can have its way with all of them: They are susceptible to mass panic. Seeking community in ritual dance and chant, they can be overcome, even the gentle among them, by an insensate brutality. They contrive, not by thought but by the inspired projection of their own darkness, a Divine Being whose malign law they interpret very well.

When *Lord of the Flies* was published in England it was reviewed with great enthusiasm by E. M. Forster, who now contributes an introduction to the handsome new edition which Coward McCann has brought out. "It is a pleasure and an honor to write an introduction to this remarkable book," Mr. Forster says, "but there is also a difficulty, for the reason that the book contains surprises, and its reader ought to encounter them for himself." Quite so, but Mr. Forster, alas, does not overcome the difficulty he notes and the reader would be well advised to read his admirable essay as a coda rather than as an introduction to the book.

It should be said on behalf of Mr. Forster that there was no way for him or anyone to write in any detail about the book without telling too much; even the little I have said about it here discloses more than should be known before reading. For the fable of *Lord of the Flies* is simple and even schematic; the power of the book, which is very considerable, lies in the masterly way in which simple events are subtly darkened before being brought into the light of comprehension. Which is to say that *Lord of the Flies,* long before it is a moral, social, and political parable, is a remarkable work of art.

—OCTOBER 1962

Music, Theater, and Fine Arts

Why Talk About Art?

Jacques Barzun

On Erwin Panofsky's *The Life and Art of Albrecht Dürer*

IN THE GRAND PASSION of our age for Art, and especially for the inarticulate arts, there is an enormous amount of talking and writing done. The budget of words runs into the billions. Every object is classified and commented upon; every artist's history is searched and recounted; every style and device compared and explained. What we know about art overflows our minds, books, libraries, and nobody can flatter himself that he has said or heard the last word.

Yet it is surprising that in so self-conscious a time so little of the discussing should be devoted to the aims and principles of discussion itself. Why talk about art? When the question is asked, it is asked rhetorically; and the answer most often implied is that we should not talk at all but only "experience"— and possibly enjoy. Despite the flood of words there is a distrust of the "literary," a suspiciousness of biography and history, and a positive resentment of any attempt to bring a little order among the clichés and catchphrases which people *will* repeat about masterpieces and their makers.

I myself have incurred polite obloquy for suggesting a distinction between technical and critical remarks, and for reminding professional interpreters that their writings, to be of any use, must be intelligible: surely the essence of an explanation is that it should explain rather than puzzle. But by saying so, it appeared that I would spoil a recognized game, in which such phrases as "rhythmic integrity," "spatial inventiveness," and "purely pictorial potentials" can be multiplied without harm and linked together rather pleasantly.

The notion that bad language may engender bad habits of thought and thus interfere with both perception and enjoyment is not generally credited; which may mean that speakers and writers attach little weight to what they themselves say, or that they do not understand the "potential" of their own frivolous business. Their skepticism amounts to answering the question "Why talk about art?" by saying: "There's no stopping it, but why bother? Talk has as little effect on art as on the weather."

The conclusion is contrary to fact. Leaving aside the influence of talk on fame or reputation, it has a direct influence on taste. Careful studies have shown that what people physically see in a painting bears a close relation to what they have been told or taught. And long before these studies, the general truth which they confirm was a matter of common observation. All teachers know that to educate is in large part to suggest, and all historians prove that the views and the blindnesses of an epoch have their source in the same tendency of the human mind to perceive according to preconception.

This is the whole point of Criticism, its glory and its menace. Why does the artist cry out when his work is badly reviewed? Not usually because of the effect on his vanity of the words "good" or "bad," words which are in fact seldom used; but because of the effect of other words, technical or vaguely critical, on his work. He knows that his piece, if misrepresented, is not presented at all. It will exist in the beholder's eye as a false image, something visible which nevertheless isn't really there. Small comfort to the creator to tell him that in fifty years' time the mistake will be straightened out. This won't happen by itself in any case: someone will have to see differently, with the aid of different thoughts and different words.

Nothing, therefore, is more important to the life of art in a secular society than tending and developing its critical vocabulary, just as nothing is more important to the connoisseur who wants to see rightly in order to increase his range of delights. I do not mean to say, of course, that merely by using the right words a person or an age will enlarge its stock of artistic pleasure and deepen its understanding of what it likes. The truth is rather that lacking those right words and true ideas, the fleeting perceptions will not sustain themselves against the flood of nonsense on the one hand, and of factual information on the other.

It is an error to suppose that the right words rise naturally to the lips of any reasonable man when faced with the object of his interest. Critical terms are rare pearls, born of the irritation that the mind feels at not being able to account to itself for something it repeatedly encounters. For example, ages went by during which people wondered how they came to put their whole faith and credit in theatrical actions which they knew to be "unreal." Then Coleridge one day coined the phrase "willing suspension of disbelief," with the result that now we can describe, test, and sufficiently explain a common literary phenomenon.

The repertory of literary criticism is, as one would expect, much richer than that of any other art. This is because literary men have the habit of analyzing and recording their sensations in words. Whereas for the same purpose graphic artists, musicians, and dancers use lines, sounds, or gestures. But this does not mean that the characteristic modes and effects of these other arts cannot also be rendered or translated into words.

If any proof of this were needed, all one would have to do is point to Mr. Erwin Panofsky's *Albrecht Dürer*. This great work has been considered a classic since its first appearance in 1943. It now reappears in its fourth edition, this time in one volume instead of two, and with certain improvements which should be mentioned before going on to consider the text in its unaltered form and excellence.

The new single volume is of slightly smaller format than its forebears, which makes it easier to hold and store, without spoiling the appearance of either the letterpress or the illustrations. These last, 325 in number as before, have benefited from recent advances in the art of reproduction, and are now beautifully clear. Light and dark and fineness of line duplicate those of Dürer's originals, with the result that a good many of the details that one formerly took on trust now stand out and let themselves be identified. The rest of the book is, with one exception, identical in style, contents, pagination, and apparatus with the original edition, and its equal in workmanship. All that is missing is the Handlist of Dürer's works, an elaborate index of great use to scholars and art dealers, but not likely to be required by the amateur.

The true amateur will probably begin by looking rather than reading—the plates are all together at the back—and if he is so true as to be honest with himself, he will end his slow perusal in wonder. What wild imaginings, he will inwardly exclaim, what mysterious meanings, what oppressive emotions, what exquisite sensuousness, what inexhaustible skill, what choking abundance, what a world, what a man! Unless the beholder is quite familiar with Dürer's century, he will be surprised by the style of a number of paintings, only to discover that some are not by Dürer but by Mantegna or Pollaiuolo, or Jacopo de' Barbari. Curiosity about their relation to Dürer's work must, if nothing else will, draw the infatuated eye to reading Mr. Panofsky's chapters. The text, in turn, continually sends one back to the pictures, and with each shuttling the wonder and admiration for Dürer's art changes in quality while growing in strength.

Mr. Panofsky uses the biographical form, that is to say the mixed mode of presenting his information and criticism. We learn about Dürer's youth, circumstances, travels, ambitions, and achievements, and also about Germany in the early sixteenth century, about other artists and schools, and—most deftly—about the techniques of the woodcut, engraving, and drypoint and the science of perspective. The sum of knowledge is supplied as we need it, chronology being the container and organizer both. On the plateaus of the narrative we find ample discussions of the great works from every point of view: that of historical styles, that of iconography or symbolism, that of intellectual or religious intention, and that of esthetic success and development. Often one such consideration is the dominant one in the treatment of a work. But in the best critical moments they are naturally interwoven, as in the description of the portrait of Dürer's father (1497) which, says Mr. Panofsky,

shows Dürer's newly acquired capacity for suggesting space without actually depicting it. The figure is turned slightly toward the spectator so that it seems to detach itself both from the frontal plane and from the background; but the resulting slight asymmetry is counterbalanced by the fact that the hands (joined in front of the belly) and the face are placed on the central axis of the panel. The head, with the fine high forehead no longer hidden by the cap, emerges proudly from a simple pyramidal mass which is enlivened, however, by a studied contrast between the rising lines of the lapels and the descending curves of the wide sleeves. The general impression is therefore one of composure without stiffness.

This is seeing—and showing. The task was simple, no doubt, but it always seems simple after someone has done it. One would like the chance to compare with this a paragraph produced offhand by any of the devout visitors to the exhibition of Dürer prints and drawings at the Morgan Library last month. And then one would like to set as the next test the Melencolia I, which everybody "knows," which everybody has "seen." Mr. Panofsky's fifteen pages upon it are his critical masterpiece. The critic's wide scholarship, subtlety of feeling, technical understanding, and independence of judgment are here perfectly displayed. He is neither over-awed by his own learning, nor dominated by the wish to make the picture "purely" this or that. He can summarize the medieval theory of the four humors without losing sight of the pictured meanings appropriate to use and to the life of the artist. For he knows that great art is at once programmatic and self-sustaining, autobiographical and detached, decorative and dramatic. And he feels free to speak about all these aspects of Dürer's work, with no thought that some of them, being moral or historical, will violate modern canons of esthetics.

The lucidity of Mr. Panofsky's prose and thought is all the more remarkable that German, not English, is his native tongue. He rarely succumbs to the bad habits of contemporary speech, though he does use "field" and "approach" in the ways of the jargoneer, and here and there he permits himself the inconsequence of the mere "appreciator," as in: "The drawing has no 'subject' except the breathing movement of the earth as such." Any connection, one asks, with the "fast thick pants" in *Kubla Khan?*

But one finds few such specks, and if one is going to quarrel with Mr. Panofsky it must be on higher ground. His subject gives him so many opportunities to make illuminating asides that one reproaches him for not making more. Think of the critical value of pointing out, in relation to a precursor: "But the act of pruning presupposes the tree." With eight words, he makes a mass of vicarious perfectionism fall away and he defines a recurrent situation in art history. Yet he should add a caution to balance the idea of pioneers and followers, and our critic does not supply this; or rather, he does not prop the assumption on which should rest a remark such as: "Her horror-stricken face, the mouth wide open with a cry of anguish, is unthinkable without such models as the mourning old woman in Mantegna's *Deposition of Christ.*" Why unthinkable? Who thought of it for Mantegna? Who are the models of the models, and to what extent, in art as in culture, does independent discovery supplement imitation and diffusion? These are not matters to let go by default.

Again Mr. Panofsky gives us, gradually and without pedantry, an excellent notion of the way in which Dürer came to the Renaissance, which is to say, how the Renaissance overtook the middle ages in northern Europe. The critic disposes of the long debate over the meaning of Renaissance and restores the reality of change, which is as common as the fact of continuity. But he could do more with a parallel which he hints at once or twice, between this same transition to the Renaissance and the later one from the dying neo-classic to Romantic. In other words it would be well to show the recurrence of decay and fresh starts within neighboring centuries of one culture, till the phenomenon becomes familiar as a variable type instead of remaining a unique event.

Oddly enough, at the threshold of his book, Mr. Panofsky ventures on a far riskier generalization based on nationality. Germany, he says, has never produced "one of the universally accepted styles." And he goes on to ascribe Gothic to France, Renaissance and Baroque to Italy "in cooperation with the Netherlands," eighteenth-century Classicism and Romanticism being "basically English." This seems to me to deny the tangible unity of cultural Christendom and I confess I do not understand the meaning of "basically" and "in cooperation with." In a Foundation Report, yes, or in the loose abstractions of small talk; but not when I visualize living artists with arms and legs and ambitions moving about the capitals of Europe, copying, gossiping, and re-inventing one another's conceptions under the pressure of spiritual supply and demand. Besides, clear cases sweep away bad "laws": if Classicism and Romanticism are English, what are we to do with David, Goya and Delacroix? If Impressionism is French, how do we fit in Whistler, Pissarro, the influence of Japanese prints and the impressionism of Velasquez? The nation state, which defines nationality, may buy art or vaguely foster it, but it has no responsibility for producing it and can therefore not be credited with styles, let alone the mirage of "universally accepted" ones.

It remains to say how admirably Mr. Panofsky recapitulates and judges Dürer's theoretical works, relating them with equal finesse to contemporary science and to the artist's quasi-mystical passion for perfection. What we required of the critic at the outset, that his descriptions describe and his explanations explain, seems with him effortless, second nature. That is why we require still more and want him to expound even the rules upon which his exposition is built. To be sure, we ask this with no guarantee that the demand for clearer and fuller formulation, for Critical Theory in the correct sense of the term, can as yet be met by any man, and we ask it with the full recognition that his account of Dürer, as it stands, is a complete work.

—MAY 1955

Wisdom, Wit, Music

W. H. Auden

On Hector Berlioz' *Evenings with the Orchestra*

EVENINGS WITH THE ORCHESTRA belongs to that literary genre which is the most difficult of all for a reviewer, "the artful hodge-podge."

To succeed in it, as Berlioz most brilliantly does, requires a combination of qualities which is very rare: the many-faceted curiosity of the dramatist with the aggressively personal vision of the lyric poet. Without the former, the result will be a monotony unmitigated by formal charm; without the latter, an arbitrary heap of fragments which, however interesting when taken separately, fail to relate into any coherent pattern. It is almost impossible for a reviewer to prove to a prospective reader that such a success has been achieved because, to do equal justice to the variety and the unity, he would have to quote the greater part of the book.

The structural idea of the book is based on the critical presupposition that bad art is boring. Night after night the orchestra of an opera house in northern Europe assemble to perform the opera appointed for that evening: when the opera is a bad one, and it usually is, the members of the orchestra, with the exception of the bass-drum player who is kept too busy, chatter among themselves, exchanging gossip and anecdotes. Occasionally, however, the opera is good—Berlioz mentions six, *Der Freischütz, Fidelio, Il Barbiere di Siviglia, Don Giovanni, Iphigenia in Tauris, Les Huguenots*—then, the orchestra keep silent and do their conscientious best. Berlioz himself appears in two roles, sometimes in his actual role of music critic (I'm not quite certain how he is able to talk to the orchestra in this capacity, but he does) and sometimes as the concertmaster and composer Corsino. The imaginative centre of the book, though we do not hear about it until the last, or twenty-fifth evening, is Berlioz' vision of Euphonia, the musical Utopia. From the viewpoint of this imaginary perfection, he surveys the realities of musical life in his time, the arrogance of patrons and the commercialism of managers, the snobbery of the fashionable and the vulgarity of the mob, the lack of professional pride among performers and the lack of artistic taste, alas, in the Fair Sex, the anatomy of claques and the psychology of tenors.

What strikes me most on re-reading *Evenings with the Orchestra* after an interval of several years is Berlioz' common sense and willingness to see what is good in the actual state of affairs, however far from perfection that may be. Most descriptions of Utopia are humorless, but Berlioz exhibits his Euphonia as a comic daydream which he knows neither can nor should become actual.

> The singers and players of instruments are grouped by categories in the several quarters of the town. Each type of voice and instrument has a street bearing its name, which is inhabited only by the section of the population which practices that particular voice or instrument. There are streets of sopranos, of basses, of tenors, of contraltos; of violins, of horns, of flutes, of harps, and so on.
>
> Needless to say, Euphonia is governed in military fashion and subjected to a despotic regime. . . .
>
> They are also trained to silence, a silence so absolute and profound that if three thousand Euphonian choristers were assembled in the amphitheatre or in any other resonant place, one could still hear the buzzing of an insect, and a blind man in their midst might think he was quite alone. . . .
>
> A minute later, each one recovering breath and voice—and in this you see again our Euphonian's musical sense—without either the prefect of the choruses or myself making the slightest signs to suggest the harmony, ten thousand voices burst out spontaneously on the chord of the diminished seventh followed by a magnificent cadence in C major.

From passages such as these, it is quite clear Berlioz knew that Euphonia was not a New Jerusalem to be realised if possible but an Eden which it is fun to imagine but madness to believe one can enter.

It would have been excusable in a musician who was a perfectionist and temperamentally passionate in his likes and dislikes had he written of the realities of musical life with a kind of Swiftian disgust but, amazingly enough, Berlioz, however savagely satirical he may be, rarely loses compassion and understanding; note, for instance, the adjective *sincere* in the following:

> I have never yet attended a first night at the Opera without finding among the judges in the lobby a large majority hostile to the new work, however

beautiful and great it may have been. Nor is there a single score, however flat and empty, null and void, that does not gather a few votes of approval or that fails to number sincere admirers, as if to justify the proverb that says there is no pot without a lid.

Popular tenors may be a pain in the neck, but Berlioz does not allow us to forget that their voices are great god-given gifts or that their end is usually disgrace and oblivion.

One of the most famous stories in the book is the tale of Adolphe, the Spontini fan, and Hortense, the brainless and vain singer, at the end of which Adolphe commits suicide after hearing a perfect performance of *La Vestale,* and Hortense, passing by at that moment, thinks he has done it out of hopeless love for her: as Berlioz tells it, the hero is made to look quite as ridiculous as the heroine. (My reading of this story may, I must admit, be influenced by my inability to appreciate *La Vestale* which I find almost as boring as works by another of Berlioz' great heroes, Gluck.)

Again, he exhibits a healthy realism and self-knowledge when he allows Berlioz-Corsini to say to Berlioz-author:

The woman singer of whom you wrote: "we thought she was in labor," retorted sourly: "At any rate, he'll never be the father of my children." Here I cannot congratulate you, for she is an enchanting little fool.

Nor is the book all fun and games; interspersed at intervals come serious and interesting studies of Spontini, Paganini and Beethoven.

Still, it is, of course, the fun and games that one remembers, the despiser of Weber whose skull was used in Freiscutz, the claque in Church:

"How do you mean? You can't applaud in church."

"I know. But you can cough, blow your nose, shift your chair, scrape your feet, hum and haw, lift your eyes to heaven—the whole bag of tricks, don't you know. We could have done a sweet job for you and given you a real success, just as we do for a fashionable preacher."

The arrival of Jenny Lind in the United States:

. . . the dolphins and whales that had for more than twenty-five hundred miles shared in the triumphal progress of this new Galatea, convoying her ship while spouting scented jets, were twisting and turning outside the port, in despair at their inability to accompany her ashore. Sea-lions shedding salt tears could be heard bellowing their lamentations . . . gulls, frigate birds, loons, and other wild inhabitants of the solitary ocean wastes, luckier than the seals, circled fearlessly about the adorable creature, perched on her pure shoulders, and hovered over her Olympian head, bearing in their bills abnormally large pearls, which they presented to her most courteously, cooing gently the while.

The political quarrel of the stage hands under the artificial storm during a performance of Adolphe Adam's *Le Fanal,* which created such a tempestuous effect, or best of all, perhaps, and certainly the most frightening, his encounter in the beautiful countryside with the crippled little girl who tried to keep a crippled swallow:

I did what grandmother told me; I cleaned her leg all up, and tied it together with matchsticks. . . . And I gave her nice flies all the time, and I only pulled their heads off so's they wouldn't fly away. And grandmother kept on saying: "That's right, you must be good to animals if you want them to get well. Only a few days more and you'll be well yourself." And just now she hears that flock of other swallows squalling up there in the steeple, and the mean thing pushes up the lid of her basket, and while I'm busy getting more flies ready for her, she—hee-hee! she—hoo-hoo! she hooked it.

"I know how you feel, my child; you loved your swallow very much."

"Me? What an idea! But she wasn't quite well yet, and now I won't be well myself at all. The others she's gone off with are going to break her leg for her again, I know they will."

"What makes you think the others will do that?"

"Because they're wicked, o'course, like all the birds are. I saw it all right this winter, when it was so cold; I plucked the feathers off a sparrow somebody gave me; I left only his wing and tail feathers; then I let him loose in front of some others. He flew to them, and they all pounced and pecked him to death. I saw it I tell you" (crying) "I never laughed so—hee-hee! And now you see my leg will never get well. Oh, if I'd known—boo-hoo! I'd have wrung her neck proper the minute I found her."

Mozart's letters are evidence of great potential literary gifts which he had no time and, perhaps no inclination to develop; there are prose works of Wagner's which are much more readable and interesting than is generally supposed, but the *Autobiography* and *Evenings with the Orchestra* are literary achievements which would have made Berlioz famous if he had never written a note, and he and his English-speaking audience are now lucky in having found in Jacques Barzun a translator who really knows his business. Not only is he accurate as regards the meaning of individual words, including technical terms (which should be easy but is not always, apparently, found to be so) but also his sentences never betray, either in their syntax or their cadence, a foreign origin and anybody who has ever tried to translate even the simplest passage from another tongue knows what constant vigilance this requires.

A frank and humorous picture of the conditions under which music is composed, performed, judged and paid for is a job which needs re-doing every twenty-five years or so. Some things, of course, never change.

A composer-pianist to-day who is foolish enough to give a concert in a fishing port on the day that the herring have come in, will be as disappointed as his nineteenth century forebear, and have no more right to complain. Food must always take precedence over art. Arrangers, alas, are still with us. Smarting under the tyranny of divas and tenors, Berlioz day-dreamed of an Eden where the conductor would be absolute master: it came to pass, and the new tyranny proved just as insufferable as the old. But now the conductor is becoming a poor old back number, slave to a new master, the evils of whose reign deserve a description by Berlioz in his most blood-thirsty mood, that sworn enemy of music and insolent corrupter of our ears, the Sound-Engineer.

—May 1956

The Nude Renewed

Lionel Trilling

On Kenneth Clark's *The Nude*

I SUPPOSE IT WOULD BE quite possible to deal with Sir Kenneth Clark's *The Nude: A Study In Ideal Form* as if it were an especially accomplished work of scholarship and criticism, delightful for the vivacities of its observation and expression, commendable for the directness of its communication, for the grace with which it involves us in ideas about the plastic arts, which are far less easily available to most of us than equivalent ideas about literature. And certainly *The Nude* deserves any praise we may want to give to its sensibility and—using the grim word in the pleasantest possible sense—its pedagogy. But beyond the intrinsic qualities of the book we have to be aware of the significance of its appearance at this moment of cultural history, of what its aesthetic assumptions, set forth with considerable authority, mean to us at the present time.

A good way to understand the particular interest and force of *The Nude* is to bring to mind the well known essay by José Ortega y Gasset, *The Dehumanization of Art.* (It is available in an Anchor reprint.) This essay was first published in 1925, when the modern movement in art was already fully formed but still had to make its way with the public. Ortega wrote in defense of the new art. He did not, it would seem, undertake the defense out of love, for there is no note of joy or of discovery in the whole essay, but rather out of intellectual conviction. What he admired in the new styles, as he says again and again, is that, as between the aesthetic elements of a work and the "human" elements, the aesthetic dominates and the "human" is sunk nearly out of sight. Of the seven qualities which Ortega discovers in modern art, he cites as the first two the tendency "to dehumanize art" and "to avoid living forms." The theory of a wholly nonrepresentational art had not yet been fully established at the time Ortega wrote, and he expresses his doubt of the possibility that there can be an art that does not make *some* reference to actual objects. But his praise of the new art consists chiefly of the reiterated declaration that, referring as it must to an actual object, it suppresses all sense of responsibility to the object as what Ortega calls a "lived reality"; it makes no appeal to the beholder which is not strictly pictorial, which is not grounded upon organization and design. Any other appeal is held to be adventitious and illegitimate—as we say, "impure" and, worse, "literary."

But beyond this positive aesthetic intention of the new art, Ortega perceives another intention to which he gives full weight and an implied approval. This is a cultural intention, a matter of conscious, embattled taste—a massive dislike of, and hostility to, the art of the past. "For about twenty years now," Ortega says, "the most alert young people of two successive generations—in Berlin, Paris, London, New York, Rome, Madrid—have found themselves faced with the undeniable fact that they have no use for traditional art; moreover, that they detest it." And what he isolates as the detestable thing in traditional art is the "human" element. "It will not be easy to interest a person under thirty in a book that under the pretext of art repeats the doings of some men and women. To him such a thing smacks of sociology and psychology. He would accept it gladly if issues were not confused and those facts were told him in sociological and psychological terms. But art means something else to him." Here, where he speaks of literature, Ortega would seem to exaggerate, but he does so in a significant way and his statement of the case can be allowed to stand for the moment without question. He is on firmer ground when he speaks of the plastic arts—"it is not an exaggeration," as he says, "to assert that modern paintings and sculpture betray a real loathing of living forms or forms of living beings." And again: "Why is it that the round and soft forms of living bodies are repulsive to the present day artist?"

Ortega's essay sums up in a very striking and accurate way the tendency of modern "advanced" taste. To be sure, as I have suggested, Ortega goes too far when he undertakes to assimilate the theory and practice of literature to the theory and practice of the plastic arts. Perhaps in 1925 Proust and Joyce could reasonably be thought of as authors whose works "satisfy the urge to escape and elude reality," and express "contempt for the old monumental forms of the soul and unhuman attention to the micro-structure of sentiments, social relations, characters." But thirty-two years later this judgment seems quite wrong. As we now read *Ulysses* and *Remembrance of Things Past,* what is likely to strike us is exactly their massive monumentality, the pathos of their commemoration and celebration of the old humanistic soul. Sooner or later, as we think about them, we murmur, "Sunt lacrymae rerum," and we do not find their pathos to be less moving because the Vergilian sadness goes along with the Lucretian desperateness. Now that we are no longer astonished by the devices and distortions of Proust and Joyce, we can scarcely fail to see how committed they are to the old humanistic soul and how they delight in all the old elements of the literary art—pathos, humor, heroism, the charm and excitement of good and evil.

But so far as the plastic arts go, Ortega's summary is substantially true. In the plastic arts, the main tendency, the significant tendency, has indeed been away from the human, from the "lived reality." And where this tendency has been resisted—I mean by artists of some power and distinction, not by mere academicians—it has produced an art that is likely to make us uneasy, as with a sense of unearned compromise. Speaking for myself, I find that although my relation with "dehumanized" painting is at best an ambiguous one, I am almost always made uncomfortable by modern representations of "lived reality." Whatever reservations I may have about, say, Jackson Pollock, I am on easier terms with him than with, say, Ben Shahn, and I think that my preference is pretty typical of the educated classes.

This being our situation, it comes as a surprise, and even as a shock, that Sir Kenneth Clark should at this time ask us to consider, of all things, The Nude, that genre of traditional art which is most extravagantly "human." Sir Kenneth says of the nude that it is not a subject of art but a form of art—"an art form invented by the Greeks in the fifth century"—and it is, of course, the form of art which has the closest relation to "lived reality." As Sir Kenneth says, "the human body, as a nucleus, is rich in associations, and when it is turned into art these associations are not entirely lost. For this reason it seldom achieves the concentrated aesthetic shock of animal ornamentation, but it can be made expressive of a far wider and more civilizing experience. It is ourselves and arouses memories of all the things we wish to do with ourselves; and first of all we wish to perpetuate ourselves."

This brings us at once to what would seem to be for Sir Kenneth—and for most of us—the central fact about the nude, its erotic implication. Sir Kenneth treats his subject under several heads—he devotes a chapter, called "Apollo," to the male nude; one to the nude as expressive of energy, chiefly spiritual; one to the nude as expressive of pathos; one to the nude as expressive of ecstasy, spiritual as well as sexual; and one to what he calls "the alternative convention," which is the tradition, chiefly Germanic, of representing the human body realistically, even satirically, and wholly without the idealization that marks the main tradition. But the aspect of the nude which involves him in as it were a definitive way is the female nude in all its erotic appeal, and for the treatment of this he needs two chapters, "Venus I," "Venus II." He makes it the very essence of his discourse that the erotic emotions are of paramount importance in our response to the nude, the nude being for him "the most serious of all subjects in art," the Word made flesh and dwelling among us full of grace and truth. (No one will want to tax him with inconsistency in the matter of whether or not the nude is a subject of art or a form of art.)

Most of us have been taught, from childhood on, that we ought to regard the nude statue or picture as having been purged of all erotic emotion in its creation, as requiring of us that we suppress all erotic emotion in our response. It is worth observing that respectability and aesthetics issue in the same attitude and rely on the same word—*purity.* Supposing the Victorian mamma or governess to be a lady of some cultivation, she would say to the young person she had in charge, "Yes, dear, don't laugh—that *is* a statue of a naked lady, although it's more polite to say *nude.* It is Greek, or, if not actually Greek, very like the statues that the ancient Greeks used to make, and educated people admire it very much. They admire it because of its artistic value and they don't think of her in the least as if she were a real lady. That is why the vicar and your Papa's friend the Professor think so highly of it, as I know they do." There is no difference between what Mamma or the governess said and what was said by the established aesthetic theory of the later nineteenth century, with its insistence on the autonomy and purity of the aesthetic emotion.

Sir Kenneth, to sum up the general tendency of this theory, quotes Professor Alexander's statement: "If the nude is so treated that it raises in the spectator ideas of desires appropriate to the material object, it is false art and bad morals." To this dictum Sir Kenneth replies by standing it on its head: "No nude, however abstract, should fail to arouse in the spectator some vestige of erotic feeling, even though it be only the faintest shadow—if it does not do so, it is bad art and false morals. The desire to grasp and be united with another human body is so fundamental a part of our nature that our judgment of what is known as 'pure' form is inevitably influenced by it."

Thus the issue is joined. But we cannot miss seeing that it is an issue not only between Sir Kenneth's aesthetics and that of the later nineteenth century but also between Sir Kenneth's aesthetics and that of the radical "dehumanized" art of our time. The latter is continuous with the former and there is no essential difference between Professor Alexander's position and that of Ortega.

In point of fact, it isn't always possible for Sir Kenneth to sustain his statement about the erotic implication of every good representation of the nude, or at least not in a direct and simple way—Rembrandt's nudes, for example, or almost any of the Pietas can be called erotic only in a negative sense. But the erotic or quasi-erotic intention is certainly a dominant one in the genre of the nude and Sir Kenneth misses no opportunity to insist upon it. "These sweet round bodies are as sensuous as strawberries," he says of Raphael's *Three Graces.* He speaks of "the landscape of the breasts and thorax, . . . the most satisfying that the eye can rest on," and takes note of the "lineaments of gratified desire" of the nude figure of Titian's *Sacred and Profane Love.* He remarks with regret the "unaphrodisiac quality of certain of Titian's nudes" and says of the figure of Truth in Botticelli's *Calumny* that she is "of all nudes that are not positively ugly, the least desirable."

Here, then, is "lived reality" being asserted with a vengeance. But this assertion, although in itself it is refreshing, is in itself not especially interesting as aesthetic doctrine—after all, there is always some grizzled, angry academician to assert that the nude is a celebration of the natural beauty of the human body. What does make Sir Kenneth's doctrine interesting and important is that it abolishes the dichotomy between desire and thought, between "the human" and "the aesthetic." Sir Kenneth speaks, for example, of what the French call the *déhanchement,* the uneven distribution of the body's weight upon the feet which has the effect of throwing one hip outward. " . . . This disposition of balance," he says, "has automatically created a contrast between the arc of one hip, sweeping up till it approaches the sphere of the breast, and the long, gentle undulation of the side that is relaxed; and it is to this beautiful balance of form that the female nude owes its plastic authority to the present day." So much for the description of the charm of the pose. But the exposition goes on: "The swing of the hip . . . is a motive of peculiar importance to the human mind, for by a single line, in an instant of perception, it unites and reveals the two sources of our understanding. It is almost a geometric curve; and yet, as subsequent history shows, it is a vivid symbol of desire."

It isn't hard to see whose pupil Sir Kenneth is. The spirit of William Blake informs his book at every point. Just as the nude figure of *Sacred and Profane Love* is said to be of peculiar charm because she shows "the lineaments of gratified desire," so the personality of Rubens is praised because his nude figures "never pause to calculate or nurse an unacted desire." If energy is the subject of discourse, it is energy as Blake understood it—"energy which is endless delight." And surely it is Sir Kenneth's commitment to Blake that makes it possible for him to speak of humanism as if the word still had interest and authority. Nowadays humanism is much discredited; it is very dull; it is downright academic. But Sir Kenneth's humanism is not that of the universities and of the universities' self-pitying praise of themselves. It is rather the humanism of *The Marriage of Heaven and Hell.* This humanism conceives of form, style, order, discipline, knowledge and control not as being opposed to passion, energy, eroticism, and ecstasy, but as growing out of the intensities of life as their natural expression. Sir Kenneth can speak of "the union of sex and geometry" which is encompassed in the nude, and remark on "how deeply the concept of the nude is linked with our most elementary notions of order and design." It is the most natural thing in the world for him to connect sex with style: commenting on Rubens' preoccupation with the female haunches, he says that Rubens "was a master of the baroque and the bottom is a baroque form." And how much we learn about the nature of style when, with some antecedent awareness of the worldwide impulse of human beings to decorate and alter and remold their bodies, we are reminded of "how much formalization the female body can undergo and still preserve some tremor of its first impact."

In short, *The Nude* challenges the whole idea of the "pure" aesthetic emotion which, all through our century, has been a prized and characteristic possession of the intellectual elite. (There are signs that this idea is not quite so powerful as it was even a few years ago. It seems to me, for example, that opera, that most impure of the musical genres, the one that relies most upon "lived reality" and makes most reference to the erotic emotions, is now again being permitted to be a source of fully legitimate pleasure; the belief, once so full of prestige, that only "pure" music, preeminently the string quartette, was appropriate to fine sensibilities no longer has its old unqualified authority.)

But if Sir Kenneth challenges the idea of purity, if he in effect establishes the aesthetic legitimacy of the "lived reality," he doesn't in the least fortify Mr. Selden Rodman, who, in his recent *Conversations With Artists*, exhibits so uneasy a yearning for an art which shall be "human" and "humanist" and shall present again, for our comfort and faith, an "image of man." Mr. Rodman's attitude is analogous to that of those scholars and philosophers and religious personalities who annually meet in Conferences to ask that mankind affirm the Western tradition, the Hellenic tradition, the Hebraic-Christian tradition. Why do we instinctively know that nothing living can come out of these demands for the establishment of the "human" and the "humanistic"? Is it not because William Blake is never invited to the Conferences, because it is always *papers* that are read, and not encausticated copper plates, because everyone speaks of "Heaven" and no one of "Hell," because the virtuousness and the explicit social idealism of the meetings have no knowledge of energy as endless delight or of the charm of the lineaments of gratified desire or of the danger of the unacted desire—of, in short, all the things that Blake knew and that Sir Kenneth takes account of when he speaks of the "human" and "humanism"?

The Nude will, in all probability, have a very considerable effect upon modern taste. I can't imagine anyone reading it and not learning to look at the art of the past with bolder and more affectionate and more demanding eyes, and an unembarrassed readiness to accept the aesthetic propriety of an avowed "lived reality." This will not necessarily depreciate our relation to the "dehumanized" art of our time, but it will almost certainly change that relation. And probably for the better, making it less inert, more active and articulate.

A Concluding Word in Protest: It puzzles me why Sir Kenneth mentions Maillol only once and briefly (although respectfully) and shows us not a single example of his work.

A Concluding Word of Praise: As a physical book, *The Nude* is most satisfactory and does credit to the Pantheon Press. It is designed with generosity but without the intention of lavishness that makes many art books oppressive and unhandleable. The type is clear, the photographs simple, clear, well-placed, and numerous; and the size of the book, although necessarily considerable, is not greater than it need be.

—JULY 1957

The Lost Glory

Lionel Trilling

On *Look Back in Anger* and *The Entertainer* by John Osborne and *Epitaph for George Dillon* by Mr. Osborne and Anthony Creighton

WHEN I VISITED LONDON in the winter of 1956–7, John Osborne's *Look Back in Anger* had come to the end of its run, but it was still a haunting presence in the mind of everyone who had seen it. The seriousness with which the English took this play could not fail to impress a stranger. I learned that during its last week the audiences had turned the little Royal Court Theater into a forum, staying on after the performances to discuss with the actors what the play was really saying. And in general the English gave the impression of having just received from Mr. Osborne the first authentic word of what their social system was like. It seemed to me that they took the news to be very grave indeed, and yet somehow exhilarating.

I was puzzled to know why they should have been stirred in this way, why the hero of *Look Back in Anger* was of so much consequence to them. From what I was told about him, it did not seem that young Jimmy Porter was a likely person to engage a universal sympathy. He is the son of working-class parents, and this seems to make a circumstance with which he cannot come to terms. Despite his presumable talents and despite a university education—red-brick, to be sure—he has elected to make his living as the proprietor of a sweet-stall in a provincial city. In this way he expresses his contempt for all that English upper-class life has to offer. Apart from a hostile, obsessed reading of the middlebrow Sunday papers, his chief intellectual occupation would seem to be the refinement of his cruelty toward his young wife. She is a perfectly nice girl and devoted to her husband, but she is a member of the upper-middle class, which Jimmy hates. His calculatedly sadistic treatment of her is his form of social protest.

I pressed my English friends to explain why they found it so especially significant. "Does it," I asked, "represent anything more than that old—that *very* old—English situation of the young man who is embittered because he is not what you people call, or used to call, a 'gentleman'? Can this really still excite so much interest?"

And I went on: "It used to be that the young non-gentleman acquired almost automatically a sort of heroic quality through his disadvantaged social position. He overcame the disabilities of his class by becoming a genius, like Dickens or H. G. Wells or D. H. Lawrence. Or he became a social revolutionary, like poor Hyacinth Robinson. Or a politician, like Paul Muniment. Or a labor leader, like many whose names you haven't yet forgotten. But your Jimmy Porter welters in self-pity and behaves—if you'll excuse the old word—like a cad. And yet he seems to have great moral weight with you. Why is this so?"

No real answer was forthcoming. My English friends were polite to my questions, but they didn't explain anything, didn't really try to. It was clear that they thought that this was a matter on which a stranger could not be enlightened.

But now that I have actually read *Look Back in Anger,* together with Mr. Osborne's two later plays, *The Entertainer* and *Epitaph for George Dillon,* I think I understand something of why the English responded as they did, and why to many people who are not English Mr. Osborne speaks so movingly.

He is, of course, a remarkably good writer. But his happy gift of poetic vivacity—his ability to make dull circumstances consequential and mere objects animate, to lay his hand on the commonplaces of speech and make them move with grace and energy—is not likely to come into a writer's possession unless it is to be put at the service of some idea about the nature of life, an idea which the writer desires to impose upon his audience.

Mr. Osborne has such an idea, and I think I can best suggest what it is by comparing Mr. Osborne with D. H. Lawrence, not in point of genius, that would not be fair, but in point of the relation of the two men to English society.

It is a commonplace to say of Lawrence that his working-class origin made a decisive element in his thought and creation. One of the chief and most obvious characteristics of modern literature is the search for the "real" which lies behind, or under, the factitious. Lawrence drew from his class-consciousness the material of a very powerful reality, which was contrived to make the life of the English middle class—especially the cultivated, urban middle class—seem thin and poor and pretentious. Mr. Osborne too comes of working-class people and, like Lawrence, he finds in his class origin the material of a reality; and against the respectable, the conventional, and the established he asserts the authority—one almost wants to say the *charm*—of what is really real, even if that is to be found in defeat and despair: perhaps especially if it be found in defeat and despair.

And just here lies the significant difference between the two realities, Lawrence's and Mr. Osborne's. For to defeat and despair Lawrence gave no credence and no quarter. The whole movement of his being is toward victory and affirmation.

If we look for a cultural—rather than a personal—explanation of this difference, we find it, I think, in the difference of the class structures which the two men experienced. Lawrence, like many writers who had been born in the 19th century, could identify himself with the aristocracy against the middle class—if not with an actual aristocracy, then at least with an ideal and legendary aristocracy, and could claim for himself the virtues that an aristocracy is traditionally said to possess, which are, I suppose, courage and self-sufficiency. Lawrence's heroes, no matter what their class, always have about them some element of an ideal aristocracy. They recognize in themselves a worth that is not at the mercy of any mere social valuation. They take themselves with a deadly seriousness, with conscious, fastidious pride. They undertake to be indomitable.

The aristocratic class, in Lawrence's day, could still lend the color of credibility to this ideal. And there is no doubt that Lawrence's religious upbringing, the importance of which he never underestimated, had the effect of reinforcing his aristocratic attitudes. His mind was suffused by the idea of *salvation*. He believed that it was possible to be saved.

It is just this that nowadays makes Lawrence seem old-fashioned to a good many readers, and unavailable to them. They find that his implied demand upon them is too exigent. And often it seems absurd, inappropriate to life as they know it. They are more at home with the reality that Mr. Osborne offers them, a reality that has no cultural sanction for indomitability and salvation, that is based on the confrontation of defeat and despair, on the admission of failure, and on the confession of inadequacy, whether it be of talent, or of will, or even of kindness or honesty.

Mr. Osborne is a writer of considerable consciousness and he seems to make virtually explicit reference to the difference between the situation of now and the situation of Lawrence's day. In his representation of Jimmy Porter's self-pity and cruelty he includes, I think, an awareness of Jimmy's misfortune in having nothing to resist—as against Jimmy's anger, which expresses itself futilely and vulgarly in the crashing of upper-class parties and the exploitation of well-fixed hosts, he might well be thought to have in mind Lawrence on his visit to King's College, consumed with rage as he confronted the best Establishment minds and resolved never to submit or yield, determined to rise above them and confound them. For Lawrence there was still enough power and authority in the "superior" classes to make an issue, a vital tension, to call forth his combative energies. Mr. Osborne takes account of the loss of that power and authority in the figure of Jimmy Porter's father-in-law, Colonel Redfern. This retired Indian officer is represented as being in all ways a decent man, and he is treated with gentle respect. But he is merely the vestige of authority. Can we fail to speculate whether Jimmy Porter's tantrums may not be the expectable behavior of a child from whom the natural restraints have been removed?—by the outrageousness of his conduct he asks for someone to check him, for some figure in command to tell him what the rules are: to tell him, in effect, who he is. Even an enemy can do that, and Jimmy Porter has not even an enemy.

It is this, I think, that the English were responding to in the play. This is what they could not explain to a stranger. They knew—not consciously—that Jimmy Porter's subversive alienation from English life was his response to the loss of an old glory, an old power, even an old internal struggle. They saw in him the response to a culture which no longer makes the demands it once made, in which the figures of authority no longer exercise their sanctions. My English friends were men of proper and mature behavior, but they overlooked or forgave Jimmy Porter's childish cruelties because they could not but see that in some way they were an appropriate response to the situation. *In some way* an appropriate response: not, indeed, a moral way, or a commendable way, or a "manly" way, but appropriate none the less.

I have given all my space and attention to the first of Mr. Osborne's plays, feeling justified in doing so because I have little doubt that *Look Back in Anger* will always serve as the prolegomenon to all of Mr. Osborne's canon of work, no matter how large it may grow. *The Entertainer* and *Epitaph for George Dillon* (the latter written in collaboration with Anthony Creighton) are somewhat less topical than *Look Back in Anger*. But they are no less immediate, no less concerned with the great social and cultural change, surely not peculiar to England, which suggests to so many people that their moral energies ought no longer go to the maintenance of strict conduct, of "ideals," of a moral "front," but to the realization of failure, defeat, and despair. To people who grew up in the bright energies of that late efflorescence of humanism which was the age of Lawrence and Shaw, this decision is not easy to comprehend. It is, however, not quite as new as we might think it. We have only to remember Chekhov to understand that the confrontation of failure, defeat, and despair has its own curious moral energy. And I don't think that I overestimate Mr. Osborne when I say that he stands in the tradition of Chekhov.

—JULY 1959

The Creation of Music and Poetry

W. H. Auden

On Valéry and Stravinsky

AFTER THE PREMIÈRE of *Persephone* in 1934, Valéry wrote Stravinsky this congratulatory note:

> I am only a "profane" listener, but the divine detachment of your work touched me. It seems to me that what I have sometimes searched for in the ways of poetry, you pursue and join in your art. The point is to attain purity through the will.

Though the poet was some ten years older than the composer, both belong to that extraordinary generation of revolutionaries who, in every medium, created what is known as "modern" art. When they talk about their experiences, therefore, they must be listened to with the utmost attention and reverence. At the same time, their statements must be viewed in the light of the polemical situation with which they were faced but which for us, their juniors, thanks to their achievements, has altered.

Furthermore, in assessing the critical remarks of any practising artist, we must remember that his primary concern is, very properly, with the works which he is making himself, and that the works of others are important to him mainly as examples to follow or avoid. What he says about his art is never false, but it may only be true of the kind of work he desires and is able to produce.

No one can appreciate an art who is not a proto-artist, who has not, that is to say, had certain experiences which, were he creative, he would be able to objectify in some artistic medium. There are proto-poetic, proto-graphic, and proto-musical experiences which are quite distinct from each other, though they may overlap. Valéry gives us an account of a proto-musical experience of his own.

> As I went along my street, which mounted steeply, I was gripped by a rhythm which took possession of me and soon gave me the impression of some force outside myself. Another rhythm overtook and combined with the first, and certain strange transverse relations were set up between them. . . . in my case walking is often conducive to a quickened flow of ideas, but this time my movements assailed my consciousness through a subtle arrangement of rhythms, instead of provoking that amalgam of images, inner words, and virtual acts that one calls an Idea. . . . This grace had descended on the wrong head, since I could make no use of a gift which, in a musician, would doubtless have assumed a lasting shape, and it was in vain that these two themes offered me a composition whose sequence and complexity amazed my ignorance and reduced it to despair.

It is revealing to compare this story with Valéry's description of the genesis of *Le Cimetière Marin:*

> My intention was at first no more than a rhythmic figure, empty and filled with meaningless syllables, which obsessed me for some time. I noticed that this figure was decasyllabic, and I pondered on that model which is very little used in modern French poetry; it struck me as poor and monotonous, of little worth compared with the alexandrine. . . . The demon of generalization prompted me to try raising this Ten to the power of Twelve. It suggested a certain stanza of six lines, and the idea of a composition founded on the number of these stanzas and strengthened by a diversity of tones and functions to be assigned to them. Between the stanzas contrasts and correspondences would be set up. This last condition soon required the potential poem to be a monologue of "self" in which the simplest and most enduring themes of my affective and intellectual life, as they had imposed themselves upon my adolescence, associated with the sea and the light of a particular spot on the Mediterranean coast were called up. . . . All this led to the theme of death and suggested the theme of pure thought. (The chosen line of ten syllables bears some relation to the Dantesque line.) My line had to be solid and strongly rhythmical. I knew I was tending towards a monologue as personal, but also as universal, as I could make it.

Just as in the case of the "musical" experience which baffled him, Valéry's initial impulse is a rhythm, but this time he recognizes it as decasyllabics—that is, a *verbal* rhythm—which draws to it images and ideas which can be formulated and only formulated in words.

So few composers have given us accounts of the process of musical composition that Stravinsky's remarks are particularly valuable. It would seem that what a word is to a poet, an interval is to a composer.

> When I compose an interval, I am aware of it as an object, as something outside me, the contrary of an impression.

Like words in poetry, intervals do not begin to become music until they are associated with a rhythm.

> I recognize musical ideas when they start to exercise a certain kind of auditive sense. But long before ideas take shape I begin to work by relating intervals rhythmically. This exploration of possibilities is always conducted at the piano. Only after I have established my melodic or harmonic relationships do I pass to composition. When my main theme has been decided on, I know in general lines what kind of musical material it will require. I start to look for my material, sometimes playing old masters (to put myself in motion), sometimes starting directly to improvise rhythmic units on a provisional row of notes (which can become a final row).

This second stage seems to be analogous to the stage at which a poet becomes conscious in a general sort of way of what his poem is to be "about." But for the poet, so far as I can see, there is no problem analogous to the composer's search for the right pitch and timbre since, in the case of words, these qualities are decided by the normal speech habits of those who speak the poet's mother tongue, whereas the composer is free and therefore obliged to choose them for himself.

> The sound (timbre) will not always be present. But if the musical idea is a group of notes, a motive coming suddenly to your mind, it very often comes together with its sound. . . . It is very important to me to remember the pitch of the music at its first appearance: if I transpose it for some reason, I am in danger of losing the freshness of first contact and I will have difficulty in recapturing its attractiveness.

Although nearly all poets think of their poems as heard speech, most of them also attach importance to how they look on the page; they associate the sound

of the words with a certain length of line and shape of stanza. It had not occurred to me, I must confess, that composers can feel the same way.

> As a composer I associate a certain kind of music, a certain tempo of music,
> with a certain kind of note unit . . . the unit of the note and the tempo ap-
> pear in my imagination at the same time as the interval itself. . . . It is diffi-
> cult for me to judge whether a work of mine, translated into larger or
> smaller note units, but played at the same tempo, would make an aural dif-
> ference. However I know that I could not look at the music in its translated
> shape, for the shape of the notes as one writes them is the shape of the orig-
> inal conception itself. . . . I do believe in a relation between the character of
> my music and the kind of note unit of the pulsation, and I do not care that
> this is undemonstrable.

Valéry and Stravinsky have many likes and dislikes in common. Both prefer the formal to the happy-go-lucky, an art which disintoxicates to an art
which would bewitch, both have a horror of the pseudo-grandiloquent. But,
as practising artists, their careers have been very different. Valéry's poetic output was small, most of it produced during a few years between the ages of
forty-five and fifty, and stylistically uniform. Having found his voice in *La
Jeune Parque,* he never felt a need to change it, and the themes which excited
his imagination were unusually limited in range. Stravinsky, on the other
hand, has composed steadily from youth till now, and is one of the most striking examples in musical history of continuous growth.

Growth does not mean, of course, that each new work is necessarily better
than its predecessors or that it supersedes them, only that each work is a fresh
departure. Musical journalism usually divides Stravinsky's works into periods—the Russian period, the Neo-Classical period and now, in his seventies,
the Serial period—but, like all journalistic labels, this is misleading: every important composition of Stravinsky's has a style, a musical language all its
own.

Lastly, while Valéry was obsessed all his life with the question of *La Poésie
pure,* Stravinsky seems never to have worried about "pure" music. More than
half his compositions so far have been ballet scores or settings of words,
about which one can say, not only that they are good to listen to, but also that
they are good to choreograph and dance to, or good settings of their text.
Beautiful, for example, as *Agon* sounds on the phonograph, it requires to be
seen with Balanchine's choreography to make its full effect; nor, whatever
Stravinsky may have said at times about treating words as syllables, has he

ever really thought of language as a mere pretext for singing. Few composers have shown better *literary* taste in their choice of texts to set, and his feelings about this can be gauged from his criticism of Schönberg:

> . . . nearly all of his texts are appallingly bad, some of them so bad as to discourage performance of the music.

Poetry is in a unique position among the arts in that its medium, language, is neither the creation and private property of poets, as musical sounds are of composers, nor passive matter upon which they can impose any significance they choose, like the stone of architects and the colors of painters.

The poet can only write his poetry after the linguistic group to which he belongs has created both the words themselves and their meanings, and these are needed for a great many other purposes than simply providing building materials for poetry. Even so peculiar a language as that of *Finnegans Wake* would be meaningless without the pre-existence of the conventional languages which it breaks up and recombines.

Poets, therefore, unlike composers, are faced with the perplexing question: "How is the poetic use of language to be distinguished from all the other uses to which language is put?" The formal distinction between metrical verse and prose is obvious enough but tells us very little.

Valéry, who was both a practising poet and a highly intelligent man, devoted more time than most to this problem, and the inadequacy of the solutions he offers—no one has suggested better and most have suggested worse—convinces me that a clear and definite answer is impossible.

The French *Symbolistes,* among whom Valéry grew up and by whom he was greatly influenced, tried to assimilate poetry to music.

> What was baptized Symbolism can be very simply described as the common intention of several groups of poets (otherwise mutually inimical) to reclaim their own from Music—our literary minds dreamed of extracting from language the same effects as were produced upon our nervous systems by sound alone. Some cherished Wagner, others Schumann. I could as well say that they hated them. In the heart of passionate interest these two states are undistinguishable.

But language can never become pure sound and tonal relations without ceasing to be language; when we listen to someone speaking a tongue we do not know, we do indeed hear it as if it were music, but as a music without any artistic significance. It is unfortunate, too, for their argument, that these French poets made statements about music, for what they said about that art makes it clear that they valued music for its capacity to induce vague day-dreams in the listener; in the structural side of music they showed no interest whatsoever.

Abandoning this theory, Valéry tried to make a division between the poetic and the prosaic based on an analogy between action with a practical purpose and play. The example which, following Malherbe, he uses as an illustration is the difference between walking and dancing.

> Walking, like prose, has a definite aim. It is an act directed at something we wish to reach. Actual circumstances, such as the need for some object, the state of my body, my sight, the terrain, etc., which order the manner of walking, prescribe its direction and speed. . . . There are no movements in walking which are not special adaptations, but, each time they are abolished and, as it were, absorbed by the accomplishment of the act, by the attainment of the goal.
>
> The dance is quite another matter. It is, of course, a system of actions; but of actions whose end is in themselves. It goes nowhere. It is therefore not a question of carrying out a limited operation whose end is situated somewhere in our surroundings, but rather of creating, maintaining and exalting a certain state, by a periodic movement that can be executed on the spot.

But is the distinction as sharp as Valéry says? A commuter may walk to the railroad station every morning, but at the same time he may enjoy the motion of walking for its own sake; the fact that his walk is necessary does not exclude the possibility of its also being a form of play. Conversely, the ritual play of dancing can be and frequently has been associated with practical ends, like securing a good harvest, without thereby ceasing to have artistic merit as a dance.

And the same is true of different modes of speech. If I call at the house of a sick peer to inquire after his health, and the butler tells me: "His Lordship is up but not down," the butler's intention may be merely the practical one of satisfying my curiosity by giving me correct information, yet I can and do relish his answer as poetry.

On the other hand, though there are certain lyrics the appeal of which lies almost entirely in their beautiful verbal play, most of the poetry we call great possesses a quality, call it vision, wisdom, what you will, which transcends the actual verbal expression. It is impossible to read a prose translation of *The Iliad* or *The Divine Comedy* without being made to feel that these are works of great value, although their "music" has been abolished.

Music, of course, has no such problem: the formal conventions of music are not, like those of verse, conventions applied *to* a language; they are more like the rules of syntax which are essential properties *of* a language. To change them, to shift, for example, from a horizontal polyphonic system of composition to a vertical harmonic system, or from a triadic to a twelve-tone, is like changing from Greek to English, or Hebrew to Russian.

The counterpart among composers to the quarrel between poets as to what use of language is and is not poetic seems to be a quarrel over the question whether a certain musical language has or has not exhausted its possibilities. Here again, I think, every composer has to answer for himself and must beware of making a dogma out of his personal needs. Stravinsky has lately taken to a serial system of composition and is therefore quite properly in its favor, but when asked if he thinks the masterpieces of the next decade will be composed in serial technique, he is sensibly cautious.

> Nothing is likely about masterpieces, least of all whether there will be any. Nevertheless, a masterpiece is more likely to happen to the composer with the most highly developed language. This language is serial at present, and though our contemporary development of it could be tangential to an evolution we do not yet see, for us this doesn't matter. Developments in language are not easily abandoned, and the composer who fails to take account of them may lose the mainstream. Masterpieces aside, it seems to me that the new music will be serial.

Practising artists, like Valéry and Stravinsky, usually prefer, when they speak of their art, to talk about technique and conscious judgment and to avoid words like *inspiration*. They know that to be inspired and to make a good work are one and the same thing; what they will not do is disclaim responsibility for what they offer to the public, or claim immunity from criticism on the grounds that messages from the Muses must be accepted on faith. They also know that technique is not, as the public is apt to believe, something that anyone can acquire, but is itself a gift of the Muses, and the one about which it is hardest for an artist to deceive others.

So Valéry says:

> The spirit blows where it will: one sees it blow on fools, and it whispers to them what they are able to hear.

And Stravinsky:

> Most artists are sincere anyway and most art is bad, though, of course, some insincere art (sincerely insincere) is quite good.

It is a pity that nobody, so far as I know, ever noted down Valéry's table talk for he, like Stravinsky, was not only an artist but also a man of the world who got around. As Stravinsky's Boswell, Mr. Robert Craft has an excellent sense of the right questions to ask the maestro but he does not—perhaps deliberately—put down the answers with the accuracy of a tape recorder. The substance is obviously correct, but the cadences and sentence structure are not always those of a speaking voice. I also suspect that Mr. Craft has at times played the tactful censor. Every genius, from time to time, talks nonsense—only minor artists are never foolish—and I suspect that Stravinsky's comments are not always as sensible as those we are permitted to hear. I would also welcome more catty remarks like the one on Pergolesi—

> Pergolesi? *Pulcinella* is the only work of 'his' I like.

or this one about the French—

> They will do absolutely anything to get theatre tickets except buy them.

We are snobbish enough to enjoy anecdotes about famous people. How fascinating it is to learn that Diaghilev died singing Puccini, and how much more convincing than Cocteau is Stravinsky's account of the evening after the scandalous première of *Sacre du Printemps.*

> I went with Diaghilev and Nijinsky to a restaurant. So far from weeping and reciting Pushkin in the Bois de Boulogne, Diaghilev's only comment was "Exactly what I wanted."

Such pleasures are of course minor compared with the privilege of hearing a great composer talk about the theoretical and practical problems of his art. And who except Stravinsky could say at the age of seventy-seven without sounding shymaking:

> I don't mind my music going on trial for, if I'm to keep my position as a promising young composer, I must accept that.

—AUGUST 1959

"The Tradition of the New"

Jacques Barzun

On Harold Rosenberg's *The Tradition of the New*

THEY BEGAN IT—Rousseau and Goethe; Blake and Wordsworth; Beethoven and Berlioz; Constable, Turner, and Delacroix; Stendhal, Hugo, and Nerval—saying: "Art is not what you suppose—beautiful and confined. The truth is infinitely wider than you think. Only look at nature and your secret thoughts, and you will discover new worlds." These reality seekers also uttered opinions about government and society, whose being they declared inseparable from the life of art. Thus was established the model of the prophet-artist; and ever since, Revolution, which is but a contest about who shall make the supreme realities, has been our habit in art, politics, and feeling.

For a hundred years after Rousseau, search and invention went on at a dazzling pace. Discoveries and masterpieces covered the ground in profusion. But by the beginning of the twentieth century there were signs that the insistent genius of analysis had exhausted its material. At the height of Symbolism, thought and sensation had been made so impalpable it was as if a fine dust overspread the universe of mind—quite like the effect predicted by the second law of thermodynamics in the universe of matter. In 1900 the heirs of European Romanticism and Impressionism were ready to call the distillation done and start afresh on new premises. The new could only be synthesis in place of analysis, the construction of wholes in place of the attenuation of parts.

Soon, true creations answered the need, especially for the eye. Cubism and the new architecture gave types and forms to which we still return in wonder. But the new artists had reckoned without politics and society, which their latest predecessors, the Symbolists, had pointedly neglected. In the guise of the first world war, politics and society scattered and confused the new century's efforts. After that war, everybody remembered a different past; hordes of new men awoke to the charm or the challenge of art; and a wide public took to it as a prop or a semi-profession. Talents and tastes were mixed with ignorances and with the disordered fragments of the tradition. Primitive, futurist, naturalist, symbolist, African, neo-classical, vers-librist, Japanese, ferro-concrete, expressionist, abstract, atonal, imagist, pastichist—all styles and stances were simultaneously alive, or at least wriggling as if alive.

They wriggle still, while a new mass audience of naive and knowing people, equally respectful, absorbs the products of a deliberate industry. The New has branches to suit all tastes: there is the plain New for the brisk vanguardians, the Near-New for the faltering, the Old-New for the laggards. A little ahead and in a seasonable haze stands the New-New, from which at times, by a tremendous effort, particles of the New-New-New detach themselves, like a helium nucleus out of radioactive material. All these arrangements have in fact been brought down to a science. Dozens of specialists will tell you about any part of the operation you care to examine.

What is so far lacking is a qualified theorist of the whole. But the desire for such a mind is growing, which is why Mr. Harold Rosenberg's *The Tradition of the New* has been received with joy and praise. Writers and painters, in particular, have seized upon the author as a source of comfort and strength, for he seems to give them principles and formulas and not merely local arguments and explanations.

This is true even though Mr. Rosenberg's book is not a treatise in form or intention. It consists of some twenty essays, short and long, grouped into four sections on, respectively: American painting today, poetry, Marxism and art, and mass culture. Some of the essays were originally book reviews, but they were from the start so ably conceived as diagnostic pieces that when reread today they give an impression at once of freshness and of permanence. No doubt this is due to the writer's double purpose: to write criticism and to prove a thesis.

The thesis appears most clearly in the section on modern American painting, a movement which Mr. Rosenberg serves as herald and champion. The originator of the phrase Action Painting, Mr. Rosenberg elaborates its meaning into a test of the genuinely new. In Action Painting at last, says Mr. Rosenberg, we have the definitive break which earlier men half achieved, spoiled, or retreated from. What is the test? It is the rejection of Art. In painting, this means repudiating any idea or image before confronting the canvas; it means the replacement of an intention by an act—the act of painting—which occurs as nothing more than a conjunction between the materials and the painter's "biography." Painting now abandons all its esthetic properties as earlier it had abandoned moral and intellectual properties. The resulting work is not even any longer quite an object, it is a process. "The big moment came when it was decided to paint . . . just TO PAINT. The gesture on the canvas was a gesture of liberation, from Value—political, esthetic, moral."

Mr. Rosenberg does not so much accept the resulting quietus of Art as rejoice in it. In this he is heavily backed by the arti—that is, by the actioneers themselves. I stumble over their proper name, but with respect. For their words and attitudes are not negligible, or singular, and in any case not whimsical. One need not be a practitioner to see that "Artists" have painted themselves into a corner. There is nothing left for them to say; everything conceivable has been tried, combined, and parodied. The careless prolongation of the Romantic century by its successor has driven these talents out of their minds and into the realm of gesture, where the most random is the truest.

The poets of the so-called "beat" generation act out of the same necessity. They lead sacrificial lives in hopes of overhearing something that shall not be remembered literature. They want to flee what Mr. Rosenberg calls a phantom of "past self-recognition." A poem then becomes an attempt to take "notes on a secret experimental activity—" and sometimes not so secret, as when a Surrealist relies on automatic writing or a Californian records on tape his severely uncensored outpourings. It is a new anti-mental education, in pursuit of Wallace Stevens's teaching that "poetry is a process of the personality of the poet"—the true, the blushful endocrine.

Meanwhile the musician, whom Mr. Rosenberg does not deal with, likewise collects city and factory noises, or entirely new electronic sounds, to find new matter, unspoiled and unevocative.

The social and political meaning of this program is obvious. It is the dream of total revolution: to start with a fresh slate, to discard even the ghosts or echoes of the past. Yet on reflection it does not seem as if Action Painting were radical enough to lead us on to the new life. Is the genre not conservative in keeping the memory and mechanics of paint as we know it—canvas, pigment, exhibition, sale? And it has so far failed to develop the Action Viewer, who would also make the canvas a process of conjunction with his biography, sometimes by putting an elbow through it.

But I am not concerned with prophecy, nor do I want to obscure by a passing irony the notable effect upon me of Mr. Rosenberg's vibrant words in Part I. The dream of a radical break and total renewal always comes from exasperation, and the author puts us in the mood to understand "Action," "Beat," and "Musique concrète" as no one else has done. And his wit and anger, while preparing us for his next subject, suggest a useful distinction. Exasperation can be of the mind or of the senses. The Romantics got rid of the old burden of words and wigs with senses perfectly fresh and eager for a world of experience they knew would open at their touch; and the new world developed new minds. But now, which is the second time around, both senses and mind are jaded; no frontier is left, no recourse but the blind movements of instinct—at least until the old ego is ground down to nothingness.

Mr. Rosenberg deals brilliantly with the Marxist phase of this attempt at self-renewal by self-annihilation. What has been taken as the moral turpitude of the Marxist, he points out, is nothing but this capacity to be new at will. "Bolshevism turned ideas into flesh—and flesh into an abstraction." The abstraction was history, which keeps common mankind in a rut, but which for the Marxist became an instrument of liberation. By magnifying purpose and obliterating motive, a man could loose himself from inherited morals, from yesterday's promises or today's convictions, and ultimately from any awareness through the sensibilities that such a thing as an individual exists. At that point the perfect Communist party member is close kin to the perfect modern artist. Both heed something which is not themselves and not anybody else, past, present, or future, and whose distant pulses they, motiveless, can confidently follow in action.

Mr. Rosenberg's plan in this book does not permit him to study the parallel I have just drawn, nor to discuss sufficiently a second likeness which comes into view when the author deals with Dr. Suzanne Langer's philosophy of art. This second likeness is that between modern art and modern science. Despite confusions and exchanges of hard words, the spirit of naturalistic inquiry has ruled both art and science since the Romantics. From Wordsworth to William Carlos Williams, the stethoscope is out to catch the heartbeat and the vernacular, and it is no modern affectation that drugs, acids, and transistors are now used in the *process* and *production* of poetry. It is indeed conclusive that both art and science use the same bad language: "experiment," "function of poetry," "rendering of experience," "process of a personality." To quote Mr. Rosenberg himself for (and with) added emphasis: "We relate Hamlet's incapacity to a *structural insufficiency,* that is, to his failure to be *part of an action-system.* . . ."

This deplorable jargon is, I am happy to say, not typical of Mr. Rosenberg's prose. On the contrary, he gives more light than most writers because, seeing the full panorama and affecting only a few secretive phrases, he describes his vision with great lucidity and force. He is thoroughly familiar with the French (he is the only critic I know of who has also read Mallarmé's perfume advertisements) and he is at home in the theoretical wrangles that have spurred the whole modern movement; sometimes he himself talks like a French manifesto-maker, and to our advantage: "Revolution in art lies not in the will to destroy but in the revelation of what already is destroyed. Art kills only the dead." Such pithy reminders of Stendhal should disabuse a gullible generation used to soft innuendo.

Having given these valuable lessons upon the Tradition of the New and a clear statement of the action principle which is to replace art, Mr. Rosenberg rests in some uncertainty about the wider question of culture. He perceives a decline, not in esthetic quality, but in a "complex of meanings larger than the meaning of any one art." He acknowledges that the "revolution with which the century began . . . the will to overthrow and discover . . . the originality, daring, enthusiasm . . ." are gone. But he does not succeed in linking these perceptions to his impressions of the unsorted present.

His chapters on mass culture are in truth the weakest part of the book. They are not improved by the sallies they contain against the sociology of Mr. Riesman and the literary criticism of Mr. Trilling. Rather, these pages suggest a petulant despair, in which the less the objections fit, the more exorbitant are the demands. It is surely captious to blame Mr. William Whyte and Mr. Ries-man for producing "sermons for their milieu rather than challenges to history in the name of mankind." One can imagine the critic's blast at the grandilo-quence of such a challenge if it were made. None but a great artist can at once defy and impersonate the world, and his work usually lies unregarded until after his death. And now the artist has debarred himself from utterance of any kind; he is "acting" and "experimenting," and presumably awaiting a brighter day to redeem his hopelessly mortgaged mind. When that day comes and art has reached another turning point, Mr. Rosenberg's essays will appear as an indelible marker along the road.

—DECEMBER 1959

The Comedy of Comedies

Jacques Barzun

On Molière's *The Misanthrope,* translated by Richard Wilbur

ONE OF THE LITERARY ILLUSIONS hardest to fight against is the belief that there exist touchstones by which to test a man's command, or alternatively, a reader's perception, of literary greatness. Matthew Arnold believed there were lines in poems that showed the poet and tested his readers, and we have all had the impulse, after being transported by a masterpiece, to exclaim: "Anybody who does not thrill at this is a clod!"

The unfortunate truth is that there are no touchstones, no means of infallibly testing sensitiveness, judgment, or taste, for the simple reason that there is and can be no absolute consensus about art. The circumstances that promote understanding—let alone enjoyment—are too numerous and elusive to permit the work of art—even the greatest—to be self-sufficient in its power. The merest glance at literary history shows how readily the perspective changes upon the grandest monuments, how inexplicable are the individual and collective blindnesses, and how futile it is to expect a forward march of appreciation, as if we were dealing with knowledge. What would five centuries of exquisite judgment say of our indifference to Cicero? And how surprised would be some of the best judges in that span to hear of our worship of Dante!

This state of affairs appears at its clearest, of course, when we attempt to cross the barrier of language, which may or may not be augmented by that of nationality. When differences of Time, Place, and Tongue are added to those of Subject and Convention, Tone and Technique, it requires a powerful motive—religion, singularity, snobbery, hatred of the age—to propel one within the presence, there to begin the preliminaries of friendship which make a given work our own. That this is possible and comes to pass, wiping out at last the irrelevant motive, is a miracle to be grateful for. But it should not breed the confidence implied by the faith in touchstones.

I tell myself these necessary truths every time I finish reading Molière's *Misanthrope,* for if there *were* touchstones, this masterpiece would be one of them. It has never been a popular work on the stage, even in France. Elsewhere, for lack of proper translations, it has tended to seem thin and dry. A cranky perfectionist who curses everybody and a coquette who flatters and maligns everybody do not get on as lovers and come to their separate griefs. What is there to admire in so contrived a situation, particularly when it is handled in the classical manner of long speeches full of deductive reasoning? Where is the good old Molière of Scapin beaten in a sack, of the bourgeois gentilhomme taken in by the imitation Turks, of the blackavised doctors with their ridiculous Latin and redoubtable syringes? Even *Tartuffe,* high-minded as the comedy is, takes hold of our carnal nature by its mixture of deceiving piety and real lust: we are breathless to see the outcome, as we should be at any play. Nothing of the kind in the *Misanthrope,* and I can hear the leading American agent for highbrow plays, saying again as she did at Becque's *La Parisienne,* "The story-line is weak."

To be sure, those parallel confidants of Alceste and Célimène, reasonable non-lovers who marry at the end, those parallel lawsuits we never really learn about, those parallel rivals, Oronte, the effusive poet, and Arsinoe, the pinched-lipped prude—how primitive in conception and predictable in action, how lacking in imagination! True, all true, but how marvelously moving just the same! The very language in which these six people challenge, reprove, conciliate one another is extraordinarily abstract, at times detached. And yet, when I think of the fictional hero most madly and desperately in love, I think of Alceste. I remember immediately afterwards that Alceste in this guise is Molière himself, married to an incurable and faithless coquette who shortly became heroically faithful to his memory. This knowledge is not what makes Célimène move me as deeply and painfully as Alceste, she being unaccountably as lovable as he thought her; but these biographical facts certainly had something to do with Molière's mysterious ability to endue the language of Descartes with such passion and sense of fatality as to produce the sublime. It is because there is *nothing to it* that the *Misanthrope* is wondrous. It is made of a nameless sentiment at the end of life, an overwhelming commonplace.

There is nothing to it, but what this vacancy leaves is room for the question, how is society—the machinery and facade of society—endurable for beings with feelings, more particularly sexual feelings? One aspect of the question gives us in essence Rousseau's *Social Contract;* the other, Freud's *Civilization and Its Discontents.* And in the play these two facets of the eternal question belong not to the realm of ideas but to the fabric of ordinary conscious selves—silly, respectable people who write sonnets because it is fashionable, who preen themselves and take advantage because they are handsome and well-dressed, who gossip about one another because they are sensitive to trifles and have the wit of words, who see themselves more or less clearly being disdained and grossly flattered, teased and driven and deceived and distracted, and who cannot help themselves because their minds and limbs are bound by the fine unbreakable chains of society. Alceste's attempt to tear himself loose fails and is comic because all he can fly to is another society, in which the pain caused by dissembled spite and hypocrisy will be replaced by the wounds of moody sincerity. There is no solution; there is no satisfaction of either instinct or reason; there is only the weary compromise of Philinte and Eliante.

IF SOME VERY GOOD JUDGES of literature are left untouched by the superb simplicity and effortless accuracy of the speeches in *Le Misanthrope,* finding in them nothing more than improbable debate, it can be imagined how rare must be the accident of someone's having both a true perception of this comedy of comedies and the power to render it in another language. This happy accident has occurred, and the English reader now has a translation deserving to bear the title *The Misanthrope* on its front. Mr. Richard Wilbur is too well-known as a poet to require introduction. As a translator he is still a poet, and one who has taken on the discipline of the original without losing the freedom afforded by his own. His version reads with complete smoothness and felicity, even though he set himself the goal of producing in rimed couplets a nearly line-by-line rendering of the sense. It is a tour-de-force whose fit reward can only be the pleasure it will give to all those for whom the play has so far remained a double enigma, linguistic and emotional.

To give a fair idea of Mr. Wilbur's unflagging rightness (and lightness) of touch would require three or four pages of varied dialogue, in short repartee and long speeches. I have only the space to give a minute sample, one of Célimène's retorts to the assaulting prude Arsinoe:

> Madam, I think we either blame or praise
> According to our taste and length of days.
> There is a time of life for coquetry,
> And there's a season, too, for prudery.
> When all one's charms are gone, it is, I'm sure,
> Good strategy to be devout and pure:
> It makes one seem a little less forsaken.

> Someday, perhaps, I'll take the road you've taken.
> Time brings all things. But I have time aplenty
> And see no cause to be a prude at twenty.

As Mr. Wilbur hopes in his excellent Introduction, his diction is as nearly timeless as it can safely be made. It is modern without affectation and yet sufficiently sprinkled with words no longer on our tongues to convey the effect of detachment which I referred to earlier as characterizing the play. There is only one word I wish Mr. Wilbur had avoided and that is "conniving" in the recent false sense of plotting and conspiring. This blemish spoils a whole page for me and I would, if I could, forget how and why it is bad, rather than find it there, the only flaw in an admirable work. Let us hope for a second edition, in which Mr. Wilbur will not be intransigent about his illicit intransitive.

The vision of a second edition puts me in mind of the ideal volume in which *The Misanthrope* should be encased, like a jewel within superfluous wrappings. The book should begin with Becque's great essay on the play, followed by Mr. Wilbur's Introduction. Then the play itself. Then a few words that another great comic writer, Georges Courteline, devoted to *Le Misanthrope,* followed in turn by a translation (if Mr. Wilbur would do it) of the additional act Courteline wrote in Molièresque verse, not as a pastiche upon the play, not as amplification of what is complete and perfect, but in veneration, as a demonstrative piece of criticism. Such a book as I ask for should have no illustrations and would need no other padding to bring it to a commercial thickness. It would be Molière-Misanthrope at last among his peers.

One last word: in reading the play as Mr. Wilbur gives it to us, do not let the lordlings and their ribbons mislead you into thinking: "Ah, yes, that was Versailles." It is not the past and it is not Washington: it is Hollywood.

—FALL 1960

Bergman Unseen

LIONEL TRILLING

On Ingmar Bergman's *Four Screenplays*

INGMAR BERGMAN is the only contemporary maker of films who figures in the mind of the public as a creative artist in his own right. I judge the mind of the public more or less by my own mind—Bergman's name is the only one that has forced itself upon my consciousness as equivalent to certain names of the past, such as Griffith, Chaplin, Eisenstein, René Clair. And, indeed, what people say about the man's work leads me to believe that it arouses a more complex enthusiasm than that of any of his predecessors. Bergman is spoken of as if he alone had risen above the confines of an art which, whatever its popularity, is always on trial, and as if he had the right to claim equality with the eminent practitioners of the traditional arts.

It is of course possible that my belief in the uniqueness of Bergman's position is an indication of the extent of my ignorance of what is now going on in the cinema. It may be that Bergman's is but one of the many names that signify at Film Festivals, that there are a score of brilliant Italians and Poles and Japanese whose talents are debated with special fineness of discrimination, the wonderful snootiness of sensibility, that marks the judgment of those who cultivate an intellectual love of the screen. But to the simple untutored laity Bergman's name stands unique.

I speak only of the man's reputation, not of his work, for the simple fact is that my cinematic ignorance extends to my never having seen a single one of Bergman's pictures. This benighted state is neither particular nor entirely accidental but is part of my general alienation from the cinema. It is a condition in which I take no pride and which did not always prevail. Indeed, I know of only one person, the late Robert Warshow, a film critic of superlative talent, who has ever described in a way that seemed adequate to my own experience what the passion of film addiction can be in a boy or an adolescent. And with me the addiction went on well into maturity. But there came a moment when the magic suddenly failed. There had been a time when I could take pleasure in almost any movie, even bad or mediocre ones—I recognized a quality of B-ishness, a sort of hopeless shabbiness, which had its own charm. But then, almost overnight, I found that I could no longer submit to what I was seeing. The beauty or extravagance of the actors' faces no longer compelled me, nor did the emotions, the moral codes, the points of honor, to which these faces were committed. Something did remain: moments of comedy (but the great tradition of film comedy came to an end); certain scenes of visual beauty (*The Bounty* getting under way, for example, and, somehow, the scene in which tea is brought out on the lawn of the old Russian estate in a picture called *Knight Without Armor,* surely the worst picture ever made); and scenes of danger, the man alone walking slowly toward his enemies, his arms held ready for the quick draw, and men going into battle, especially on horseback. But of the old visionary gleam, how little this is—mere embers!

Not long after my disaffection, I was given to understand that the movies were being animated by a new spirit, that great things were being done. I was willing to believe this, to suppose that the new *mystique* of the film which I heard buzzing in the cultural atmosphere was very fine indeed and that some-day I would go to the movies again, perhaps not in my old neurotic way in which the plunge into the fetid dark was half sickness, half therapy, and wholly satisfying, but calmly, as a rational man ought to take his aesthetic pleasures. That day may still come, but it isn't here yet. And so Mr. Bergman has grown into fame and I have no knowledge of his talents as they manifest themselves on the screen.

But it is just this ignorance that makes it possible for me to write about the present volume of Mr. Bergman's screenplays as a book to be read, as a species of literature. In another part of the forest John Simon will be found in a state of high enthusiasm over Mr. Bergman as what he really and essentially is, a maker of films. Mr. Simon, I know, writes from a long and intense experience of his subject—he has seen the Bergman films again and again and he means to see them as many more times as opportunity allows. But all that I expect he will be saying about the visual beauty or the dramatic subtlety or force of the actual films is apart from my purpose, which is not at all cinematic but quite strictly literary.

Mr. Bergman does not think of himself as being in the least literary. "I my-self," he says in his engaging introduction to this volume, "have never had any ambition to be an author. I do not want to write novels, short stories, essays, biographies, or even plays for the theater. I only want to make films . . .

I am a film-maker, not an author." And Mr. Bergman undertakes to support this avowal of his non-literariness by a description of how he conceives a film. "A film for me begins with something very vague—a chance remark or a bit of conversation, a hazy but agreeable event unrelated to any particular situation. It can be a few bars of music, a shaft of light across the street. . . . These are split-second impressions that disappear as quickly as they come, yet leave behind a mood—like pleasant dreams. It is a mental state, not an actual story, but one abounding in fertile associations and images. Most of all, it is a brightly colored thread sticking out of the dark sack of the unconscious. If I begin to wind up this thread, and do it carefully, a complete film will emerge. . . . This primitive nucleus strives to achieve a definite form, moving in a way that may be lazy and half asleep at first. Its stirring is accompanied by vibrations and rhythms which are very special and unique to each film. The picture sequences then assume a pattern in accordance with these rhythms, obeying laws born out of and conditioned by my original stimulus."

I do not think that this statement actually serves to substantiate Mr. Bergman's belief in his non-literariness. The process he describes would seem to be the process of artistic conception in general—or at least of *modern* artistic conception in general—and if the composer of music (to whom Mr. Bergman says the film-maker has the closest affinity) or the painter would assent to it, so too would the poet or the short-story writer and perhaps even the novelist. But if what Mr. Bergman says about his way of composing a film does not in fact show him to be as devoid of the literary impulse as he says he is, it is nevertheless true that only a small part of the process he describes has reference to or can be expressed in words. "The only thing that can be satisfactorily transferred from that original complex of rhythms and moods is the dialogue, and even dialogue is a sensitive substance which may offer resistance. Written dialogue is like a musical score, almost incomprehensible to the average person. Its interpretation demands a technical knack plus a certain kind of imagination and feeling—qualities which are so often lacking, even among actors."

The declaration of independence from literature that Mr. Bergman makes is not a new thing. It is common to all the modern arts, and no doubt the cinema must insist upon it with especial vehemence because its bondage to literature is so great, if only because the cinema still needs story and is still drawn to think of story in the same way that literature does, and even to borrow its stories from literature. Mr. Bergman speaks with great cogency of the difficulty and disadvantage of maintaining a connection between the cinema and literature in the practice of making films out of books: "The irrational dimension of a literary work, the germ of its existence, is often untranslatable into visual terms—and it in turn destroys the special irrational dimension of the film." This, of course, is true, and it explains why it often happens that a good picture is made from a bad novel, while it seldom if ever happens that a good picture is made from a great novel. And in their hearts, and quite without taking thought about the matter, people know that Mr. Bergman is right, and I feel sure that one reason they respond to him with so much enthusiasm is to be found in their sense that in the making of a film the director of a picture ought to be, as Mr. Bergman is, the sole creative force, and that the story ought to be wholly of his own devising.

And yet the cinema, even as Mr. Bergman conceives it, is not free of literature, and perhaps can never be free. In arguing this I put no great weight on the kind of writing that Mr. Bergman relies on to make clear either to himself, or to his collaborators, or, eventually, to the public that now reads his screenplays, what his visual and modal intentions are. Thus, the screenplay of *The Magician* begins in this fashion: "On a summer evening pregnant with thunder in July of the year 1846, a large coach stops beside a road just south of Stockholm. The hot sun slants down mercilessly on the marshes, the forest and the black clouds in the eastern sky." Then, after a retreat to a more neutral language to describe the coach and its sufficiently strange occupants: "In the forest, sunbeams tremble in the trees like hurled spears, but the twilight is heavy." This might be called literary with a vengeance, but it isn't this reliance on words quite intensely used that I have in mind when I speak of the cinema's inability to separate itself from literature. As long as the cinema makes use of story, it is captive to the concepts that control story in literature, it is bound by Beginning, Middle, and End, and by the criterion of "truth." (I put it in quotation marks to prevent the pedantic jesting Pilates from asking what it is.) And exactly because this is so, the texts of Mr. Bergman's four screenplays can be read as we read any other presentation of story.

The statement needs modification. The kind of imagination we exercise in reading the screenplays is not the same as that which we use when we read stories or novels (or plays either, but the proportion of dialogue to narration and description suggests comparison with novels and stories rather than with plays). We do not, that is, make reference directly to reality, we do not conjure up before our mind's eye actual people, but make reference to another art, to people conceived in a stylized way, as they are acted on the screen. To the details of this stylization the photographs which accompany each screenplay do indeed contribute, but that they are not decisive in this process I can attest from having first read two of the screenplays in typescript—even without the photographs my imagination worked in cinematic rather than in "real" images. There is a peculiar pleasure in this form of imagination, a satisfaction that comes from using the imagination in another mode than that of "reality" and yet finding reality of some sort at the end of the process. That is to say, one is never permitted to forget that one is dealing with an art, with a form of playing; and the pleasure, the curious sense of freshness that one experiences, lies in the interfusion of the non-seriousness of play with the seriousness of the matters that are being played with.

This effect is heightened, or made the more readily possible, by one or another degree of fantasy which marks Mr. Bergman's stories. Of the four screenplays, only one, *Wild Strawberries,* is contemporary in its setting, and this matter-of-factness is modified by the dreams, memories, and imaginings of the aged protagonist. *Smiles of a Summer Night* is set at the turn of the century and its erotic comedy is given a fuller liberty by the costumes of the period (in this instance the Scandinavian *chic* of the costumes does come to the aid of the text). *The Seventh Seal* is medieval; *The Magician* is set in Stockholm in 1846. In each instance the fact that the people do not support worries or wear clothes like our own gives license to the freedom of fancy.

And it is in part because of this license that Mr. Bergman is able to satisfy the demand which literature and cinema must alike acknowledge, the demand of truth. The cinema is always under the imputation of not telling the truth, even of downright lying, the more so, perhaps, because it has at its disposal a more intense way of telling certain kinds of truth than any other art: the camera, which can be made to lie at will, can also be made to show truths of a kind that are almost unendurable. And because no other art has been so conscious in its intention of evading the truth, so brazen in its avowal of its commercial reluctance to shock or startle its audience, the cinema, whenever it undertakes a flier in veracity, as even the commercial cinema does now and then, cannot do so without a great huffing and puffing and groaning of the spirit, turning up its eyes, laying its hand upon its heart, and calling for a stack of Bibles. But truth seems to come naturally to Mr. Bergman and as a matter of course. Thus the erotic comedy *Smiles of a Summer Night* conforms to the rules of a genre which are as strict as those of a minuet, and like every other such comedy relies on the beauty and charm and purposefulness of the women, on the swaggering self-deception of the men, and exploits to the full all the elements of titillation, breathless urgency, sudden lyric discovery of the erotic fact; but few such comedies go through their delighted game as unafraid as this one is to take account of the remorselessness and wilfulness that figure in the erotic game, or to play it out in the shadow of the inevitability of old age, or to make discriminations among the various kinds of love that may be involved. *Wild Strawberries* is as exposed to sentimentality as a story could be—it is about a curmudgeonly old man who, by memories, dreams, and fortuitous encounters, is enlightened about himself and learns to repent his coldness. Actually the story is not sentimental, its tone is that of reasonable kindness; it is kept within good limits by its willingness to involve the gentle theme with certain bitter, complex truths of human behavior, such as are represented by the recall of the perverse and brutal sexual scene between the protagonist's wife and her lover, or the insane hatred-in-love of the married couple met on the road (it is not for nothing that Mr. Bergman pays homage to Strindberg as a chief influence upon him). Apart from the other virtues of *The Seventh Seal,* how right it is that the broken young girl, about to be burned as a witch, really is a witch, a loving partisan of the devil, who might have stepped right out of the pages of Marguerite Murray's *The God of the Witches,* or that the figure of Death, represented as an actual person of the play, should be of truly terrible, although not of horrible, aspect. And the same uncompromisingness, the same hardness in gentleness, marks *The Magician.*

I have spoken of Mr. Bergman's introduction to this volume as being engaging; it is so because of the author's modest willingness to tell the truth about himself. One of the most attractive passages is that in which Mr. Bergman ventures into autobiography. His father, he tells us, was a clergyman, and of his parents he says that they were "of vital importance, not only in themselves but because they created a world for me to revolt against." He goes on: "In my family there was an atmosphere of hearty wholesomeness which I, a sensitive young plant, scorned and rebelled against. But that strict middle-class home gave me a wall to pound on, something to sharpen myself against. At the same time they taught me a number of values—efficiency, punctuality, a sense of financial responsibility—which may be 'bourgeois' but are nevertheless important to the artist. They are part of the process of setting oneself severe standards. Today as a film-maker I am conscientious, hard working and extremely careful; my films involve good craftsmanship, and my pride is the pride of the good craftsman." This avowal is pleasant in itself and it perhaps took a certain courage to make, but it does not tell us as much about Mr. Bergman as what follows upon it. "I have been asked, as a clergyman's son, about the role of religion in my thinking and film-making. To me, religious problems are continuously alive. I never cease to concern myself with them; it goes on every hour of every day. Yet this does not take place on the emotional level, but on an intellectual one. Religious emotion, religious sentimentality is something I got rid of long ago—I hope. The religious problem is an intellectual one to me: the relationship of my mind to my intuition. The result of this conflict is usually some kind of tower of Babel." I don't know what Mr. Bergman means when he says that the relation of his mind to his intuition makes a religious problem, or what he means by the tower of Babel that results. But I think he is right in a general way when he connects his artistic powers with his religious upbringing. From that rearing, I think, he derived his sense of immanent or present crisis in human lives, which makes his dramatic imagination, even as one knows it from the printed page, so momentous.

—DECEMBER 1960

"Curtains"

Lionel Trilling

On Kenneth Tynan's *Curtains*

THE OTHER DAY a young colleague said to me with a sweet, musing, pedagogic smile, "I shall have to do something about your hatred of the theater."
He is a scholar of the drama and a very gifted dramatic critic; he had once
been a student of mine and of course I was touched by his wish to lead his
former teacher out of the darkness into the light.

He is mistaken—it is not true that I hate the theater. Actually, indeed, I can
believe that I love the theater, not simply and directly, but in one of those
complex modern ways of love that every playwright knows so well. Yes, that
is surely the truth of the matter—I love the theater *really*, which is to say unconsciously, deep down, angrily, bitterly. And some day again the theater will
hold out its arms to me as once it did in my childhood, before the intervening
years—and some dreadful traumatic episode which in due dramatic course
will be brought to consciousness—seared and hardened this all too sensitive
heart of mine. There will come—there cannot fail to come—a moment in the
third act when everything will be made clear in a terrible scene of revelation
and reconciliation. Not, to be sure, that we can ever live happily together. Too
much has occurred for that. But in the wild and wonderful scene of confrontation we shall at last *understand*, and, purged of confusion and falsifica-
tions, we shall be able to face life maturely, as whole people, clear-eyed and
strong. I look forward to that.

But the time for the playing of that scene is still far off, and I am at the moment firmly established in the negative part of my ambivalent passion. I seldom go to the theater. Most actors make me nervous, and I find that the
conjunction of actors and plays, one of the theater's necessities, is likely to
cause me embarrassment. Plays make me nervous too—nine times out of ten,

when I read the text of a play, I am bewildered by the process of thought through which the playwright came to conclude that he had anything to say that anyone would want to listen to. And my bewilderment turns into anxiety when I realize, as I must, that plenty of people do want to listen. The playwright, with an air of fearless dedication to truth, gives us the intellectual, emotional, psychological, and political clichés of twenty years ago, and a quite significant part of the world responds as if he were as *farouche* and original and cogent as a new William Blake and a new Friedrich Nietzsche rolled into one. I know what my mistake is, it has been pointed out to me many times—I expect the wrong things, I expect the theater to have intelligence, when everyone knows that it contracts only to have truth of passion. Quite so, quite so—that is why I go to the opera.

Feeling as I do about the theater, it will scarcely be thought that I am well-disposed to Kenneth Tynan's *Curtains* because of its subject, which is, God help the man, the theater. Mr. Tynan has gathered together his writing about the theater for the last ten years, the reviews he has contributed to *The Spectator,* the *Evening Standard,* the *Daily Sketch,* and *The Observer* in England, and to *The New Yorker* in this country, together with various essays and notes, and the sheer amount of it suggests how intensely, how compulsively, how obsessively, he is committed to the theater. And yet with all my murky prejudice against Mr. Tynan's subject, I found great pleasure in Mr. Tynan's book and substantial reason for admiring it.

I like it, first, as writing. As I set down the word, it comes to me how little it is used nowadays, how seldom we express our pleasure in a work because it is well written, because, that is, quite apart from our agreement or disagreement with its ideas, we enjoy the force or the speed or the flexibility of the writer's prose. It is a category of criticism, or of literary conversation, that seems old-fashioned. There was a time, not out of memory, when a part of the secondary school curriculum was the study of the masters of English and American prose. But the teaching of what is now called "formal" writing fell into disuse, and Burke, Macaulay, Hazlitt, and Ruskin, and Emerson and Thoreau, have been banished from the course of study, and with them, we might almost say, the whole conception of prose style and a taste for it and in it. The "prose masters" were likely to be expository writers of one kind or another, and this is, to be sure, a narrow conception of the province of prose, but it did make the point that artistry has a part not only in "creative" art, not only in the arts of expression but also in the arts of communication. Now, however, the ever-growing authority of creative art is such that the college student who is all alert to every device of Joyce will be a little puzzled why you should ask him to consider the prose style of Swift—once taken for granted as being the finest in the language and one of the glories of literature—and quite at a loss if you should refer to the virtues of the prose of Bernard Shaw.

Shaw is on point in speaking of Mr. Tynan as a writer, for some of Shaw's best prose is to be found in his reviews of musical and dramatic events. At the moment, Shaw the dramatist is rather behind the clouds, but Shaw the critic is probably better known and more admired than ever before. What readers seem to be conscious of in their pleasure in Shaw's reviewing is his intelligence, fairness, and cogency, but I have no doubt that, without saying so or quite knowing why, they are responding to the marvel of his style, that wonderful effortless run of language, natural without condescension, personal and vivacious without coquetry, rapid, flexible, true in pitch. Mr. Tynan does not have the lightness and delicacy which go along with Shaw's unremitting energy and gusto, but he does have the energy and gusto, a delight in communicating experience, a ceaseless impulse to say when things are good and when they are bad. He is witty, although sometimes with more effort than should appear, and, like Shaw, he *likes* to write, his prose never shows any sense of doing its author a favor in getting written; it is glad to get on paper.

Mr. Tynan has another of the qualities that make Shaw so attractive a critic, a notable good nature in exercising the rights of criticism. Inevitably criticism is an aggressive trade, it cannot be otherwise. But it may or may not be hostile, according to the nature of the critic. There is—let us as readers admit it—a pleasure to be found in the critic's display of hostility or malice, which usually takes the form of his implying not only that the offending author or performer has not succeeded in doing what he should have done but that he has failed because of some deep deficiency in his character or personality, some lack of honesty and integrity and that his failure is a threat to decency. Failure in the arts is more humiliating, or can be made to seem more humiliating, than failure in any other line of endeavor. But Shaw never tried to make it humiliating. He was concerned only with the job to be done, not with the person who did the job. He could condemn what had been done yet treat the person with the gentlest courtesy, on the assumption that what he was commenting on was but a single occasion and that there would be other and better ones. He lectured, he scolded, he teased, but he never undertook to wound, there was no malice in him. Mr. Tynan has, as I say, a similar freedom from malice, which, going along with a high standard of judgment, serves to create the pleasant sense that there is a civilized community of the arts in which, on the whole, everyone does the best he can and in which failures are mistakes and not corruptions.

What I have said about Mr. Tynan's prose manner will perhaps suggest what his mode of criticism is. He is neither highbrow, nor lowbrow, nor middlebrow. In part because he is a journalist—in the good sense of that unhappy word—and in part because he is an English critic, he operates with a minimum of theory. Like Hazlitt as a theater reviewer, or like G. H. Lewes, or Shaw, or James Agate, or—I suppose I should add, but I am heretic in my inability to find him interesting—Max Beerbohm, his basis of judgment is pragmatic, his appeal is to taste and to common sense. Here, for example, is the way he deals with the most vexing of theatrical vices, stylistic affectation:

> What is style in the theater? A happy consonance of manner with matter, of means with end, of tools with job. Style is the hammer that drives in the nail without bruising the wood, the arrow that transfixes the target without seeming to have been aimed. It makes difficult things—and on the stage everything is difficult—look simple. When a strenuous feat has been performed without strain, it has been performed with style. The essence of it all is tact. *"La perfection du style,"* said Taine, *"c'est la disparition du style."* I would not labor the point in this unstylish way if it were not for the fact that a new definition of style has lately been plaguing the theater. According to this, style is a special kind of galvanic treatment to be meted out to all artificial comedies written before World War I. Having picked your play, you first overdress it and then overstress it, so that unimportant lines are delivered as if they were italicized, and important ones as if they were printed in capitals and followed by three exclamation marks; finally, you keep the characters whirling about the stage like the ingredients in a Waring Blender. When the show closes after five performances, you are apt to become a sage, shaking your head wisely and pitying the inability of the modern audiences to recognize style when they see it. The truth, of course, is that what you have offered them is not style at all but its antithesis. Your production said, in effect, "See how hard it is to be entertaining!" Style, on the other hand, would have shown how easy it is, and kept its mouth shut.

Mr. Tynan makes it a characteristic of a great critic of the drama that, like Shaw and Agate, he shall instruct the audience and bend its taste to his, leading or coercing it to overcome the failures of its sensibility, seeing to it that Ibsen or Chekhov is first accepted and then admired, and for the right reasons. Mr. Tynan, it seems to me, is at the disadvantage of having no battle to wage with the audience. This is by no means his fault—he writes for an audience that is, from the point of view of the critic, all too eager to accept the new, or the apparently new. The Philistinism of our day is likely to manifest itself in ready acceptance rather than in stubborn resistance. If I had more awareness of or more feeling for Berthold Brecht, I might utter the wish that Mr. Tynan carry his undoubted admiration for him in a more militant way, but apart from Brecht I don't know—but how ignorant I am of such things has been established!—of any urgent dramatic talent that is being resisted by the contemporary audience.

Yet I must not leave the impression that Mr. Tynan is without militancy. He is militant by temperament and he expresses his natural pleasure in battle by taking what is to be called, I suppose, a social-political position. I knew of this from other writings of his that I had come across and it led me, as I began this book, to wonder what effect it would have on his critical judgments. It is a position that is pretty common among English intellectuals of Mr. Tynan's generation, consisting of a sort of Thirtyish radicalism, no doubt as generous in its intention as it is uncertain in its substance, which allows him to express quick indignation at social and political conditions, a truculent demand for something that he calls "socialism," a word he uses in the fond belief that it refers to a specific simple thing, and the supposition that America is, or shortly will be, in the grip of reaction. It is this position which permits Mr. Tynan to give fuller credence than they deserve to the critical views of Arthur Miller, and to share the excessive admiration that some English intellectuals give to the writings of Christopher Caudwell, the English Marxist critic who was killed in the Spanish war at a lamentably early age. But it must in fairness be said that my uneasiness proved quite unjustified—Mr. Tynan's position, which is deplorable not because it is "radical" but because it is not enough developed intellectually, does very little in the way of affecting the accuracy and justice of his critical judgment. It does indeed sometimes lead Mr. Tynan to suggest that the only questions that the mind can ask are social questions and the only answers that can be given to all questions are social answers. I am sure that neither *J.B.* nor *Sweet Bird of Youth* is a play that I should admire and yet I think they deserve the right to deal with "man in relation to forces, either cosmic and external . . . or neurotic and internal . . . that are utterly beyond his control," and that they are not necessarily wrong in not considering the possibility that man "might, in some madcap Utopia, be able to shape the circumstances in which he lives." At this rate, Mr. Tynan will be telling us that Oedipus would not have got into so much trouble if it had not been for that bad experience at his public school at Corinth, or if he had not neglected the sewage system of Thebes and thus been responsible for the plague that was the beginning of his troubles. On the other hand, Mr. Tynan is not misled by that position of his into supposing that Arthur Miller's *The Crucible* is the strong political play that some American criticism took it to be—he thinks it a pretty dim affair. And I like and respect his ability to draw from his opinions a degree of positive energy which is becoming all too rare.

Cyril Connolly once said, once and wanly, that it was closing time in the gardens of the West; but I deny the rest of that suavely cadenced sentence, which asserts that "from now on an artist will be judged only by the resonance of his solitude or the quality of his despair." Not by me he won't. I shall, I hope, respond to the honesty of such testimonies, but I shall be looking for something more, something harder; for the evidence of the artist who is not content with the passive role of a symptom, but concerns himself, from time to time, with such things as healing. Mr. Ionesco correctly says that no ideology has yet abolished fear, pain, or sadness. Nor has any work of art. But both are in the business of trying. What other business is there?

On only one matter of actual judgment will I take issue with Mr. Tynan, his adverse view of the performance, some eighteen months ago, of the three editors of Mid-Century on the television program "Open End." I am quite willing to accept with meekness the bad notice I received from Mr. Tynan in *The Observer* after my performance as chairman of the *Partisan Review* meeting on the Thirties—I thought that none of the cast, not Arthur Schlesinger, not Norman Mailer, not Mary McCarthy, not Norman Podhoretz, not myself, was up to reasonable expectation. But Mr. Tynan is quite wrong about the "Open End" occasion. It is plain to me that he did not understand it—in his comment on it he makes no mention, for example, of Mr. David Susskind, and unless the critic realizes what is involved in responding to one of Mr. Susskind's wide-eyed questions, he is not competent to judge the meaning of any single line or gesture, he cannot know the significance of a blank expression, or an embarrassed smile, or a long silence. And Mr. Tynan deals with the performance with no comprehension of its genre: he takes it to have been a problem drama, when actually it was wild, grim comedy. I should have thought that the author of the enthusiastic essays on James Cagney and W. C. Fields could have done better by Mr. Auden, Mr. Barzun, and me than Mr. Tynan has done.

—APRIL 1961

The Artist in Public Life

Jacques Barzun

On Bernard Shaw's *Platform and Pulpit*

HE REMAINS THE MOST ASTONISHING mind in two centuries. Despite the temporary eclipse of his artistic reputation, he is still the greatest master of English prose since Swift. His plays still furnish the Anglo-American stage whenever the short productive span of his successors gives out, or when the comedy of laughter is wanted in preference to that of sadism and despair. As for the posthumous collections of his letters or other fugitive writings, they confirm the strength of the qualities that make him astonishing—the range of his mental powers, the variety of his knowledge, the candor of his polemics, the depth of his passionate understanding of men in society.

I refer to Bernard Shaw. We tend, of course, to like our literary masters more specialized and less lucid. We think the revelation greater in proportion as it is less revealed, and we nurse the illusion that the mind we read easily is superficial. The true test of ultimate worth is not so simple and mechanical, for there at least are two variables to judge—the complexity of the message and the degree of art in its communication. In Shaw much of what is said is still to be absorbed by a generation that has enjoyed but not understood his radicalism, and that has taken to itself the credit which is due to his miraculous powers of expression.

The new volume of his speeches, entitled *Platform and Pulpit* and admirably edited by Mr. Dan Laurance, makes the most orthodox Shavian wonder all over again how through this one man the diversity of leading ideas since the French Revolution managed to concentrate themselves into a coherent European tradition. It was at a public meeting that Shaw was accused by a heckler of talking like two different people. "Why only two?" was Shaw's reply. The sally shows his usual self-knowledge, coupled with the sense of a mission that so far only he has accomplished. This most partisan of men, this indefatigable debater and corrector of our minds and mores is, take him for all in all, the only reconciler and expositor who could conceivably deserve the title of "Western man." No one since Rousseau, at any rate, has approached so close to a total grasp of the intellectual inheritance, the present reality, and the nascent collective purpose. Turn, in the present book, to the speech on socialized medicine and read the date: 1909. Or scan the brilliant sketch on Ruskin's politics, which sounds like parts of *Growing Up Absurd*. Or clear your own mind about art and the state by reading "The Needs of Music in Britain (1920)." If you prefer to delve into the self, consult "Acting, By One Who Does Not Believe in It"—and who yet was giving in 1889 the religious interpretation of the histrionic art which it has taken three quarters of a century to make familiar.

It is the baffling mixture in Shaw of originality with subsequent obviousness that makes the definition of his role difficult. When he was delivering these speeches, the originality was discounted as lack of seriousness and the solid grounding in tradition was thought superfluous. Now that the "frivolous" part has done its work, it is the knowledge of Europe's thought and destiny that seems extraordinary and the new vision that seems too familiar. For we have voluntarily drifted away from the moorings and float among the wreckage, looking for decorative grotesques in the jetsam. Shaw points out how this predicament of the artist in the city of men comes about:

When at last I made a plunge into London, I soon found out that the artistic people were the shirkers of the community. They ran away from their political duties to portfolios of etchings; from their social duties to essays on the delicacies of their culture; and from their religious duties to the theatre. They were doing exactly what I had done myself, in short—keeping up a Fool's Paradise in order to save themselves the trouble of making the real world any better. Naturally, they hated reality; and this involved some awkward consequences for them. For since the climaxes of Art are brought about by the successful effort of some powerful individuality or idea to realize itself in an act of some kind, whether picture, book, or stage impersonation, these artistic skulkers had to be continually dodging great works of art, or else devising ways of discussing and enjoying their accidental methods, conditions, and qualities so as to ward off their essential purpose and meaning. And they, or rather we, did this so effectually that I might have remained in my Fool's Paradise of Art with the other fools to this day, had I not, to preserve myself from the dry rot of idleness, attempted to realize myself in works of Art.

This was uttered in February 1889—seventy-three years ago—when the Nineties were still an era in the future, like the two periods of postwar "artism" in which one might echo the self-reproach beginning, "And they, or rather we—" without much confidence that we could finish it as Shaw did, in the promise of self-realization through works.

But Shaw's plays were not his sole means of escaping idleness and fulfilling his duty. Though an extremely shy and ignorant youth, he had forced himself to speak in public on all occasions, on all subjects, in little societies and large halls, on street corners and in political committees. It was for this mode of self-realization that he learned to project his voice and spent long hours at the British Museum mastering the substance and the history of every subject related to his political and social duties. It is thanks to that oratorical effort and scholarly research that we owe the present collection of hitherto unpublished talks.

They have, in addition to their intrinsic and historical interest, a special value for the student of style, for several of them are transcripts of unrevised and unwritten remarks. They thus give the movement of Shaw's mind before it was subjected to the discipline of his exhaustive literary expression. The most striking thing about these improvisations, as those will remember who heard Shaw at the Metropolitan Opera in 1934, is not so much the range of diction (compare the transcript of any literary conference today) but the art of modification through successive advances and rephrasings of the thought. For a good sample, see in this book "The Need for Expert Opinion in Sexual Reform."

Toward the end of the volume, and corresponding chronologically to the end of Shaw's life, come certain statements that have led some critics to doubt the wisdom of Shaw's prescription for the artist in public life. As in his late essays he seems to be advocating dictatorship and showing indiscriminate partiality for Soviet Russia. Some have attributed these remarks to senility, others to despair, and still others to the wish to shock. I think none of these explanations true. Shaw's political position is more complicated than single points and detached sentences suggest. He never "abjured democracy"; he only preached the indispensability of government, which in his latter days the western democracies were in one way or another giving up. This is not the place to go into this intricate question, but the present condition of France under De Gaulle, like the huge development of "agencies" under Franklin Roosevelt, will remind the thoughtful of those difficulties of parliamentary government which Shaw, once again, was among the first to bring home to his generation. As for socialism applied by bureaucracy, his lifelong adherence to it was equally prophetic and apt, as we may see in the nationalizations of wartime and since. It is a Fabian and Shavian England that we behold today, even though it has not gone so far toward equality as he proposed.

No, it is not his political past that Shaw renounced in old age, nor his political sense that failed him. What he had lost by the time he was ninety was his zest for the demonstration, through his unique versatility, that the man of the future should be like himself a determined generalist, a completed mind—political, social, religious, and artistic. The pathos of a diminished purpose is heard in the concluding words of the famous "Goodbye, Goodbye" speech of July 26, 1946. That note is found nowhere else in Shaw, and it is one which only proves that even supermen feel the weariness of the repeating years:

> If your son or your daughter—if they inform you, the son that he wants to be a great artist or a great musician—I was going to say a great politician but there may be something in that—he may try that if he likes—but if he wants to be a great artist and so on, do your utmost to prevent him; don't let him . . . and if your daughter tells you that she wants to be a very great actress and thinks that she is the only person in the world who can play my Saint Joan, try to prevent her. Tell her . . . instead of being great people to have the great fun of celebrating great people, admiring them, reading their books and looking at their pictures and listening to their music and all that. . . .
>
> If you knew all I have had to put up with in my life you would say 'Heaven defend me from living *that* man's life.' However, I don't complain. . . .

Shaw had the best reasons for not complaining: he had been used exactly as he wished—used in the literal sense he had himself defined: used up and thrown on the scrap heap. That ending was from the start his religion, and he lived for it with the perseverance of an artist and the gaiety of a saint.

—MARCH 1962

Poetry

T. S. Eliot So Far

W. H. Auden

On *The Collected Poems* of T. S. Eliot

IT IS HIGH TIME that the book-buying public started protesting against a practice of publishers which borders on the dishonest, namely, their habit of labelling a collection of past work by a still living author as *the* collected etc., or "complete." In the case of the volume before us, for instance, the title will be a lie by the fall of this year. Apart from the misrepresentation, such titles encourage the tendency of most readers to forget that no judgment about a contemporary work can be more than tentative. The more important a writer, the more his separate productions are, like the movements of a symphony, subordinate parts of his whole "oeuvre" and cannot be seen in proper perspective until that is complete. *The Waste Land,* for example, read very differently in 1925 when its only successor was *The Hollow Men* than it reads today in the light of *Four Quartets.*

> . . . every sentence is an end and a beginning
> Every poem an epitaph.

The trouble is that, at the time, no one, not even the poet himself, can tell exactly what birth and what death it signifies. The poet, at least, knows this; his critics are apt to be less diffident.

To become a poet of the first rank, great talent is not enough; one must also get born at the right time and in the right place. To become a great revolutionary innovator, for example, a man must come to manhood just as historical circumstances have created a real break in sensibility; those who are born earlier have no stimulus to break with their immediate past, those who are born later find the innovations already made.

To have had a chance of becoming a real explorer in the arts, it would seem that one had to be born between 1870 and 1890; the eighties were particularly favorable, producing, among others, Picasso, Stravinsky, Joyce and Eliot. Those of us who were born later have to put up with the less heroic but, I hope, useful role of colonisers.

Further, so far as English poetry was concerned, it was important *not* to be born in England itself and, of all other places, the United States seems to have been the best. Leaving Eliot's influence aside, we should not have had the poetry of Edward Thomas without Robert Frost, the later poems of Robert Graves without Laura Riding and, probably, not even the later poems of Yeats without Ezra Pound.

The poets in England at the turn of the century lay imprisoned in the poetic conventions, both of sensibility and technique, created by the Romantic Movement, confined to the territory opened up by Wordsworth, Coleridge, Keats and Shelley and colonised by Tennyson, Browning and Arnold. They sensed that they were in bondage, that these conventions no longer corresponded to their real needs, but they were too habituated to be able to see where true liberation lay. Swinburne and the Pre-Raphaelites had tried to escape into an aesthetic universe where the novelty consisted in a total divorce from the contemporary material universe. Three very remarkable poets, Hardy, Hopkins and Doughty, had found other routes, but for themselves alone; their work, fine as it is, is cranky.

American writers, just because they inherit no long indigenous tradition, have always been more curious than their English cousins about the poetry of other traditions than just the English; compare, for example, the interest shown by even so genteel a poet as Longfellow, in the poetry of Europe, with the insularity, tempered only by his classical education, of Tennyson. Further, they could look at even the English tradition with a fresh detachment. The impact of *The Sacred Wood*, for example, was caused not so much by the critical remarks it contained, as by its revelatory quotations. Mr. Eliot has told us that the chief influences in forming his style were the late Elizabethan dramatists like Webster and the French Symbolists like Laforgue. Many British poets had sought inspiration in the Elizabethan drama but without success because they could only hear the verse through the ears of the Romantics, just as they could only hear Baudelaire through the ears of Swinburne.

Prufrock came upon English poetry like a bombshell (it is difficult now to realise how great the shock was, to remember that one outraged critic referred to Mr. Eliot as "a drunken helot"). Here, in one poem, a satisfactory solution had been found to the three main problems that were baffling poets:

the prosodic problem of how to escape from the iambic convention, the organisation problem of how to escape from stanzaic succession, and the problem of diction and imagery, of how to integrate the traditional "poetic" properties with the properties of contemporary industrial civilisation.

What has struck me most on re-reading his poems straight through is how little, stylistically, Mr. Eliot has changed. (In the plays, of course, there is a change, but it is mostly a technical one, an adaptation of the style to the stage.) We already find, fully developed in *Prufrock* and *Portrait of a Lady,* the imagery, the elderly hero in whom desire has failed, the nostalgic vision, the intimate voice—no other poet so gives a reader the sense that he is alone in the room with it—and even such little tricks as epanorthosis on words like *time.* The change in the later poems is not stylistic but a change brought about by a steady maturing and purification of the poet's vision of life, in particular a conquest of the aesthetic dandy in him.

In most of the poems up to and including *The Waste Land,* we find two figures opposed to each other as hero to churl, the sad elderly sensitive cultural observer—Prufrock, the Lady's Friend, Gerontion, Burbank, Tiresias—and the vulgar active greedy man of this world—Sweeney, Bleistein, the carbuncular house agent, whom the former is at once disgusted by and envious of. What is disagreeable about this hero is his mixture of self-pity and conceit. Sweeney steals his girl, he is very upset, but he comforts himself that he is better educated and wears cleaner linen. One is sometimes tempted to say, even to Tiresias: "Really, why don't you stop moping and go out and play with the other boys."

But the "I" of *Ash-Wednesday* and *Four Quartets,* the "chosen" individuals of the plays, Becket, Harry, Celia, no longer masochistically indulge their pain but accept it as a means of grace and a hope of glory, a signpost pointing to a special vocation: the old Tiresias had to do nothing but shore up fragments against his ruins, the new Tiresias has to become an explorer,

> . . . still and still moving
> Into another intensity

a journey which may end in a martyr's death.

Sweeney, if he appears at all, appears transformed, no longer a monster without feeling, but just an average human being, the Johns and Edwards who carry on, making the best of a bad job,

> Maintain themselves by the same routine,
> Learn to avoid excessive expectation,

> Become tolerant of themselves and others,
> Giving and taking, in the usual actions
> What there is to give and take.

If in *Family Reunion* and *The Cocktail Party,* one hears an occasional discordant snobbish note, I believe that this is not a matter of sensibility but of technique. While concentrating upon the problem of how to write dramatic verse which shall not be "Little Theatre" and arty, Mr. Eliot has postponed the problem of dramatic convention, i.e., he has simply taken on unchanged the conventions of English "High" Comedy that have existed from Congreve down to Noel Coward, under which the decor and the main characters are aristocratic. So long as the dramatic subject is one of the various worldly self-affirmations, like love between the sexes, and the moral values implied are social, the convention is perfectly satisfactory; wealth and good-breeding are quite adequate symbols for gifts and virtues. But when the theme becomes one of spiritual election, of the radical gulf between the Christian faith and *all* worldly values, the symbolism breaks down. I am absolutely certain that Mr. Eliot did not intend us to think that Harry is called and not John because John is stupid, or that Celia is called and not Lavinia because she is of a higher social class, but that is exactly what the comedy convention he is using is bound to suggest. Now that he has pretty well solved his verse problem, he has time to consider, as I am sure he is, the problem of "setting." That is one reason, surely, why we look forward so eagerly to *The Confidential Clerk*.

—1953

John Betjeman's Poetic Universe

W. H. Auden

On John Betjeman's *Collected Poems* and *The Golden Treasury of John Betjeman*

THIRTY-THREE YEARS AGO, when undergraduates wore double-breasted waistcoats and flannel trousers that flapped around their ankles like skirts and—believe it or not—could give extravagant luncheon parties in their rooms lasting till five o'clock, I first met John Betjeman, and the mixture of admiration and envy he aroused in me then has never altered. I felt exactly the same last year when he asked me to meet him at the buffet in Marylebone Station, "the only railway terminus in London," as he informed me, "where you can hear birds singing." (It was true. You could.)

For most young men, particularly if they are intellectual and ambitious, the years between eighteen and twenty-one are, subjectively, rather awful. One has become aware of such questions as "Who am I? What do I like and dislike? What manners of conversation and behavior, eccentric or conventional, are proper to me?" But one cannot answer them. So one alternates between gaucheness and affectation.

But occasionally one runs across the exception. John Betjeman stood out among his fellow freshmen in the mid-nineteen-twenties as Max Beerbohm seems to have done among those of the eighteen-eighties; he was the extraordinary phenomenon, the boy who, because he knows exactly who he is, is already mature.

In a little essay on *Topographical Verse*, written in 1945, he states his tastes in poetry; they were already his taste in 1925.

> I find hardly any pleasure in the Elizabethans, less in the seventeenth century (but this may be due to an excessive reverence for those ages from unsympathetic "tutors") and almost the only early poet I can enjoy is Chaucer.

In the eighteenth century Dr. Watts, Swift, Robert Lloyd, Thomson, Dyer, Shenstone, Mickle, Cowper and Burns are easily among my favorites, not for their finer flights, but for their topographical atmosphere. In the nineteenth century Crabbe, Praed, Hood, Clare, Ebenezer Eliot, Capt. Kennish, Neale, Tennyson, Charles Tennyson Turner, Clough, William Barnes, Meredith, William Morris and a score or so more. I find great pleasure in what is termed minor poetry, in long epics which never get into anthologies; topographical descriptions in verse published locally at Plymouth, Barnstaple, Ipswich or Northampton, Mullingar, Cork, Dublin, Galway.

As one could guess from such a list, his poetry has very little in common with what is generally thought of as "Modern Poetry," the ancestors of which are the English metaphysicals and the French *symbolistes*. (I do not know if Mr. Betjeman has ever read any poetry written in a foreign tongue, but I should doubt it.) There is complexity of feeling in his verse, but no ambiguity of image or metaphor; he has an exceptionally sensitive ear and great metrical virtuosity, but he has never felt the slightest need or desire to write free verse or experiment with unconventional prosodies.

At the same time, let me hasten to add that he has never been a prig who makes a dogma out of his personal taste and talent. Now that he has had such a tremendous success in England, his name will undoubtedly be taken in vain as a stick with which to beat his "difficult" contemporaries. Indeed, it already has been; as a life-long admirer, I hope Mr. Betjeman regrets as much as I do, having himself described by the Earl of Birkenhead as

one who has always stood aloof and alien among the modern poets upon many of whom the autumnal blight of obscurity seems finally to have settled.

Since I have struck a slightly sour note, let me make the few criticisms I have to make of Mr. Betjeman's poetry straightaway so that I can get on as soon as possible to the more important and pleasant task of appreciation. From time to time, he tries his hand at satire, but in my opinion, whenever he does, he is unsuccessful. His failure as a satirist is to his credit as a human being. Mr. Betjeman's universe is made up of a number of sacred objects, most of them dating from the Age of Gaslight and Steam Locomotives (as do my own) to which he is passionately devoted. Upon this universe, a number of profane objects, glass-and-steel architecture, progressive education, electronic industries, etc., keep imposing themselves from the present outside world. Naturally, he dislikes these intrusions upon his devotions, but he does not hate them; he only wishes they were not there. Hatred, like love, can only be felt for what is, to the hater, a sacred object and therefore demands the same concentration of attention as a sacred object which is loved. Mr. Betjeman fails as a satirist because, since they are to him merely profane, the objects of his satire do not fascinate him sufficiently. When he is writing about one of his loved sacred objects, suburban Surrey, for example, his eye for detail is unerring:

> Her father's euonymus shines as we walk,
> And swing past the summer-house, buried in talk,
> And cool the verandah that welcomes us in
> To the six-o'clock news and a lime-juice and gin.

> The scent of the conifers, sound of the bath,
> The view from my bedroom of moss-dappled path,
> As I struggle with double-end evening tie,
> For we dance at the Golf Club, my victor and I.

But when he would satirize Progressive Education, the particulars he mentions are commonplace generalities and even inaccurate. For example:

> The children have a motor-bus instead,
> And in a town eleven miles away
> We train them to be "Citizens of To-day."
> And many a cultivated hour they pass
> In a fine school with walls of vita-glass.
> Civics, eurhythmics, economics, Marx,
> How-to-respect-wild-life-in-National-Parks.

I will bet Mr. Betjeman five pounds that he cannot find a high school in England where the pupils study either eurhythmics or *Das Kapital*.

There is one, only one, object in his world which is at once sacred and hated, but it is far too formidable to be satirizable; namely, Death, and it has been the inspiration for many of his best poems. I am glad to learn from his phonograph record that *Remorse* is one of his own favorites, as it is one of mine.

> The lungs draw in the air and rattle it out again;
>   The eyes revolve in their sockets and upwards stare;
> No more worry and waiting and troublesome doubt again—
>   She whom I loved and left is no longer there.

The nurse puts down her knitting and walks across to her;
    With quick professional eye she surveys the dead.
Just one patient the less and little the loss to her,
    Distantly tender she settles the shrunken head.

Protestant claims and Catholic, the wrong and the right of them,
    Unimportant they seem in the face of death—
But my neglect and unkindness—to lose the sight of them
    I would listen even again to that labouring breath.

Hardy is the only other English poet I know who can so employ triple rhymes in a serious poem with triumphant success. Equally moving and metrically interesting is his elegy on an Oxford don:

Dr. Ramsden cannot read *The Times* obituary to-day
    He's dead.
Let monographs on silk worms by other people be
    Thrown away
    Unread
For he who best could understand and criticise them, he
    Lies clay
    In bed.

* * * * *

They remember, as the coffin to its final obsequations
    Leaves the gates,
Buzz of bees in window boxes on their summer ministrations,
    Kitchen din,
    Cups and plates,
And the getting of bump suppers for the long-dead generations
    Coming in,
    From Eights.

A great many of Mr. Betjeman's poems are expressions of topophilia. As an emotion, topophilia differs both from the peasant's possessive passion for his home soil and the regional novelist's self-conscious limitation of attention to a chosen area; though he generally has some places which he adores above all others—in Mr. Betjeman's case, Cornwall, East Anglia, and North London, because he spent his childhood in these places—the practised topophile can find objects to worship in a district he is visiting for the first time.

He is not, however, what is usually meant by a lover of nature; that is to say, wild nature lacking in human history has little charm for him, unless he is a geological topophile, fascinated by the history of the earth itself. Though he may often, like Mr. Betjeman, know a lot about architecture, the genuine topophile can always be distinguished from an educated tourist or an art historian by the uniquely personal character of his predilections; a branch railroad can be as precious to him as a Roman Camp, a neo-Tudor tea-shop as interesting as a Gothic cathedral. As for Proper Names, whether of people or of things, he ignores completely that poetic convention, starting with Vergil, according to which certain names are "beautiful" and certain others are "ugly" or comic and therefore unusable in a serious poem; if he loves a person or thing he loves their actual name and would not change it.

Most readers of poetry are so under the spell of this convention that they may be tempted to think that Mr. Betjeman is poking fun or being ironic when he is simply speaking the truth. A poem like Burns's *The Cottar's Saturday Night* seems serious poetry to them because the social life of the peasantry is unreal and romantically distant—most readers of poetry are middle class—but when they read *North Coast Recollections,* in which Mr. Betjeman describes English middle-class life in about 1922, they have difficulty in taking him seriously.

> Within the bungalow of Mrs. Hanks
> Her daughter Phoebe now French-chalks the floor.
> Norman and Gordon in their dancing pumps
> Slide up and down, but can't make concrete smooth.
> "My Sweet Hortense . . ."
> Sings louder down the garden than the sea.
> "A practice record, Phoebe. Mummykins,
> Gordon and I will do the washing up."
> "We picnic here; we scrounge and help ourselves,"
> Says Mrs. Hanks, and visitors will smile
> To see them all turn to it. Boys and girls
> Weed in the sterile garden, mostly sand
> And dead tomato plants and chicken-runs.
> To-day they cleaned the dulled Benares ware
> (Dulled by the sea-mist), early made the beds,
> And Phoebe twirled the icing round the cake
> And Gordon tinkered with the gramaphone
> While into an immense enamel jug
> Norman poured "Eiffel Tower" for lemonade.

The odd thing about the reaction to lines like these of many people who call themselves lovers of poetry is that if Mr. Betjeman had said the same things in a prose novel, they would have no difficulty in accepting them; it must be such people, whether as relatives or schoolteachers, who are responsible for the low esteem in which poetry is held by the average man.

I myself have some difficulty, I must confess, with a feminine figure who keeps turning up in Mr. Betjeman's poems.

> Pam, I adore you, Pam, you great big mountainous sports girl,
>> Whizzing them over the net, full of the strength of five;
> That Old Malvernian brother, you zephyr and khaki shorts girl,
>> Although he's playing for Woking,
> Can't stand up to your wonderful backhand drive.

Such a type of beauty is so remote from my personal critical taste that I find it hard to believe that there are men who admire it, and I get no help from conventional love poetry or fashion magazines. But I am as sure that the poets and fashion editors have concealed the attractions of this type as I am certain that it holds none for me, and that Mr. Betjeman is not trying to be funny except insofar as, like all people who are capable of serious emotions, he knows that their objects can seem funny to others.

Mr. Betjeman's poetic universe, verbally, architecturally, and ecclesiastically, is so British that when I first began introducing his poems to American friends, I was afraid that they might not be able to make head or tail of them. To my surprise and delight, even those who had never visited England in their lives seemed to "get" them quite easily. It proved to me that the human capacity to translate alien experience, provided it is genuinely and truthfully expressed, into its own terms is much greater than one sometimes fears.

In the Spoken Arts recording, Mr. Betjeman reads fifteen of his poems and prefaces each of them with a few remarks explaining the background and genesis.

Among records of poets reading their own work, this is one of the best I have ever heard, and certainly *the* most enjoyable. Listeners to his comments will understand why Mr. Betjeman has become a T.V. star in England, for he is a born performer. His choice of poems gives a just idea of his poetic range and styles, and his diction and tempi could not be bettered. Recording excellent.

P.S. I SHOULD LIKE to complain that The Earl of Birkenhead, who compiled the collection of Mr. Betjeman's poems in the book, has omitted several poems which I like very much, in particular, *South London Sketch, 1944*. I have therefore asked The Mid-Century Book Society to secure the rights for the publication of the poem, and it appears on the next page.

—JULY 1959

The Word as Heard

LIONEL TRILLING

On the audio recordings of T. S. Eliot's poetry

Four Quartets

WHEN THE WASTE LAND was a new poem, the first thing about it that any reader would be aware of, after sensing its curious authority, was its difficulty. This is in some measure still true, but the difficulty of now is not the same as the difficulty of thirty-five years ago. Now the poem has its existence in a communal comprehension created by decades of explication, exegesis, discussion, and sheer habituation. Every reader will still be puzzled by one or another aspect of the poem, by this passage or that, but we all know what the poem "is about," we all know its beginning, its middle, and its end. Whatever difficulty we do still encounter is not a barrier to our pleasure but actually one of its causes. It is an element of the poem's life, of its living resistance to being dominated by our comprehension. But formerly this was not the case; when the poem was new, the difficulty did stand in the way of comprehension and pleasure. In my own experience of the early difficulty of *The Waste Land,* a remark by I. A. Richards proved to be of decisive usefulness. Richards said that the poem should be first apprehended as music. This seemed a strange thing to say in the face of its textual thickness, the elaborateness of its reference, its extreme verbal ingeniousness. And I think that what Richards meant was not that we should listen to the music *of* the poem but that, hearing the poem, we should let it affect us as music does, immediately, directly, and with-

Originally published as two separate essays: "The Word as Heard" and "Practical Cats More Practical Than Ever Before."

out any effort to formulate its effect. I read the poem aloud as best I could and I had at once the aesthetic equivalent of what William James calls the sentiment of rationality—I felt that I knew what the poem was up to; I had a rudimentary sense of its style, which is the natural beginning of our relation to a person or a poem.

Then, some time later, I heard Mr. Eliot's own reading of the poem on a phonograph record. I call it a reading but it was actually a performance—I was quite taken aback by its overt histrionism. My own way of reading the poem aloud had been controlled by all the attention that had been fixed upon its reconditeness, which Mr. Eliot had emphasized by the notes he supplied, so solemn and so unsatisfactory, and which made the poem the inevitable object of academic interest. In the face of this, it was shocking to hear the manifest pleasure that the poet took in *doing* every scene, with gusto, right up to the hilt, using the broadest Cockney for the colloquy in the pub, representing with a strangulated voice the desperateness of the husband and the wild febrility of the wife in The Game of Chess. This was anything but the scholarly and esoteric poem it was said to be, and if it was a poem that ought to be heard as music, it was also a poem that ought to be heard as drama. As the record and the voice advanced, one had no time to fret over uncomprehended detail.

And yet, despite the help toward pleasure which I had received from my aural experiences of *The Waste Land,* I have maintained a long resistance to the growing tendency to make poetry a thing of the ear, the platform, and the record-player, rather than a thing of the book and the mind.

One reason for my intransigence is that, although I lay claim to no special acuity of hearing, I set great store by what I hear in the human voice. (I think I learned to do this from Bernard Shaw.) If I consider my feeling about the most obvious example of spoken poetry, the performance of Shakespeare, I can say that I am not of the school of Charles Lamb, who thought that a performance of any of the plays was inevitably a traduction of it, an opinion that he held in spite of his passion for the theater. I go gladly and gaily to any production of Shakespeare that is reputed to be spirited. But when I am in the theater I spend half the evening in a wince and a shudder at what I hear—the pinched voice, the flat voice, the over- or under-modulated voice, the vulgar-plausible voice (so *real!*), the voice dripping with explication. I take refuge from present reality in the memory of the few great voices that are exceptions from the general awfulness: Maurice Evans in his first great production of *Richard II*—an indescribably beautiful performance, quite unlike anything else I have ever seen Evans do—or the Hamlets of Barrymore and Gielgud, or the Hotspur of Olivier—I shall never cease regretting that I missed his Oedi-pus—or Judith Anderson in almost any tragic role, or some of the old Abbey Theatre actors, their names now, alas, forgotten. I am not talking about act-ing in general, only about the speaking of dramatic poetry, to which the voice and its use—and its training—are as essential as to opera. The same is true of the speaking of non-dramatic poetry, and not the less so when it is spoken by the poet himself. On most of the poetry-speaking records I have listened to, the *persona* that the poet assumes is either the wrong one or he carries it badly. There are of course exceptions, such as Mr. Eliot and Mr. Frost, but all too many poets read their own work either affectedly, or with embarrass-ment, or with excessive diffidence; the most prevalent fault is gentility, per-haps a by-product of the effort to enunciate clearly—I don't know how Dylan Thomas sounded on the platform; on the only record of his I ever heard he sounded like someone representing the popular idea of an Oxford don.

Another reason for my resistance to poetry as an oral-aural art is my sense that the contemporary interest in it is part of the growing hostility to print. More and more we come to believe that nothing can be learned without what is called an audio-visual aid. Of all audio-visual aids for the teaching of liter-ature, the best is thought to be an actual writer; universities are at great pains to provide occasions on which the student can have the direct, unmediated experience of a practitioner of literature. The student sees the writer, hears the writer, feeds the writer, pokes the writer by asking the questions which the writer has contracted to answer or to wittily evade; he thus comes to believe that the writer is actually actual, is human, is contemporary, and in conse-quence understands that literature is real, a living force, not a mere abstrac-tion as he had supposed from having experienced writers only in print. A modern secondary-school textbook in history is a mass of ingenuities—sketches, cartoons, graphic charts, typographical devices—designed to coun-teract the hieratic incommunicativeness of print. The staff of the *New York Times Book Review* shudders at the thought of a page of text without a pic-ture, and much prefers two: it is perfectly plain that no one will read a review of a book about The Modern Dilemma unless it is conjoined with a paint-ing—it may be of whorls or of transfixed people or of a cluttered desk—which shows what The Modern Dilemma looks like. Anything, anything to mitigate the arrogant silence of print.

The modern feeling for eye-mindedness, ear-mindedness, hand-minded-ness, as against the mind-mindedness that print implies is ground that Mr. Barzun has covered very thoroughly in *The House of Intellect* and there is no need for me to go over it again. I refer to it, and with what I mean to be due pejoration, only to suggest the kind of resistance that Robert Speaight's reading of Mr. Eliot's *Four Quartets* had to overcome to win the enthusiastic admiration I have for it.

The first thing to say about the record is as simple a thing as that it is beautiful. On two occasions when I was listening to it, people walked into the room and, either without knowing or without quite knowing what they heard, stood entranced and said, "How beautiful." Mr. Speaight, who is both an actor and a literary scholar, reads in a voice that is remarkably like Mr. Eliot's own when Mr. Eliot was younger, and Mr. Eliot's voice, unlike that of many poets, is exactly right for his own poetry. Mr. Speaight renders with subtle accuracy the interplay between the two dominant tones of the poems, that of an apparently objective, apparently affectless precision of statement and that of a controlled but intense despair and bitterness which move toward the energy of an effort to understand what is not to be understood—*Burnt Norton* begins as if it were a university lecture on the nature of time delivered by the most impersonal and fatigued of lecturers who, as he proceeds, discovers that he is talking about his own life under the aspect of eternity.

In their own way, the *Quartets* are quite as difficult as *The Waste Land*. I have to be aware of this difficulty whenever I undertake to deal with them in a college course—it has never seemed to me possible to assign more than two of the poems, both because of the amount of time the students will need to read them properly and because of the number of class hours that I will need to say anything about them that will even approach adequacy. There is always the question of which two of the four should be chosen as at once the most representative and the most easily comprehensible. I ought to add that my sense of the difficulty of the poems has reference not only to my students but to myself. But when I heard Mr. Speaight's reading for the first time, I found myself wondering what all the pedagogic fuss had ever been about. The poems seemed so readily available to understanding that I saw no reason for not assigning all of them, and I saw no necessity for me to say anything at all about them—except in an impressionistic way, it seemed no more possible for me to comment on them than on Beethoven's late quartets, to which they are often, and appropriately, compared.

When the record had come to its end and a little time had passed, I was able to emerge from my beglamoured state and consider that my profession and the printed page had not lost their reason for being. I had of course been the readier to respond to the word well spoken because of my having read it in cold type, because of my struggles with its difficulties, because of what I have read about it, and thought about it. (And of course Mr. Speaight was able to speak it so well because he had gone through much the same process.)

Yet with all my wish to defend the Word As Print, I have to admit that there was added to my experience of the poems a new element of closeness of communion with them which I am very glad to have.

—FALL 1960

Old Possum's Book of Practical Cats

THEY ARE CALLED Practical Cats for the obvious reason that they are manifestly not Theoretical Cats. A certain amount of *theoria* is mixed in with the *praxis,* which is as it should be—as the Comrades used to say in the old days, "Comrades, there can be no *praxis* without *theoria*." Thus, for example, we are instructed in "The Naming of Cats": this is *theoria* or nothing, and the same can be said of "The Addressing of Cats," which establishes the principle, "A CAT IS NOT A DOG," or, put another way, "A Dog's a Dog—A CAT'S A CAT." But most of the book is devoted to *praxis,* to the actual Mungojerrie and Rumpelteazer, to Jennyanydots, who is a Gumbie Cat, to the Rum Tum Tugger, to the great Macavity, The Napoleon of Crime, all as they exist in their intense particularity. Yet to think of them as Existential Cats would be going too far. Cats are, if anything, creatures of essence.

How great the Practical Cats are as poetry, even how good they are, we must wait for the Judgment of History to decide, and the docket of that court is a crowded one—it may be several years before a decision is handed down. I have met adult readers who say they are not good, by which, of course, they mean nothing more objective than that they don't like them, or don't like cats. On the other side of the question, I can report that no child reader has, to my knowledge, ever said that they are *not* to be classed among the great treasures of literature, or, for that matter, has ever expressed a doubt of their right to be compared with *The Waste Land.* It is my experience that children like them very much, and I know of no more compelling evidence of their value than this.

As for myself, I have no way of making a truly critical judgment. Practical Cats came into my life about a year after the advent of Actual Cats. These included the transient, because Impractical, Kittens, as well as the two permanent residents. The latter are the objects of worship of a domestic cult, from which I hold aloof, being by temperament a Dog Person, but I observe it with sympathy and I have learned from it a great deal about the civilization of Ancient Egypt. The youngest member of the family was illiterate in the early days of the cats, and one of the pressing problems of life was how to find books that would please him and that could be read aloud without fatiguing my soul. Practical Cats proved a step toward the solution of the problem, thus removing any lingering doubt of their practicality. My young analphabetic liked them, perhaps first because he liked anything that was cattish—the adjective *feline* does not accurately apply to cats most of the time—and then apparently for their literary value; and I found them pleasant to read aloud and became rather proud of my renditions. They could not be read, I found, in the rather menacing quiet tone in which I generally read poetry aloud—they invite a certain hammish richness of utterance. For example, the couplet

Bark   bark   bark   bark
Bark   bark   BARK   BARK

requires to be read with a variety of inflections and emphases or it amounts to nothing; and I fancied that there were few who could bring it to as complex a crescendo as I did.

But now the author himself has read the Practical Cats for records. I have no wish to institute a comparison between Mr. Eliot's manner of reading, and its degree of success, and my own. In some respects our interpretations differ. It seems to me that Mr. Eliot inclines to a bold dramatic manner, while I incline to lyricism—or did so incline, for the passing years have relieved me of the necessity of performance and have freed me to pursue other interests closer to my heart. This being the case, it would be fruitless for anyone to concern himself with the question, tempting though it is, of which rendition is the better. I am glad to yield to Mr. Eliot, not because he is the poet himself and knows whereof he speaks—it is well understood that the poet knows nothing of his own meaning—but because, of the two performances, his is the only one that anyone will now ever hear. And I am happy to say that it is very good.

—NOVEMBER 1959

Two Ways of Poetry

W. H. AUDEN

On Philip Larkin's *The Less Deceived* and Geoffrey Hill's *For the Unfallen*

To WRITE ABOUT A POET for others who have not yet read him is not criticism but reviewing, and reviewing is not really a respectable occupation. When a critic examines the work of a well-known poet, he may, if he is lucky, succeed in revealing something about it which readers had failed to see for themselves: if, on the other hand, what he says is commonplace or false or half-true, readers have only themselves to blame if they allow themselves to be led astray, since they know the text he is talking about. But a reviewer is responsible for any harm he does, and he can do quite a lot. A "good" review urges the public to buy a book, a "bad" one tells them that it is not worth reading. It does not matter very much if a reviewer praises a bad book—time will correct him—but if he condemns a good one the effect may be serious, for the public can discover his mistake only by reading it and that is precisely what his review has prevented them from doing.

But a reviewer can do worse harm than that. Let us suppose that he has to review four poets in the same article and that they are all of them quite good, which means that the work of each is unique. If he treats them as such, then his article has no focus. But an article must have a focus. So he invents one. He looks for some characteristic which they have in common—it may be something as trivial as their age—and gives this a label—the X School, the Y Generation, the Z Young Men, etc.—and writes his article around it. The Publishers are delighted—it is easier to sell packages—and so is the Public delighted—labels save it from thinking and provide it with party conversation. Everybody, in fact, is pleased except the unfortunate poets. Having suffered from this sort of thing myself, I know that nothing is more insulting to a writer than to have his work lumped together with that of others (particularly if they happen to be his personal friends).

When I read a review of a poet whose work I don't know, I never read what the reviewer says; I only look at his quotations. This is very unsatisfactory. In the first place, there are seldom enough of them and, in the second, it is almost impossible for the reviewer to be just in his selection. If he likes the work, he chooses the best passages; if he dislikes it, the worst. If this were a sensible world, I should now give extensive quotations from Mr. Philip Larkin and Mr. Geoffrey Hill without any comment whatsoever, but this is not a sensible world.

When I read a poet for the first time, I proceed from the part to the whole. Thus, I begin by skimming through the pages, waiting for my eye to be caught by single lines which, so to speak, say themselves. One could not imagine their length, their arrangement of words, their sound and rhythm being other than they are. Single lines, of course, do not by themselves make a poem, but they are the basic evidence of the poetic gift and, if I cannot find any, I read no further.

Skimming through Mr. Larkin, I am stopped by

> But superstition, like belief, must die,
> And what remains when disbelief is gone?

Glancing through Mr. Hill, I come across

> A busy vigilance of goose and hound
> Keeps up all guards. Since you are outside, go,
> Closing the doors of the house and the head also.

So I do read further.

This time, if the poet writes lyrics, I look for single stanzas which seem to me "right," that is to say, the number of lines, their contrasting lengths, their rhyme arrangement and so forth exactly embody the structure of meanings they have to convey. Anybody who has ever written verses has had the experience of beginning a poem and then getting hopelessly stuck until he suddenly realized that his choice of stanza has been wrong—it should have five lines, not four, or the last line should have two feet, not three. Again, I find much in Mr. Larkin and Mr. Hill to please me.

> The cross staggered him. At the cliff-top
> Thomas, beneath its burden, stood
> While the dulled wood
> Spat on the stones each drop
> Of deliberate blood.
>
> (HILL)

> Since we agreed to let the road between us
> Fall to disuse,
> And bricked our gates up, planted trees to screen us,
> And turned all time's eroding agents loose,
> Silence, and space, and strangers—our neglect
> Has not had much effect.
>
> (LARKIN)

Mr. Larkin is, I think, the more interesting craftsman; he shows more formal curiosity and variety. For example, the formal structure of his poem *I Remember, I Remember,* in which the succession of five-line stanzas is regular but the rhyming is not, being used both within the stanza and as a link across the stanza break, gives me great pleasure as a device, irrespective of the poem's particular contents. I have to remind myself, however, that my fascination with devices of this kind may be excessive, and that there have been many good poets who have not felt it. What always matters is sureness of hand; a good poet always convinces one that his results are exactly what he intended. Here again the critic must beware of his own prejudices. The correct question is: "Has this poet succeeded in writing the poem he set out to write?" All too frequently critics have in their heads some imaginary poem of their own and then condemn the poet for having failed to write it.

After looking for lines and stanzas, I pick out a poem here and a poem there and read it through to see if its parts are successfully articulated into a whole. If I feel that the number of stanzas and their order could be different or I cannot see a necessary relation between one stanza and the next, then I suspect that there is something wrong with the poem.

There are many possible principles of poetic organization and some of them are much harder to grasp at a first reading than others. The easiest to perceive, though in poetry they are not, perhaps, the most essential, are logical sequences like If-Then, Because-Therefore, and temporal sequences like I-start, I-continue, I-end. If I say that Mr. Larkin's poetry is more "traditional" and Mr. Hill's more "modern," I am using these detestable adjectives as descriptive, not as value judgements. I mean that Mr. Larkin in his organization of a poem makes use of logical and temporal sequences as, until recently, nearly all poets have done, while Mr. Hill dispenses with them: his organization is based almost entirely on associations of feeling-states, a way of composing which has only been adopted by poets as a *conscious* principle during the past seventy years or so.

The difference between them in this respect is, in part, a reflection of the difference between their poetic worlds. After satisfying myself that a poet can write a good poem, I read through his whole volume, comparing one poem with another, to discover if he possesses what I value most of all, a world and tone of voice of his own.

In poetry as in religion there is a *via positiva* and a *via negativa*. Poets who follow the first find their inspiration in the temporal and spatial flux of events; poets who follow the second seek for a vision of permanent and universal truth behind the phenomena. As examples of the two types at their most extreme, I think of Praed and Mallarmé. Neither way can entirely ignore the other without becoming trivial or meaningless. The most ascetic of poets must at least use words which have concrete physical properties and a social history; and the most worldly must at least find some beings and events more sacred, more charged with undefinable significance, than others.

One can recognize most easily which way a poet is following on the occasions when he uses the first personal pronoun.

> I detest my room,
> Its specially-chosen junk,
> The good books, the good bed,
> And my life, in perfect order.

Reading this I can visualize the speaker quite easily; he lives in England in the twentieth century, he has had a good education and the name in his passport might very well be Philip Larkin.

> And I renounced on the fourth day,
> This fierce and unregenerate clay,
> Building as a huge myth for man
> The watery Leviathan. . . .

To this "I," the fact that there is a living individual called Geoffrey Hill to whom one might be introduced at a party is totally irrelevant.

Another indication can be found in the way each kind of poet titles his poems. I read these lines without looking at their title.

> Caught in the centre of a soundless field
> While hot inexplicable hours go by
> *What trap is this? Where were its teeth concealed?*
> You seem to ask.
>
>   I make a sharp reply,
> Then clean my stick. I'm glad I can't explain
> Just in what jaws you were to suppurate:
>   You may have thought things would come right again
> If you could only keep quite still and wait.
>   (LARKIN)

If I now ask myself what would be a suitable title, I think the chances are quite good that I would hit on Mr. Larkin's, *Myxomatosis*. But when I have read these lines

> They sat. They stood about.
> They were estranged. The air,
> As water curdles from clear,
> Fleshed the silence. They sat.
>
> They were appalled. The bells
> In hollowed Europe spilt
> To the gods of coin and salt.
> The sea creaked with worked vessels
>   (HILL)

I should have to guess for a very long time indeed before I came up with *The Apostles: Versailles 1919*.

One must not judge either kind of poetic world by standards which only apply to the other. To say that a vision is true is not the same thing as saying an observation is true. One cannot, of course, deny one's personal preferences—I myself like my poetry worldly rather than ascetic—but temperament must not masquerade as principle. There is only one question which must be put to all poems without exception: "Is this authentic?" It is required of observer and visionary alike that he shall have seen with his own eyes and not have made it up or looked through someone else's spectacles.

Mr. Larkin and Mr. Hill look for and see two very different worlds, but both, I believe, have looked and seen for themselves.

—OCTOBER 1960

A Poet Newly Given

Lionel Trilling

On *The Complete Poems of Cavafy,* translated by Rae Dalven

RAE DALVEN's translation of the complete poems of C. P. Cavafy gives to the English-speaking world a new poet. Not, to be sure, that Cavafy's work has been unknown until now. In his admirable introduction to Miss Dalven's volume, Mr. Auden speaks of first becoming acquainted with it in English and French translations some thirty years ago. The intervening time has brought more and more translations, fugitively published, and a constant increment of reputation. And recently both the poems and the poet himself have been given a sort of legendary fame by Lawrence Durrell's *Alexandria Quartet.* But it makes a difference to have a poet's whole canon of work, to become aware of the things that occupy or obsess him, to learn to recognize his characteristic intonation, his personal idiom.

To recognize his characteristic intonation, his personal idiom? Is this possible with a poet in translation? Almost always it is not, and that we can take it to be possible in the case of Cavafy is one of the remarkable things about him. I have said that Miss Dalven's translation gives to the English-speaking world a new poet, but that is not quite enough to say—the truth is that Miss Dalven's translation gives to the English-speaking world virtually a new poet of the English language. This is the more remarkable because the work of Cavafy stands in a peculiarly subtle and intense relation to its own native language. The poet, a man of the widest erudition, a devoted student of the Greek classics, chose to write in demotic Greek, the daily and developing language of the people, rather than in purist Greek, the language of the academy and of official occasions, which bases itself upon the grammar and the vocabulary of the ancient language; yet he did not wholly reject the purist language, and we are told that much of the charm of his work lies in the complex interplay between the two linguistic traditions, whose opposition has been the occasion of the fiercest cultural and political passions in modern Greece. This special charm we shall never experience, and even so Cavafy is a poet uniquely available to translation. To say this is not to slight Miss Dalven's powers as a translator. If I compare, for example, her version of one of Cavafy's best-known poems, "The Gods Forsake Antony," with the version in which I first read the poem, that of George Valassopoulo, I can say that Miss Dalven's translation is, as a poem in English, the better of the two, the more direct, the more elegantly economical. But the version of Mr. Valassopoulo still moves me, still seems to me to be a fine poem in English.

To this availability of Cavafy's to the English reader, Mr. Auden gives the strongest possible testimony in his introduction. "Ever since I was first introduced to Cavafy by the late Professor R. M. Dawkins over thirty years ago," he says, "C. P. Cavafy has remained an influence on my own writing; that is to say, I can think of poems which, if Cavafy were unknown to me, I should have written quite differently or perhaps not written at all. Yet I do not know a word of modern Greek, so that my only access to Cavafy's poetry has been through English and French translations." This, as Mr. Auden goes on to say, is perplexing and disturbing. "Like everybody else, I think, who writes poetry, I have always believed the essential difference between prose and poetry to be that prose can be translated into another tongue but poetry cannot. But if it is possible to be poetically influenced by work which one can read only in translation, this belief must be qualified."

For whatever the experience of a non-poet is worth, I can offer mine in substantiation of Mr. Auden's. My own first acquaintance with Cavafy came later than his, some eighteen years ago, when I was writing a book about E. M. Forster. We have lately been reminded of Mr. Forster's sojourn in Alexandria during the First World War by the fortunate reissue, in Anchor Editions, of his pleasant and useful guidebook of the city. Another outcome of Mr. Forster's Alexandrian years is the little volume of essays, *Pharos and Pharillon,* published here in 1923 by Alfred Knopf and now hard to come by. Between the group of essays that deal with the city in antiquity and those of more recent reference, Mr. Forster placed the Antony poem I have mentioned, and to the poet himself he devoted a brief essay—it is reprinted elsewhere in these pages—in which, in his light, unpressing way, he suggests Cavafy's quality and quotes several poems in Mr. Valassopoulo's translation. Cavafy claimed me at once, and I him. I wondered as Mr. Auden wonders how any poems in translation could speak to me so directly, more directly, indeed, than most native poems do. I may as well confess the extent of my response—they led me to believe what I had never before believed, that I could write poetry, and that if I could, I should! Good sense prevailed over belief—I never did make the attempt. And very likely all that I was responding to were the virtues that Cafavy's poetry has in common with good prose: transparency, modulation, subtlety of cadence, of the cadence of language coming to us as the cadence of thought.

The cadence of thought: this, I suppose, is what Mr. Auden is saying he responds to in Cavafy's work. Having dismissed any hope of understanding what is implied by the conscious mixture of the two kinds of Greek, and having remarked that it cannot be the imagery of Cavafy that we are engaged by ("for simile and metaphor are devices he never uses; whether he is speaking of a scene, an event, or an emotion, every line of his is plain factual description without any ornamentation whatsoever"), Mr. Auden asks: "What, then, is it in Cavafy's poems that survives translation and excites?" He answers: "Something I can only call, most inadequately, a tone of voice, of personal speech. I have read translations of Cavafy made by many different hands, but every one of them was immediately recognizable as a poem by Cavafy; nobody else could possibly have written it. Reading any poem of his, I feel: 'This reveals a person with a unique perspective on the world.' That the speech of self-disclosure should be translatable seems to me very odd, but I am convinced that it is. The conclusion I draw is that the only quality which all human beings without exception possess is uniqueness; any characteristic, on the other hand, which one individual can be recognized as having in common with another, like red hair or the English language, implies the existence of other individual qualities which this classification excludes. To the degree, therefore, that a poem is the product of a certain culture, it is difficult to translate it into the terms of another culture, but to the degree that it is the expression of a unique human being, it is as easy, or as difficult, for a person from an alien culture to appreciate as for one of the cultural group to which the poet happened to belong."

This is true, and excellently said. And yet we must see that Cavafy's existence as a unique human being is conditioned by his particular relation to his culture, of which we may understand at least something from the facts of his life as set forth in Miss Dalven's extended biographical note.

Constantine Cavafy was born in 1863 in Alexandria. He was the youngest of the nine children of Peter John Cavafy and Chariclea Photiady. The parents were originally of Constantinople, of well-to-do families. They had come to Alexandria in 1850, where the father established a branch of the Constantinople firm of Cavafy & Sons specializing and prospering in the growth and export of Egyptian cotton. Constantine grew up in what Miss Dalven calls the aristocracy of Alexandria, although it should perhaps rather be thought of as an elegant oligarchy or patriarchy. Cavafy's father died in 1870, leaving the family in straitened financial condition. There were branches of the family business in several English cities, and in 1872 the widowed mother took her sons to England, where they sojourned seven years. Constantine's fluency in English remained with him through life. He commanded also French, Italian, Latin, and Arabic, but his linguistic passion was for Greek, both the ancient language, which he studied diligently at all times, and the demotic, becoming, as we have seen, a partisan of its appropriateness for literary use. In 1882, following upon disorders in Alexandria, he went with his mother and brothers to Constantinople, where he became deeply devoted to his maternal grandfather, and, through him, to the old Greek community of the city, the so-called Phanariots. It was at this time that he began to apply himself to the study of Byzantine and Hellenic history which was to be of such consequence to his poetry and also began to acquaint himself with the demotic literary tradition.

In 1885 he and his mother returned to Alexandria. The disorders of 1882 had been the beginning of political upheavals which destroyed the commercial life of the Greek community; the old amenity of existence was no longer to be hoped for. Constantine lived for a time upon the willing bounty of a brother, Peter, who was not alone among the several brothers in being sympathetic with the young poet's career. But Peter died in 1891 and Constantine was thrown upon his own resources. He became a provisional clerk in the Ministry of Irrigation—a permanent appointment was not available to him because he had some years before become a Greek citizen—and remained in the post until his retirement in 1922. He supplemented his small salary by acting as a broker on the Alexandrian stock exchange. His mother died in 1899, and for the next few years his existence was somberly punctuated by the deaths of his brothers. From 1908 until his own death twenty-five years later, he lived alone.

Cavafy composed freely, writing some seventy poems a year, but of this number he would destroy all but four or five. He was extravagantly diffident of public opinion and published nothing until it had won the approval of a group of friends on whose judgment he relied. In his lifetime he published only two volumes, one in 1904, when he was forty-one, containing fourteen poems, and one in 1910, adding twelve more. But from 1908 onward his poems appeared frequently in Greek magazines. They gained fame for him in the Greek world, and, as I have noted, were widely translated.

Miss Dalven does not speak of a circumstance of Cavafy's life which certain of the poems make plain, his homosexuality. All his loves were what he calls again and again, as if making sure that there shall be no mistake about their nature, "deviate." And all of them were unabashedly sensual. The possibility of remorse seems always immanent in his consciousness, but it is always put to flight: the ancient dispensation of love never fails to assert its rights. Sometimes the threat of remorse is routed by the thought of time's winged chariot and the misery that must inevitably attend renunciation, as in "An Old Man":

> In the inner room of the noisy café
> an old man sits bent over a table;
> a newspaper before him, no companion beside him.
>
> And in the scorn of his miserable old age,
> he meditates how little he enjoyed the years
> when he had strength, the art of the word, and good looks.
>
> He knows he has aged much; he is aware of it, he sees it,
> and yet the time when he was young seems like
> yesterday. How short a time, how short a time.
>
> And he ponders how Wisdom had deceived him;
> and how he always trusted her—what folly!—
> the liar who would say, "Tomorrow. You have ample time."
>
> He recalls impulses he curbed; and how much
> joy he sacrificed. Every lost chance
> now mocks his senseless prudence.
>
> . . . But with so much thinking and remembering
> the old man reels. And he dozes off
> bent over the table of the café.

Sometimes it is the idea of art being nurtured by sensuality that makes the ground of guiltless acceptance, as in "Understanding":

> The years of my young manhood, my sensual life—
> how plainly I see their meaning now.
>
> What needless repentances, how futile . . .
>
> But I did not grasp their meaning then.
>
> Deep in the dissolute life of my young manhood
> the designs of my poetry took shape,
> the scope of my art was being plotted.

This is why even my repentances were never stable.
And my resolutions to restrain myself, to change,
lasted for two weeks at the very most.

But behind all reasons is the certitude of the law of his own being:

The joy and essence of my life is the memory of the hours
when I found and sustained sensual delight as I desired it.
The joy and essence of my life for me, who abhorred
every enjoyment of routine loves.

He was but little, if at all, a Christian. When he lay dying of cancer of the throat, his friends summoned the Patriarch of Alexandria to administer Holy Communion, which Cavafy, in a rage, refused to accept. For a time he resisted stubbornly; in the end, however, he submitted and received communion, but, we are told, "with compunction."

Must one not have, even from this bare outline, the sense that Cavafy's relation to his culture was unique, or, indeed, that the thing he was related to was not really, in the sense in which we ordinarily use the word, a culture at all, that it was both something less and something more? If we consider how many homes in the world his spirit had, Alexandria, Constantinople, Athens, not to mention London; and of how many different Greeces he was a citizen; and how much less important to him than existence in space was existence in time—is it any wonder that he can speak to us in a voice which is so clear because it carries so little of the alloy of any particular national culture with its imperatives and sanctions, its customs and taboos? Cavafy once said of himself in conversation, "Many poets are exclusively poets. . . . I, I am a poet-historian. I, I could never write a novel or a play, but I feel in me a hundred and twenty-five voices that tell me that I could write history. But now there is no more time." Probably he judged the situation inaccurately—I suspect he could not have written history in the simple sense he seems to mean. But he was right enough in calling himself a poet-historian. The history that presides over his imagination is not the one that has charge of the famous Dust-bin, but an older kind of history, akin to tragedy, ruthless enough, as is to be expected, yet in some degree tenderly concerned with the honor and dignity of man in his inevitable failure. It is this history that speaks in "The God Forsakes Antony":

When suddenly at the midnight hour
an invisible troupe is heard passing
with exquisite music, with shouts—
do not mourn in vain your fortune failing you now,

your works that have failed, the plans of your life
that have all turned out to be illusions.
As if long prepared for this, as if courageous,
bid her farewell, the Alexandria that is leaving.
Above all do not be fooled, do not tell yourself
it was only a dream, that your ears deceived you;
do not stoop to such vain hopes.
As if long prepared for this, as if courageous,
as it becomes you who are worthy of such a city;
approach the window with firm step,
and listen with emotion, but not
with the entreaties and complaints of the coward,
as a last enjoyment listen to the sounds,
the exquisite instruments of the mystical troupe,
and bid her farewell, the Alexandria you are losing.

It speaks the bitter mocking wisdom of "Expecting the Barbarians," surely one of the great political poems of all time (and one of the poems, I would guess, that had a particular effect upon Mr. Auden):

What are we waiting for, assembled in the public square?

The barbarians are to arrive today.

Why such inaction in the Senate?
Why do the Senators sit and pass no laws?

Because the barbarians are to arrive today.
What further laws can the Senators pass?
When the barbarians come they will make the laws.

Why did our emperor wake up so early,
and sits at the principal gate of the city,
on the throne, in state, wearing his crown?

Because the barbarians are to arrive today.
And the emperor waits to receive
their chief. Indeed he has prepared
to give him a scroll. Therein he engraved
many titles and names of honor.

• • •

Why have our two consuls and the praetors come out
today in their red, embroidered togas;
why do they wear amethyst-studded bracelets,
and rings with brilliant glittering emeralds;
why are they carrying costly canes today,
superbly carved with silver and gold?

Because the barbarians are to arrive today,
and such things dazzle the barbarians.

Why don't the worthy orators come as usual
to make their speeches, to have their say?

Because the barbarians are to arrive today;
and they get bored with eloquence and orations.

Why this sudden unrest and confusion?
(How solemn their faces have become.)
Why are the streets and squares clearing quickly,
and all return to their homes, so deep in thought?

Because night is here but the barbarians have not come.
Some people arrived from the frontiers,
and they said that there are no longer any barbarians.

And now what shall become of us without any barbarians?

Those people were a kind of solution.

It speaks superbly of the ancient virtue of magnanimity—large-mindedness—
in "Thermopylae":

Honor to those who in their lives
are committed and guard their Thermopylae.
Never stirring from duty;
just and upright in all their deeds,
but with pity and compassion too;
generous whenever they are rich, and when
they are poor, again a little generous,
again helping as much as they are able;
always speaking the truth,
but without rancor for those who lie.

And they merit greater honor
when they foresee (and many do foresee)
that Ephialtes will finally appear,
and in the end the Medes will go through.

And in the accents of the first of poet-historians it speaks of human sorrow in "The Horses of Achilles":

When they saw that Patroclus was slain,
who had been so stalwart, and strong, and young,
the horses of Achilles started to weep;
their immortal nature was indignant
at the sight of this work of death.
They would shake their heads and toss their manes,
    stamp the ground with their feet, and mourn
Patroclus who they realized was lifeless—undone—
worthless flesh now—his spirit lost—
    defenseless—without breath—
returned from life to the great Nothing.

Zeus saw the tears of the immortal horses
and grew sad. "At the wedding of Peleus,"
he said, "I should not have acted so thoughtlessly;
    it would have been better my hapless horses
if we had not given you! What are you doing down there,
among woebegone humanity, the plaything of fate?
    You for whom neither death nor old age lie in wait,
you are harassed by transitory calamities.
Men have implicated you in their troubles."—Yet the two
    noble animals went on shedding their tears
for the never-ending calamity of death.

—MAY 1961

A Poet of Honor

W. H. Auden

On *The Collected Poems of Robert Graves*

I FIRST CAME ACROSS Robert Graves's poems in the volumes of *Georgian Poetry* when I was a schoolboy, and ever since he has been one of the very few poets whose volumes I have always bought the moment they appeared. There were many others, no doubt, who did the same, but, until recently, Mr. Graves was not a Public Name in the way that Mr. Eliot, for example, was. Individuals who had discovered his poetry for themselves would talk about it to each other, but his name was not bandied about at cocktail parties to show that the speaker was *au courant,* nor was he made the subject of critical articles in little magazines or of Ph.D. theses.

But now the situation has changed.

> . . . though the Otherwhereish currency
> Cannot be quoted yet officially,
> I meet less hindrance now with the exchange
> Nor is my garb, even, considered strange;
> And shy enquiries for literature
> Come in by every post, and the side door.

wrote Mr. Graves a few years ago, and already the first two lines are out of date. I do not know whether to be glad or sorry about this. One is always glad when a writer one has long admired gains wide recognition—publicity at least means bigger sales—but public fame has its dangers, not so much for the poet himself, particularly if he has Mr. Graves's years and strength of character, as for his public. With his consent or without it, he becomes responsible for a fashion and, though some fashions may be better than others, in all there is an element of falsehood. No poet has been more concerned than Mr. Graves with poetic integrity, with being true, at all costs, to his real self. The difficulty is that it is precisely the man who is most obviously himself who can be the greatest threat to those who have not yet found themselves, for instead of taking him as an *example,* inspiring them to do in their way what he has done in his, they are all too apt to take him as a *model* whose style of writing and literary tastes they blindly follow.

As an example, nothing could be more admirable than the way in which, at a time when most of his seniors and juniors were looking to the French poets of the post-Baudelaireian period or to the English metaphysicals for their poetic models, Mr. Graves had the courage to ignore them and remain faithful to his personal preferences—nursery rhymes, ballads, Skelton, Caroline poets like Lovelace and Rochester, even romantic poets like Blake, Coleridge, and Christina Rosetti—or that, in an age obsessed with experiment and innovation in meter and poetic organization, he should have gone on quietly writing genuine contemporary poetry within the traditional forms. It would not be equally admirable, however, if Pope and free verse, say, were to become taboo because Mr. Graves does not like the one or write in the other. But to turn to his poems themselves is enough to make one forget all such gloomy forebodings.

The kind of critic who regards authors as an opportunity for displaying his own brilliance and ingenuity will find Mr. Graves a poor subject. A few of his poems, it is true, can benefit from a gloss, but this Mr. Graves has provided himself in *The White Goddess.* For the rest, though he happens to be a learned scholar, he demands no scholarship of his readers; his poems are short, their diction simple, their syntax unambiguous and their concerns, love, nature, the personal life, matters with which all are familiar and in which all are interested. About public life, politics, the world situation, etc., he has nothing to say.

This does not mean that he regards public events as of no significance—he could never have written his excellent historical novels if he did—only that it is not a realm with which he believes poetry should be concerned. He also believes, I suspect, that in our age the Public Realm is irredeemable and that the only thing a sensible man can do is ignore it and live as decently as he can in spite of it. I can picture Mr. Graves, under certain circumstances, as a guerilla fighter, but I cannot see him writing pamphlets for any cause.

Like nearly all writers worth reading, Mr. Graves is a moralist, and the artistic merits of his poems cannot be divorced from the conception of the good life which they express. Though Horace is not one of his favorite poets—Horace is unpassionate and easygoing, Graves passionate and puritanical—they both attach great importance to measure and good sense, and have a common dislike for willful disorder and theatrical gestures. If Mr. Graves is the more convincing advocate, it is because one feels that measure and good sense are values he has had to fight to achieve. It is hard to believe that Horace ever suffered from nightmares or some passion so violent that it could have destroyed him, but he would have approved, I think, of Graves's description of the climate of thought.

> Wind, sometimes, in the evening chimneys; rain
> On the early morning roof, on sleepy sight;
> Snow streaked upon the hilltop, feeding
> The fond brook at the valley-head
> That greens the valley and that parts the lips;
> The sun, simple, like a country neighbor;
> The moon, grand, not fanciful with clouds.

Graves's good man, leaving aside the special case of the good poet, is somebody who leads an orderly, hard-working, independent life—a good husband and father who keeps his word and pays his debts; outwardly, in fact, a good bourgeois, but inwardly never losing his sense of his personal identity or his capacity for love and reverence.

On the subject of love, no poet in our time has written more or better. Most of Hardy's love poems are elegies, most of Yeats's are concerned with unrequited love, but Graves's deal with the joys and griefs of mutual passion. He shares with D. H. Lawrence a contempt for those who would deny the physical element in love and call

> . . . for a chaste
> Sodality: all dead below the waist.

But that is the only point on which they agree. He has none of Lawrence's hysterical aversion to conscious understanding between the sexes; on the contrary, any sexual relationship that does not lead to personal understanding and affection is, for him, base. Nothing could be further from Lawrence than Graves's priapic poem *Down, Wanton, Down!* In this, as in many others, he shows his distaste for the vulgarity and crudeness of untamed male sexuality. Woman, to Graves, is the superior sex, and only a woman can teach a man the meaning of true love.

For the poet, as the messenger of the Mother Goddess, there is an additional obligation to speak no more and no less than the truth, and each poet, according to his nature and the time in which he lives, has his own kind of temptation to lie. Mr. Graves has told us of his. He was born—the term is inaccurate but convenient—with a natural faculty for writing verse. Ask him to improvise a poem on any subject, and in ten minutes he can turn out something competent and mellifluous. This is a very valuable gift, and a poet like Wordsworth who lacks it is deficient, but it is a dangerous one, for the poet who possesses it can all too easily forsake the truth for verbal display.

> But you know, I know, and you know I know
>   My principal curse:
> Shame at the mounting dues I have come to owe
>   A devil of verse,
> Who caught me young, ingenuous and uncouth,
>   Prompting me how
> To evade the patent clumsiness of truth—
>   Which I do now.

It is of this devil and not of another poet, I think that Graves is speaking in *In Broken Images*.

> He is quick, thinking in clear images;
> I am slow, thinking in broken images.
> He becomes dull, trusting to his clear images;
> I become sharp, mistrusting my broken images. . . .
> He in a new confusion of his understanding;
> I in a new understanding of my confusion.

A comparison between his individual volumes and the *Collected Poems* which follow it, and then between the successive *Collected Poems* of 1926, 1938, 1947, 1955 and 1961 reveals how stern with himself Mr. Graves has been in discarding any poem that contained a trace of smartness. Among them, I remember a pastiche of *Speke Parrot,* which was an amazing tour de force. Personally, I regret its omission, but I can see why it has been excluded. The only virtuoso pieces he has retained are comic poems like *Welcome to the Caves of Arta* and *Apollo of the Physiologists,* for a comic poem must almost necessarily be a virtuoso performance. If I have a greater fondness for bravura in poetry than Mr. Graves, I suspect that we only differ in our notion of what is comic or what may be comically treated. To me, for example, *Lycidas* is a "comic" poem which I can learn "by heart not by rote" as I can learn a poem by Edward Lear. It seems to me a verbal arcadia in which death, grief, religion, and politics are games which cannot possibly be taken seriously. On the other hand, because I am convinced of the reality of their emotions, there are religious sonnets by Donne and Hopkins in which I feel that the virtuosity of expression comes between them and the truth.

Mr. Graves's other temptation has been the tendency of the romantic imagination to regard the extraordinary and remote as more "poetic," more luminous than everyday events.

> The lost, the freakish, the unspelt
> Drew me: for simple sights I had no eye.
> And did I swear allegiance then
> To wildness, not (as I thought) to truth—
> Become a virtuoso, and this also,
> Later, of simple sights, when tiring
> Of unicorn and upas?

Again, a reading of his collected poems will show how successful he has been in disciplining his imagination and his tongue. Occasionally, perhaps, he indulges his subjective feelings at the expense of objective fact. Among his more recent poems is one entitled "Turn of the Moon" which concludes as follows:

> But if one night she brings us, as she turns,
> Soft, steady, even, copious rain
> That harms no leaf or flower, but gently falls
> Hour after hour, sinking to the taproots,
> And the sodden earth exhales at dawn
> A long sigh scented with pure gratitude,
> Such rain—the first rain of our lives, it seems,
> Neither foretold, cajoled, nor counted on—
> Is woman giving as she loves.

The lines are beautiful and, at first reading, I was carried away. But, then, a tiresome doubt obtruded itself: "Are drought and rainfall *really* caused by the moon? What would a meteorologist say?"

In addition to discarding many poems, Mr. Graves has revised some, and, to anyone who writes verses himself, nothing is more instructive than a poet's revisions.

In Mr. Graves's case, they are particularly important because they prevent his doctrine of the subordination of art to truth from being misunderstood. It is all right for him to say

And call the man a liar who says I wrote
All that I wrote in love, for love of art.

But we all know the kind of poet who, when one points out to him that a certain line is obscure or clumsy and should be rewritten, replies: "But that is how it came to me." Art without love is nothing, but love without art is insufficient. Here for comparison are two versions of *The Sea Horse*.

Tenderly confide your secret love,
For one who never pledged you less than love,
To this indomitable hippocamp,
Child of your element, coiled a-ramp,
Having ridden out worse tempests than you know of:
Make much of him in your despair, and shed
Salt tears to bathe his taciturn dry head.

(1953)

Since now in every public place
Lurk phantoms who assume your walk and face,
You cannot yet have utterly abjured me
Nor stifled the insistent roar of sea.

Do as I do: confide your unquiet love
(For one who never owed you less than love)
To this indomitable hippocamp,
Child of your elements, coiled a-ramp,
Having ridden out worse tempests than you know of;
Under his horny ribs a blood-red stain
Portends renewal of our pain.
Sweetheart, make much of him and shed
Tears on his taciturn dry head.

(1961)

Only a craftsman as meticulous as Mr. Graves can afford to speak lightly of his art.

To read his poems is both a joy and a privilege; they are passionate, truthful, and well-bred.

—JULY 1961

A Round-robin

Three Memoranda on
"The New Arden Shakespeare"

The Editors

On *The New Arden Shakespeare*

From W. H. Auden:

SHAKESPEARE, as every schoolboy knows, is Top Bard. In high school the student "does" two or three of his plays, and at college two or three more are required reading. He may also be taken to see some performances—he may even act in one.

Every sensible young person has an instinctive antipathy to what is Officially-Approved-Of, and, in Shakespeare's case, this is reinforced by the fact that, of all the major English writers, no one is less a writer for the young, for persons, that is, under the age of thirty.

No young man who cares for poetry reads Shakespeare with the same passion that he reads the Romantics or the Metaphysicals; no young man with an interest in the theatre enjoys Shakespeare's plays as he enjoys those of Congreve, Ibsen, Chekhov, or Shaw.

On the other hand, almost anyone *over* thirty who cares for poetry or drama, will find, if he can once get himself to read him, that the more he reads Shakespeare the more he becomes convinced that Shakespeare really *is* Top Bard, that between him and every other English writer there is an immense gulf.

Shakespeare wrote a lot and each work of his is utterly different from all the others. Dickens is one of my favorite authors and I wouldn't be without a single one of his novels, but it is fair to say, I think, that after you have read three or four of them, you know the Dickensian world: you may not yet have met all its inhabitants, but you already know pretty well what they will be like when you do. But to have read, let us say, one comedy, one tragedy, one chronicle play and one non-dramatic poem of Shakespeare's, will not give you any proper idea of the Shakespearean world: that can only be got by reading everything he wrote.

Shakespeare's work is not only very good and very varied: his enormous vocabulary and extraordinary handling of metaphor and imagery also make him a very difficult writer. So far as his language is concerned, I find Dante easier to follow than an Italian newspaper but, though English is my native tongue, there are many passages in Shakespeare which, despite many readings, still perplex me. It is never sufficient to read a Shakespeare play once.

To be good, an edition of Shakespeare must therefore satisfy the following demands:

I) It must be designed for reading by the middle-aged and the old. If they like an author, the young will put up with cheap paper, atrocious print, double columns, *anything*. The middle-aged and the old will not. They demand volumes of the right size and the right weight, and a page which is a visual pleasure to behold.

II) It must be designed for frequent re-reading. It must, that is to say, be sufficiently stoutly made to last a lifetime, but it must not be a de luxe masterpiece of bookmaking craftsmanship which is much too valuable to be constantly picked up and put down and read with unwashed fingers.

III) It must be so designed that one play can be read at a time, but in any order. This means one play, one volume.

IV) It must contain critical notes to assist the reader when either the meaning is difficult to make out or the correct text is in doubt. These must be so placed that a) when a reader wants to confine himself to the text, his eye is not drawn to the notes willy-nilly and b) when he does wish to consult a note he can do this immediately and without losing his place. There is only one way of meeting these two demands—to place the critical apparatus at the bottom of the page to which it refers and to set text and notes in unmistakably different type.

How much critical apparatus to supply is debatable. I am inclined to believe that too much is better than too little. The reader can always skip it, and my experience has been that the more familiar I become with the text, the sharper grows my appetite for emendations and explications, not only because some of them are very helpful but also because so many provide superb entertainment as exhibitions of human folly.

I have looked at many editions of Shakespeare and own a number myself, but the only one which completely satisfies me is the Arden. The format is right, the paper is right, the print is right, the notes are in the proper place, the discussions of source material are all I need, and the introductions by the various editors, though I may sometimes disagree with them (which is, anyway, as it should be), are neither too elementary nor misbegotten Ph.D. theses.

From Jacques Barzun:

YOU ASK ME to jot down some reasons why I chose the *New Arden Shakespeare* for my own use and as a selection for our readers. That is quite a simple task, though perhaps I cannot be as brief as I should like.

I subscribed to the volumes as soon as they began coming out, one at a time, partly because I knew and liked the format of the old Arden edition, which the new in general reproduces, and partly because I wanted a modern edition whose scholarship would be up to date yet not extravagant. In a word, I found the New Arden an edition for readers. Given the state of Shakespeare studies today I can think of no higher praise.

To begin with, the books are tall and thin, made to hold in one hand; the paper is of a pleasant cream tint, flexible, and trained from birth (doubtless by Juliet's nurse) to lie flat; the ink is black and, as I said, the editors are discreet. They have not peppered the page with reference marks, nor split it into two columns, nor broken many verses. The footnotes tell you what you need to know about vocabulary, and the substance cited in them is, as often as not, literature—other poets and plays—not commentators to the cube (c. upon c. upon c.).

The extremists will tell you that all this makes an edition for amateurs, ignorant people who have only a love of literature to save them from futility, mere children in the arts and sciences of our golden age. A *real* edition would deal with such difficulties as which typesetter of the First Folio composed a given portion of a play and by what reasoning it follows that his habits and his mistakes should divert us from our original desire to read the play. Even such a scholar's edition, however, fails to tell you whether, to get its full benefit, you should absorb this valuable matter between lines or between speeches.

Anyhow, in this business of mining into Shakespeare, of undermining Shakespeare, the present generation has gone farther than anybody else and the result is that no one today knows Shakespeare as Hazlitt or even Bowdler knew him. I think it is an evil pendulum that swings so far from the center. Two hundred years ago, at the University of Oxford, the Professor of Poetry, one William Hawkins, could think of little else to justify his title than to improve *Cymbeline* for Covent Garden. He "endeavoured," he said, "to new-construct this Tragedy, almost upon the plan of Aristotle himself, in respect of the Unity of Time; but whilst presuming to regulate Shakespeare's design, I have endeavoured to imitate his Stile with the humility and reverence of a son. With this in view, I have retained in many places the very language of the original author, and in *all* others endeavoured to supply it with a diction similar thereunto."

You may consider this an instance at the other end of the swing, but this Bill Hawkins of 1759 is much more my friend than his modern descendants. To do all he did, he had to read Shakespeare and even to like him. I believe Bill when he says he felt like a son. The reputation of the plays mattered to him. I can imagine him "sporting the oak" of his unheated rooms during long hours of work pursuing and finally catching Shakespeare's Stile. Our contemporaries no longer soil their hands with such direct contacts of a pre-scientific age. They use microphotography and ultraviolet rays to learn about typesetters. The president of the scholarly immortals in this country reports that he can no longer keep up with the contents of Shakespeare research. There is too much, and he must confine himself to its bibliography. If he sampled this scholarship, he would find some of it laborious, rediscovering what Coleridge and Bradley knew by inspection. Meanwhile, the worldly way to disguise that bitter pill, Shakespeare, is to stage him with lyrics and music by Cole Porter, to direct him out of recognition à la Webster (Margaret, not John), or to transmoviefy him under a coating of Freud and philosophy spoken sepulchrally by Laurence Olivier.

For all these reasons I say what the voice in the garden told Saint Augustine: *tolle et lege:* take up and read. Read Shakespeare. Read him in the most attractive edition. Read him in bed, while shaving, at lectures, during parties, in the dentist chair. Read him in whole and in bits. Read him until you possess him so well that nobody—no editor, producer, or critic—can poison your pleasure. Read him in his new leafy forest of Arden: it is as good a spot as you will find. True, one small final perfection is missing. I will not tell you what it is. That is my secret. But the flaw is only a reminder that we are still on earth, where Shakespeare and his monument are both imperfect, the one not more than the other.

From Lionel Trilling:

I HAVE NO DOUBT that the Arden is the best of all the editions of Shakespeare. Yet, oddly enough, I find that I am embarrassed when I undertake to urge its merits. Whatever one says about an edition of Shakespeare for the general reader must bear upon one consideration only—whether or not it makes the reading of Shakespeare pleasanter and easier. And I find that I am reluctant to bring into public view the matter of reading Shakespeare: it is one of the few really private things in the world and it ought to remain so. Shakespeare in the theater is one thing, a very good and right thing, conceivably the only thing that Shakespeare ever intended. Along with it go all the usual pleasures of the theater—companionship, community, the sense of event, the satisfaction of an interest that can be formulated and expressed—at each entr'acte, and for hours after the performance, one can talk at will about the play at least tangentially, by saying whether or not this or that detail of the production was appropriate and adequate. But to *read* Shakespeare is virtually a secret act. It is by no means socially licensed. Anyone is permitted to say, "I saw *Measure for Measure* last night and it was a vulgar performance." (If he has in mind the production of the Stratford, Connecticut company, he says the truth.) But no one, unless he lives in unusually fortunate circumstances, is free to say, "Last night I read *Measure for Measure* . . ." Modesty forbids. All one's social instincts make plain that the imputation of priggishness lies in wait. Society allows one *to have read* Shakespeare, and to that act of the past it even gives a frank admiration. It understands that one might *study* Shakespeare, and it is much interested in anyone who *teaches* Shakespeare. But to *read* Shakespeare—that is to say, for no good reason, for pleasure—is on all sides thought to be an act of cultural *hubris*. "Last night I read *Measure for Measure*": painful hush; dropped eyes; sweet smiles of difficult understanding. And because no one may in decency report the act of reading Shakespeare, no one is likely to commit the act for reasons of pride and prestige—one reads Shakespeare for personal and private reasons or not at all.

And now, in explaining my reluctance, I've done exactly what I was reluctant to do—I've praised the reading of Shakespeare, written a bit of high-minded advertising copy for it, given it a touch of prestige-value by saying that it has none (ploy of Inconspicuous Consumption), suggesting that it was a sign of non-conformity, that it was maybe in the same class of freedom-indicators as buying Modern Paintings.

Well, it can't be helped. . . .

The first good thing about the Arden Shakespeare is that each play is in a separate volume. There is of course something to be said for a one-volume Shakespeare, including the convenience of taking it away with you in the summer, but there's not much point in saying it because everyone has at least one such one-volume. But we shouldn't have to read Shakespeare, or any writer, in double columns. If the double columns approach legibility, the volume is too heavy to hold—the most readable of the three one-volume editions I own is as large as my desk dictionary; they both tip the bathroom scale at 2½ pounds.

Apart from the physical difficulty of a one-volume edition, there is the inappropriateness of having to deal with "Shakespeare." No doubt all his plays can be thought of as making one great single work, as do the novels of Dickens or Dostoyevsky, but this is a thought that we should have to entertain only now and then—it is better and safer to take the plays as separate entities, as we take the novels of Dickens and Dostoyevsky.

At the other extreme from the one-volume complete edition, there are the editions of the plays in separate volumes, pocket-size. But the idea of the pocket volume is at best a pleasant affection, except in the case of the *Sonnets;* it is based on a vanished ideal of English pedestrianism, of a volume to be slipped into the pocket of a tweed jacket to be read in the evening at an inn after a long day's tramp. At home one feels rather foolish holding the little thing.

The Arden edition gives us volumes of full size, gracefully proportioned. The type in which the text is set is full and clear. The type of the notes is of course smaller but very bright.

As for the notes and other apparatus, they are as full as anyone could want, but not fuller. Not all readers are interested by the problems of establishing a correct text of Shakespeare—that is to say, the problems of ascertaining what in a confusing passage Shakespeare really meant to write—but some are, and certainly the subject is of intrinsic interest. On this the remarks of Mr. M. R. Ridley in the Preface to his edition of *Antony and Cleopatra* are indicative of the general practice of the editors. "In constructing the apparatus, and deciding what to include and what to omit, I have tried to keep in mind two main types of reader, the student who is in the early or prentice days of his study of textual problems, and the ordinary reader who is mainly concerned with reading the plays as plays, who relies therefore on his edition primarily for discussion of points of meaning of dramatic presentation, but who is prepared every now and again to be interested in a technical problem. For both classes it is desirable to let the important things stand out, and not embed them in a mass of minor ones."

The notes are very full indeed. Not all readers will want all the notes on every reading, for while some are directly explicative, others serve to expand or deepen the meaning of a word or a phrase by reference to contemporary meaning. But all are relevant to one sort of interest or another.

Each of the volumes is edited by a different hand but in a uniform way. Each editor in his introduction sets forth the stage history of the play, and summarizes the scholarship and criticism that has dealt with it. In the extensive appendices he discusses difficult or debated points of interpretation or production and provides the texts of the chief sources of the story.

In short, it is difficult to imagine a more complete and satisfactory edition.

—JANUARY 1961

Jameschoice for January

THE EDITORS

On not writing about *Finnegans Wake*

THE AMERICAN PUBLISHER of *Finnegans Wake,* the Viking Press, has just issued a new printing of the famous work, and the Editors of The Readers' Subscription offer it as their selection for January in what might appear to be the most nearly unprincipled choice of a book they have ever made.

Unprincipled? Or nearly unprincipled? Harsh words. But the possibility must be considered that some adjective of extreme moral disapprobation ought to be used to characterize our choice. For not one of the three editors has read the book through.

And this despite the fact that each of us made a first acquaintance with *Finnegans Wake* a long time ago. Excerpts from *Work in Progress* began to appear not long after the publication of *Ulysses,* and it is now seventeen years since the completed work was published. Yet none of us has come to its end, or, if any of us has, he did not get there by the usual legitimate stages.

What is more, none of us is certain—or even resolved—that some day, in a long vacation, or in a distant unhurried place, or in the severe and studious calm of superannuation, he will, at long last, really read the book as most books are read, from cover to cover, beginning at page 1 and ending at page 628.

In short, we have chosen a book that none of us feels competent to review, or that we cannot review without an effort we have no wish to make. That is why our choice might seem unprincipled. But really it is not.

James Joyce is one of the great geniuses of our time. There is no doubt in the minds of any of the Editors on this score. And *Finnegans Wake* is a work of genius. The awareness that a writer is a genius or that a book is a work of genius isn't the end of judgment, nor is it necessarily the beginning of love or accord. James Joyce is not a central or even an especially influential figure in the life of any of the Editors. Perhaps if any of us were to deal with him in an extended and fully considered way, the judgments made upon him would be largely adverse. But what a gratification lies in dealing adversely with a mind that one knows to be that of a genius! What a relief to resist what one can entirely respect and even admire! What a comfort it is to be not always defending oneself from vulgarity, or enlightened stupidity, or the masked cliché, or smallness of aim, but sometimes to stand out against the force of greatness. To resist the slouching assertiveness of the latest "serious" novel serves but to delude us that we are defining our lives. But to maintain a quarrel with, say, Dostoevsky or Kafka, to withhold full assent from Baudelaire, or to question Joyce—this is salutary. And especially in view of the piety and academic prestige with which such authors are now surrounded.

James Joyce, as everybody knows, moved from the studied simplicity of his early short stories to the extravagant complexity of *Finnegans Wake.* The stages of this development seem calculated, almost predetermined. *Ulysses,* when it first appeared, seemed the last possibility of difficult complexity. But it really did not take long for *Ulysses* to lose much of its reputation for difficulty. To be sure, scholars are still at work on this scene or that. Difficulties still remain. The work must be read with a dedicated attention. But it can be read. At a second or a third reading one should be able to take it at a quite rapid pace, and with more pleasure than effort; what sense the reader may have of mysteries as yet unsolved is an element of the pleasure.

It was not unreasonable to expect that *Finnegans Wake,* with time and our habituation, would become as accessible, or nearly so, as *Ulysses.* This has not proved true.

Yet there it stands, a fact in the literary life of our age, and a great fact. Joyce may have been wrong in his assumption that no amount of difficulty could ultimately interfere with the achievement of the aesthetic and moral effects he intended. Stanislaus Joyce, a great admirer of his brother's work through *Ulysses,* has passionately proclaimed the error of *Finnegans Wake* and the waste of James's gifts and life—eighteen years of life—that it entailed. Others have not agreed, as we know from the devoted criticism and explication which the book has received. "Provoked by the sheer magnitude of the work," say the authors of *A Skeleton Key to Finnegans Wake,* "we felt that if Joyce had spent eighteen years in its composition we might profitably spend a few deciphering it."

Deciphering it? Then one does not read it? No, one does not. "Its texture is so close, its structure so organic," says Harry Levin, "that it cannot yet be considered readable in the sense of an ordinary novel." Cannot yet, and perhaps never will be. As for the years that are necessary to spend in deciphering it, each reader must decide for himself how many he can afford, just as each reader must answer for himself the temperamental question of the extent to which he can submit himself to the demands of an author.

The book, of course, is decipherable and has been deciphered. Edmund Wilson in his essay in *The Wound and the Bow* has set forth the outline and intention of the work, and the *Skeleton Key* of Joseph Campbell and Henry Morton Robinson explicates the work in further detail. Mr. Campbell and Mr. Robinson, referring to the rewards of sincere efforts to unravel the meaning of the book, speak also of the "unimaginable prize of complete understanding." Unimaginable indeed, for the book, we feel, is addressed to no human reader but to the Logos itself, for whose pleasure and amusement this eighteen years meditation on history and language—on man in the universe—was contrived. But we overhear what is addressed to the Logos, and we know that the Logos is pleased and amused because we, whose inadequate philology bars us from a complete understanding of the huge pun, are pleased and amused. *Finnegans Wake* is a funny book and a witty book—this much we can easily know. As Mr. Levin reminds us, "by printing certain fragments in pamphlet form . . . Joyce seems to have recognized that they were especially attractive." These are the famous "Anna Livia Plurabelle" (pp. 196–216) and "Tales Told of Shem and Shaun" ("The Mookse and the Gripes," pp. 152–159, and "The Gracehopper and the Ondt," pp. 414–419). With these the reader might begin and see what happens.

At any rate, here is the book. Ask it a civil question and it will return you a sybil answer. We have made our Choyce and we stick to it.

—JANUARY 1956

EDITOR'S NOTE

OF THE 173 review-essays that Auden, Barzun, and Trilling published in *The Griffin* and *The Mid-Century*, only about a fifth have been reprinted (see Appendix 2). Twelve of Trilling's were included in *A Gathering of Fugitives* and another eight in *Speaking of Literature and Society*. Five of Auden's can be found in *Forewords and Afterwords;* and his essay on Kafka (*The Mid-Century*, Fall 1960, no. 17) appears in *The Dyer's Hand* (reprinted as "The I Without a Self"). Three of Barzun's are in his *Critical Questions*. Various other essays—Auden's on Sydney Smith and Barzun's on John Jay Chapman—were first written as introductions to books and, unfortunately, these too had to be omitted. (Trilling's review of *The Adventures of Augie March*, included here, was written for *The Griffin* and reprinted later in the 1956 Modern Library edition of Bellow's novel.) This still leaves some 135 pieces.

Presented with the task of choosing fifteen from each author, a few criteria immediately presented themselves. Length, for one. Some seemed too short (the exception here is Auden on *The Ring Trilogy* because—well, because it's Auden on *The Hobbit*). Other reviews reproduced too much of the book in question—i.e., lengthy extracts from letters, poetry, and diaries, thus disqualifying Auden on Robert Graves's *Anger of Achilles* and Barzun on Robert Lowell's *Life Studies*. Nonetheless, I included Trilling's piece on Cavafy, despite its many citations, because of the poet's relative obscurity at the time. I also tended to exclude those pieces that dealt with anthologies, collections of stories, or histories of literature (which are only compilations from various sources) unless the occasion spurred the editor to perform some elegant mental arabesques.

Naturally, the main consideration was given to the significance or timeliness of the book under review. Is the book or its author still read? Alternatively, has one or the other been forgotten or neglected, and does either deserve to be resurrected? While it seemed obvious to include Auden on Muriel Spark—she's still at it—what does one do with Barzun's piece on Marchette Chute's long-out-of-print *Two Gentle Men?* In the end, I was swayed by Barzun's enthusiasm for the book, which made me want to find it. Other essays gained entry because, but not only because, the books' authors have remained newsworthy. For example, Kenneth Tynan's journals were published in 2000, and the past few years have seen new biographies of Colette and Proust. As to whether to include pieces on such canonical writers as Shaw, Wilde, Henry James, and Dostoevsky, it was, as the kids like to say, "a no-brainer."

Then there are the obvious and the not-so-obvious pairings of reviewer and book. Certain books clearly played into an editor's strengths, while others seemed so uncharacteristic of one or another of the trio that to omit them seemed somehow irresponsible, like discovering that Hegel liked to bob for apples and keeping it to yourself. So here is Trilling on Ingmar Bergman's screenplays and Kenneth Grahame's *The Wind in the Willows;* Auden on drug addiction and Faulkner; and Barzun on Japanese history.

More difficult was the matter of overlap. Sometimes, an editor wrote about an author more than once, or, as happened more often, two or all three editors wrote about the same author, if not the same book. Thus Barzun's good piece on Edmund Wilson gave way to Auden's, and Trilling's review of Dostoevsky's shorter works was nudged aside by Auden's reflections on *The House of the Dead.* On one occasion all three did write about the same book—*The New Arden Shakespeare*—and though it was essentially three quick takes on the 1960 edition of Shakespeare's plays, it seemed proper to include it, if only to get the three of them together on the stage at the same time. On two other occasions, all three editors refrained from commenting on a book that they were recommending to their readers. The first of these was James Joyce's *Finnegans Wake;* the second, Arthur Schopenhauer's *The World as Will and Representation.* With regard to Schopenhauer's opus, there was simply too little time to write a proper review. With Joyce's work, other considerations prompted them not to review it. Happily, the reasons they give become something of a comment in themselves.

It should also be said that I have allowed the reviews and essays to stand by themselves. Aside from fixing the original typos (where I noticed them) and fiddling with obstreperous punctuation, I have not attempted, except where it was unavoidable, to clarify the meaning of a phrase or sentence. This is not *hubris*. Not all these pieces were carefully proofed at the time of composition. Auden, for one, was notoriously lax about going over his copy. As a result, the attentive reader may on occasion be grounded by bizarre punctuation or else swept along by run-on sentences. Since editorial interference is often just a matter of preference, I have kept my distance.

Finally, there is the matter of the editor's preference for the poet or novelist under discussion. Although John Bayley's two recent memoirs about his wife Iris Murdoch provided some incentive to include Trilling's piece on Murdoch's *An Unofficial Rose,* I'm afraid that given the choice between reading a poem by Philip Larkin and a novel by Iris Murdoch, the more misanthropic one gets the nod. Readers interested in books and reviews not selected are directed to Appendix 1. Readers wishing to read more in the work of the critics themselves are urged to look up copies of *The Griffin* and *The Mid-Century* at their nearest college or university library.

Complete List of Essays and Reviews from
The Griffin and *The Mid-Century*

Articles Published by W. H. Auden in *The Griffin*

"Short Novels of Colette" (1951, vol. 1, no. 2)

"Our Italy" (1952, vol. 1, no. 5): Eleanor Clark's *Rome and a Villa*

"T. S. Eliot So Far" (1953, vol. 2, no. 3): *The Collected Plays and Poems of T. S. Eliot*

"Verga's Place" (July 1953, vol. 2, no. 6): Giovanni Verga's *The House by the Medlar Tree*

"Selected Essays of T. S. Eliot" (Oct. 1953, vol. 2, no. 9)

"In Memory of Sigmund Freud" (Dec. 1953, vol. 2, no. 11): poem

"Handbook to Antiquity" (March 1954, vol. 3, no. 3): Moses Hadas's *The Ancilla*

"A European View of Peace" (April 1954, vol. 3, no. 4): Raymond Aron's *The Century of Total War*

"The Freud–Fliess Letters" (June 1954, vol. 3, no. 6): *Sigmund Freud's Letters: The Origin of Psychoanalysis*

"The Private Diaries of Stendhal (1801–1814)" (Nov. 1954, vol. 3, no. 11): Robert Sage, ed., tr. *The Private Diaries of Stendhal*

"Authority in America" (March 1955, vol. 4, no. 3): Leslie Fiedler's *An End to Innocence*

"A Review of the Alternate" (March 1955, vol. 4, no. 3): J.R.R. Tolkien's *The Fellowship of the Ring*

"Man Before Myth" (April 1955, vol. 4, no. 4): James Clifford's *Young Sam Johnson*

"The History of an Historian" (Nov. 1955, vol. 4, no. 11): Ernest Jones's *The Life and Work of Sigmund Freud: Years of Maturity, Vol. 2*

"Am I That I Am?" (Dec. 1955, vol. 4, no. 12): Nigel Dennis's *Cards of Identity*

"A Self-Policing People" (Dec. 1955, vol. 4, no. 12): Response to a letter in *The People*

"Stimulating Scholarship" (March 1956, vol. 5, no. 3): C. S. Lewis's *English Literature in the Sixteenth Century*

"Wisdom, Wit, Music" (May 1956, vol. 5, no. 5): Hector Berlioz's *Evenings with the Orchestra*

"D. H. Lawrence as a Critic" (Sept. 1956, vol. 5, no. 9): Anthony Beal, ed. *D. H. Lawrence: Selected Literary Criticism;* F. R. Leavis's *D. H. Lawrence: Novelist*

"Sydney Smith" (Oct. 1956, vol. 5, no. 10): W. H. Auden, ed. *The Selected Writings of Sydney Smith*

"Dostoevsky in Siberia" (Nov. 1956, vol. 5, no. 12): F. M. Doest, ed. *Memoirs from the House of the Dead*

"Just How I Feel" (April 1957, vol. 6, no. 3): *The Oxford History of English Literature;* H. S. Bennett's *Chaucer and the Fifteenth Century*

"West's Disease" (May 1957, vol. 6, no. 4): *The Complete Works of Nathanael West*

"The Great Divide" (Oct. 1957, vol. 6, no. 9): Erich Heller's *The Disinherited Mind*

"Reflections Upon Reading Werner Jaeger's *Paideia*" (March 1958, vol. 7, no. 3): Gilbert Highet, tr. *Paideia: The Ideals of Greek Culture*

"The Kitchen of Life" (June 1958, vol. 7, no. 6): M. F. K. Fisher's *The Art of Eating*

"Thinking What We Are Doing" (Sept. 1958, vol. 7, no. 10): Hannah Arendt's *The Human Condition*

Articles Published by W. H. Auden in *The Mid-Century*

"John Betjeman's Poetic Universe" (July 1959, no. 1): Earl of Birkenhead, ed. *John Betjeman's Collected Poems;* Spoken Arts recording *The Golden Treasury of John Betjeman*

"Agee on the Movies" (July 1959, no. 1): reprinted letter to *The Nation* from Oct. 1944

"The Creation of Music and Poetry" (Aug. 1959, no. 2): Paul Valéry's *The Art of Poetry;* Robert Craft, ed. *Conversations with Stravinsky*

"Calm Even in the Catastrophe" (Sept. 1959, no. 3): *The Complete Letters of Vincent Van Gogh*

"The Private Life of a Public Man" (Oct. 1959, no. 4): W. B. Yeats's *Mythologies*

"Miss Marianne Moore, Bless Her!" (Fall 1959, no. 5): Marianne Moore's *O to Be a Dragon*

"Secondary Epic" (Dec. 1959, no. 7): a poem

"The Magician from Mississippi" (Jan. 1960, no. 8): William Faulkner's *The Mansion*

"A Children's Anthology" (Jan. 1960, no. 8): *A Treasure Chest of Tales*

"*Apologies to the Iroquois*" (Feb. 1960, no. 9): Review of Edmund Wilson's book

"An Unclassical Classic" (March 1960, no. 10): Robert Graves's *The Anger of Achilles*

"Calm Even in the Catastrophe" (May 1960, no. 12): reprinted from Sept. 1959, *The Complete Letters of Vincent Van Gogh*

"Greatness Finding Itself" (June 1960, no. 13): Erik Erikson's *Young Man Luther*

"K" (Fall, 1960, no. 17): Franz Kafka's *The Great Wall of China* and Max Brod's revised and enlarged *Franz Kafka: A Biography*

"Two Ways of Poetry" (Oct. 1960, no. 18): Philip Larkin's *The Less Deceived;* Geoffrey Hill's *For the Unfallen*

"The Problem of Nowness" (Nov. 1960, no. 19): Wylie Sypher's *From Rococo to Cubism in Art and Literature*

"Il Faut Payer" (Feb. 1961, no. 22): Ford Madox Ford's *Parade's End*

"Two Cultural Monuments" (April 1961, no. 24): Robert Lowell, tr. *Phaedre and Figaro.*

"The Case is Curious" (June 1961, no. 26): Barzun's *The Delights of Detection*

"A Poet of Honor" (July 1961, no. 28): *The Collected Poems of Robert Graves*

"A Universal Eccentric" (Christmas 1961, no. 33): Andre Chastel's *The Genius of Leonardo da Vinci*

"The Conscience of an Artist" (Dec. 1961, no. 34): Caesare Pavese's *The Burning Brand: Diaries 1935–1950*

"The Chemical Life" (Jan. 1962, no. 35): David Ebin, ed. *The Drug Experience*

"Review of *A Marianne Moore Reader*" (Feb. 1962, no. 36)

"A Marriage of True Minds" (March 1962, no. 37): Correspondence of Richard Strauss and Hugo von Hofmannsthal, *A Working Friendship*

"A Disturbing Novelist" (May 1962, no. 39): *A Muriel Spark Trio*

"'The Geste Says This and the Man Who Was on the Field . . .'" (May 1962, no. 39): David Jones's *In Parenthesis*

"The Justice of Dame Kind" (Midsummer 1962, no. 42): Lorus and Margery Milne's *The Senses of Animals and Men*

Articles Published by Jacques Barzun in *The Griffin*

"Why Not the Third Cheer?" (1951, vol. 1, no. 1): E. M. Forster's *Two Cheers for Democracy*

"Lorenzo the Magniloquent" (1952, vol. 1, no. 4): W. Y. Tindall, ed. *The Later D. H. Lawrence: The Best Novels, Stories, Essays, 1925–1930*

"Four Portraits" by Colette (1952, vol. 1, no. 4): Translated by Jacques Barzun

"Time Out of Mind" (1952, vol. 1, no. 7): Noel Annan's *Leslie Stephen: The Godless Victorian*

"Berenson and the Boot" (1952, vol. 1, no. 10): Bernard Berenson's *Rumor and Reflection*

"The Inexhaustible Bernard Shaw" (1953, vol. 2, no. 2): *The Selected Prose of Bernard Shaw*

"The Three Faces of the Drama" (1953, vol. 2, no. 5): Eric Bentley's *In Search of Theater*

"The Secretary's Turban and the Story Behind It" (Nov. 1953, vol. 2, no. 10): E. M. Forster's *The Hill of Devi*

"Dr. Freud of Vienna" (Dec. 1953, vol. 2, no. 11): Ernest Jones's *The Life and Work of Sigmund Freud, Vol. 1*

"*Flaubert's Dictionary*" (Jan. 1954, vol. 3, no. 1): Translated by Jacques Barzun

"Rereading Santayana" (Feb. 1954, vol. 3, no. 2): George Santayana's *The Life of Reason*

"As Uncomfortable as a Modern Self" (July 1954, vol. 3, no. 7): Virginia Woolf's *A Writer's Diary*

"Modern Life Begins at *Forte*" (Sept. 1954, vol. 3, no. 9): Arthur Loesser's *Men, Women and Pianos*

"O'Casey at Your Bedside" (Oct. 1954, vol. 3, no. 10): *Selected Plays of Sean O'Casey*

"The American and His Gadgets" (March 1955, vol. 4, no. 3): J. K. Galbraith's *The Great Crash of 1929*

"Why Talk About Art?" (May 1955, vol. 4, no. 5): Erwin Panofsky's *The Life and Art of Albrecht Dürer*

"Japan—Roads to Interpretation" (Oct. 1955, vol. 4, no. 10): Thomas Raucat's *The Honorable Picnic;* Donald Keene, ed. *Anthology of Japanese Literature*

"Proust's Way" (April 1956, vol. 5, no. 4): Gerard Hopkins, tr. Marcel Proust's *Jean Santeuil*

"The Blest Group of Us" (June 1956, vol. 5, no. 6): Henry James's *Autobiography*

"The Rain in Spain Etc." (July 1956, vol. 5, no. 8): Nancy Mitford, ed. *Noblesse Oblige;* Francis Meynell, ed. *The Week-End Book*

"Himself When Older" (Nov. 1956, vol. 5, no. 12): Edmund Wilson's *A Piece of My Mind*

"The Wondrous Kind" (Dec. 1956, vol. 5, no. 14): William H. Whyte, Jr.'s *The Organization Man*

"Two French Poets" (March 1957, vol. 6, no. 2): William Jay Smith, ed., tr. *Selected Writings of Jules Laforgue;* Bradford Cook, tr. *Mallarmé: Selected Prose, Poems, Essays and Letters*

"Intellect and the Hungarian Revolution" (Aug. 1957, vol. 6, no. 7): Melvin J. Lasky, ed. *The Hungarian Revolution—A White Book*

"On First Looking Into Our Own Chapman" (Sept. 1957, vol. 6, no. 8): Jacques Barzun, ed. *The Selected Writings of John Jay Chapman*

"The Man-Mountain" (Nov. 1957, vol. 6, no. 10): Donald M. Frame, tr. *The Complete Works of Montaigne, Essays, Travel Journal, and Letters*

"Lawrence in Life and Letters" (Feb. 1958, vol. 7, no. 2): D. H. Lawrence's *Twilight in Italy;* Diana Trilling, ed. *The Selected Letters of D. H. Lawrence*

"The Literary Mind" (April 1958, vol. 7, no. 4): William and Elizabeth Friedman's *The Shakespearean Ciphers Examined*

"The Sense of History" (May 1958, vol. 7, no. 5): Hugh Trevor-Roper's *Men and Events;* Jacob Burckhardt's *Judgments on History and Historians*

"Two Letters" (June 1958, vol. 7, no. 6): an exchange between Enid Starkie and Jacques Barzun

"The Truth at Any Cost" (Summer 1958, vol. 7, no. 8): Walter Kaufmann's *Critique of Religion and Philosophy*

"The Artistry of Discontent" (Christmas 1958, vol. 7, no. 12): William Morris's *Kelmscott Chaucer*

"The Esthetic Society" (Jan. 1959, vol. 8, no. 1): George Sansom's *A History of Japan to 1334*

Articles Published by Jacques Barzun in *The Mid-Century*

"The Artist as Scapegoat" (July 1959, no. 1): Frank Harris's *Oscar Wilde*

"The Ages of Man" (Aug. 1959, no. 2): George Rylands's *The Ages of Man*

"Life Into Words" (Sept. 1959, no. 3): Marchette Chute's *Two Gentle Men*

"The Siege at Peking" (Oct. 1959, no. 4): Peter Fleming's *The Siege at Peking*

"The Poet as Man in a Box" (Fall 1959, no. 5): Robert Lowell's *Life Studies*

"Out of Many, One" (Nov. 1959, no. 6): Oskar Morgenstern's *The Question of National Defense*

"The Tradition of the New" (Dec. 1959, no. 7): Harold Rosenberg's *The Tradition of the New*

"On the Death of an American Artist" (Jan. 1960, no. 8): obituary of Anne Goodwin Winslow

"Tragedy à la Shakespeare" (April 1960, no. 11): Garrett Mattingly's *The Armada*

"Not All Are O.O.O." (May 1960, no. 12): Eric Partridge's *Origins*

"The Charge of the Light Brigade" (Aug. 1960, no. 15): Burton Lowrey's *Twentieth Century Parody*

"The Comedy of Comedies" (Fall 1960, no. 17): Molière's *The Misanthrope*

"Found: A Novel With a Hero" (Nov. 1960, no. 19): C. P. Snow's *Strangers and Brothers*

"The Narrator in Command" (Jan. 1961, no. 21): Heinrich von Kleist's *The Marquise of O*

"Trial Now or by Posterity" (May 1961, no. 25): Sibylle Bedford's *The Faces of Justice;* Edward Radin's *Lizzie Borden: The Untold Story*

"An Answer to Mr. Auden's Questions" (June 1961, no. 26)

"The Playwright as Critic—of Music" (June 1961, no. 26): George Bernard Shaw's *How to Become a Musical Critic*

"When Thought is Air-Borne" (Summer 1961, no. 27): Rosalind Heywood's *Beyond the Reach of Sense*

"Ultima Thule" (Aug. 1961, no. 29): Peter Freuchen's *Book of the Eskimos*

"The Cutting of an Agate" (Sept. 1961, no. 30): *James Agate: An Anthology*

"High Jinks and Pathos" (Nov. 1961, no. 32): Eric Partridge's *A Dictionary of Slang and Unconventional English*

"The Grand Pretense" (Jan. 1962, no. 35): Richard Southern's *The Seven Ages of the Theatre*

"Modern Mores and the Law" (Feb. 1962, no. 36): Norman St. John-Stevas's *Life, Death and the Law*

"The Artist in Public Life" (March 1962, no. 37): Bernard Shaw's *Platform and Pulpit*

"Unknown? Misknown? Worth Knowing?" (June 1962, no. 40): *The Collected Tales of Henry James* Vols. I, II

"Exploring the Space of Time" (Midsummer 1962, no. 42): Leo Deuel, ed. *The Treasures of Time*

"The Spectre of Decadence" (Aug. 1962, no. 43): Oswald Spengler's *The Decline of the West*

Articles Published by Lionel Trilling in *The Griffin*

"A Change of Direction" (1952, vol. 1, no. 3): David Riesman's *The Lonely Crowd*

"Fiction and History" (1952, vol. 1, no. 6): Godfrey Blunden's *The Time of the Assassins*

"Adams at Ease" (1952, vol. 1, no. 8): Newton Arvin, ed. *Selected Letters of Henry Adams*

"The Early Edmund Wilson" (1952, vol. 1, no. 9): Edmund Wilson's *The Shores of Light*

"The Measure of Dickens" (1952, vol. 2, no. 1): Edgar Johnson's *Charles Dickens: His Tragedy and Triumph*

"The Personal Figure of Henry James" (1953, vol. 2, no. 4): Leon Edel's *Henry James: The Untried Years*

"Zola's Quality" (Aug. 1953, vol. 2, no. 7): Emile Zola's *Restless House*; Angus Wilson's *Emile Zola*

"A Triumph of the Comic View" (Sept. 1953, vol. 2, no. 8): Saul Bellow's *The Adventures of Augie March*

"Flaubert's Encyclopedia" (Jan. 1954, vol. 3, no. 1): Gustave Flaubert's *Bouvard and Pécuchet*, Jacques Barzun, tr.

"American Portrait" (May 1954, vol. 3, no. 5): David Riesman's *Individualism Reconsidered*

"Art and the Philosopher" (Aug. 1954, vol. 3, no. 8): Louis Reid's *A Study in Aesthetics*

"Measuring Mill" (Dec. 1954, vol. 3, no. 12): Michael St. John Packe's *The Life of John Stuart Mill*

"The Novel Alive or Dead" (Feb. 1955, vol. 4, no. 2): C. P. Snow's *The New Men*; Nancy Hallinan's *The Rough Winds of May*

"A Ramble on Graves" (June 1955, vol. 4, no. 6): Robert Graves's *Collected Poems*

"Product of the Revolution?" (July 1955, vol. 4, no. 7): Isaac Babel's *Collected Stories*

"Profession: Man of the World" (Sept. 1955, vol. 4, no. 9): James Pope-Hennessey's *Monckton Milnes*

"That Smile of Parmenides Made Me Think" (Feb. 1956, vol. 5, no. 2): Daniel Cory, ed.
The Letters of George Santayana

"Mr. Forster's Aunt Marianne" (Summer 1956, vol. 5, no. 7): E. M. Forster's *Marianne
Thornton*

"Preface to *A Gathering of Fugitives*" (Sept. 1956, vol. 5, no. 9): preface to a collection
of essays, many reprinted from *The Griffin*

"The Farmer and the Cowboy Make Friends" (Fall 1956, vol. 5, no. 11): Douglas
Bush's *English Literature in the Earlier Seventeenth Century, 1600–1660; The Oxford History of English Literature, Vol. 5*

"Mr. Colum's Greeks" (Christmas 1956, vol. 5, no. 13): Padraic Colum's *The Golden
Fleece* and *The Children's Homer*

"Old Calabria" (Feb. 1957, vol. 6, no. 1): Norman Douglas's *Old Calabria*

"Impersonal/Personal" (June 1957, vol. 6, no. 5): Stuart Gilbert, ed. *Letters of James
Joyce*

"The Nude Renewed" (July 1957, vol. 6, no. 6): Kenneth Clark's *The Nude*

"Last Years of a Titan" (Dec. 1957, vol. 6, no. 11): Ernest Jones's *The Life and Work of
Sigmund Freud: 1919–1939, The Last Phase, Vol. 3*

"The Story and the Novel" (Jan. 1958, vol. 7, no. 1): Isak Dinesen's *Last Tales;* James
Agee's *A Death in the Family*

"Proust as Critic and the Critic as Novelist" (July 1958, vol. 7, no. 7): Marcel Proust's
On Art and Literature

"The Last Lover" (Aug. 1958, vol. 7, no. 9): Vladimir Nabokov's *Lolita*

"Mind and Market in Academic Life" (Dec. 1958, vol. 7, no. 13): Paul Lazarsfeld and
Wagner Thielens, Jr.'s *The Academic Mind;* Theodore Caplow and Reece McGee's
The Academic Marketplace

Articles Published by Lionel Trilling in *The Mid-Century*

"The Lost Glory" (July 1959, no. 1): John Osborne's *Look Back in Anger* and *The Entertainer;* John Osborne and Anthony Creighton's *Epitaph for George Dillon*

"The Rational Enchantress" (July 1959, no. 1): Geoffrey Scott's *The Portrait of Zélide*

"An Investigation of Modern Love" (Aug. 1959, no. 2): Lawrence Durrell's *Justine* and
Balthazar

"All Aboard the Seesaw" (Sept. 1959, no. 3): William Gibson's *The Seesaw Log*

"Paradise Reached For" (Fall 1959, no. 5): Norman O. Brown's *Life Against Death*

"Practical Cats More Practical Than Ever Before" (Nov. 1959, no. 6): Recording by
T. S. Eliot of *Old Possum's Book of Practical Cats*

"Angels and Ministers of Grace" (Dec. 1959, no. 7): *The Henry Miller Reader*

"The Mind of an Assassin" (Jan. 1960, no. 8): by Isaac Don Levine

"Love and Death in the American Novel" (March 1960, no. 10): by Leslie Fiedler

"Lawrence Durrell's *Alexandria Quartet*" (April 1960, no. 11): Durrell's *Mountolive* and *Clea*

"Fifty Years of *The Wind in the Willows*" (June 1960, no. 13): by Kenneth Grahame

"The Inimitable as an Immortal" (July 1960, no. 14): F. W. Dupee, ed. *The Selected Letters of Charles Dickens*

"*The Poem Itself*" (Aug. 1960, no. 15): Stanley Burnshaw, ed.

"An American Classic" (Sept. 1960, no. 16): James Agee and Walker Evans's *Let Us Now Praise Famous Men*

"The Word as Heard" (Fall 1960, no. 17): Recording of T. S. Eliot's *Four Quartets*

"*Masterpieces of Greek Art*" (Oct. 1960, no. 18): Father Raymond V. Schoder

"Bergman Unseen" (Dec. 1960, no. 20): *Four Screenplays of Ingmar Bergman*

"*Looking at Pictures*" (March 1961, no. 23): by Kenneth Clark

"*Curtains*" (April 1961, no. 24): by Kenneth Tynan

"A Poet Newly Given" (May 1961, no. 25): Rae Dalven, tr. *The Complete Poems of Cavafy*

"Yeats as Critic" (Summer 1961, no. 27): W. B. Yeats's *Essays and Introductions*

"Beautiful and Blest" (Sept. 1961, no. 30): *The Great Short Novels of England, The Great Short Novels of France, The Great Short Novels of Russia* (3 vols.)

"Angels and Ministers of Grace" (Oct. 1961, no. 31): partial reprint of earlier review on Lawrence Durrell, ed. The *Henry Miller Reader*

"A Comedy of Evil" (Nov. 1961, no. 32): *The Short Novels of Dostoevsky*

"Rimbaudelaire" (Dec. 1961, no. 34): Two biographies by Enid Starkie, *Rimbaud* and *Baudelaire*

"No Mean City" (March 1962, no. 37): Jane Jacobs's *The Death and Life of Great American Cities*

"What a Piece of Work is Man" (April 1962, no. 38): Claude Lévi-Strauss's *A World on the Wane*

"The Wheel" (July 1962, no. 41): Christopher Isherwood's *Down There on a Visit;* Iris Murdoch's *An Unofficial Rose*

"James Baldwin" (Sept. 1962, no. 44): Baldwin's *Another Country*

"*Lord of the Flies*" (Oct. 1962, no. 45): by William Golding

* * *

"Jameschoice for January" (*The Griffin*, Jan. 1956, vol. 5, no. 1): The Editors on James Joyce's *Finnegans Wake*

"Three Memoranda on *The New Arden Shakespeare*" (*The Mid-Century*, Jan. 1961, no. 21): The Editors

Essays from *The Griffin* and *The Mid-Century* Published Elsewhere

W. H. Auden

"A Review of the Alternate" (*The Griffin,* March 1955, vol. 4, no. 3). Appeared in *The New York Times Book Review* (Oct. 31, 1954) as "The Hero is a Hobbit," and in *Encounter* (Nov. 1954).

"Am I That I Am?" (*The Griffin,* Dec. 1955, vol. 4, no. 12). First appeared in *Encounter* (April 1955).

"Sydney Smith" (*The Griffin,* Oct. 1956, vol. 5, no. 10) is part of the introduction to *The Selected Writings of Sydney Smith* (Farrar, Straus, & Cudahay, 1956).

"West's Disease" (*The Griffin,* May 1957, vol. 6, no 4). Reprinted in *The Dyer's Hand* by W. H. Auden (Random House, 1962).

"The Kitchen of Life" (*The Griffin,* June 1958, vol. 7, no. 6). Published as the introduction to *The Art of Eating* by M. F. K. Fisher (Faber & Faber, 1963). Reprinted in *Forewords & Afterwords,* edited by Edward Mendelson (Random House, 1973).

"Agee on Film" (*The Mid-Century,* July 1959). First appeared in *The Nation* as "Agee on Film" (Nov. 18, 1944).

"Calm Even in the Catastrophe" (*The Mid-Century,* Sept. 1959, no. 3). First appeared in a longer version in *Encounter,* April 1959; reprinted in *Forewords & Afterwords.*

"Greatness Finding Itself" (*The Mid-Century,* June 1960, no. 13) in *Forewords & Afterwords.*

"K" (*The Mid-Century,* Fall 1960, no. 17). Reprinted as "The I Without a Self" in *The Dyer's Hand.*

"A Marriage of True Minds" (*The Mid-Century,* March 1962, no. 37). First appeared in a longer version in the *Times Literary Supplement* (November 10, 1961). Reprinted in *Forewords & Afterwords.*

"The Justice of Dame Kind" (*The Mid-Century,* Midsummer 1962, no. 42) in *Forewords & Afterwords.*

Jacques Barzun

"Modern Life Begins at *Forte*" (*The Griffin,* Sept. 1954, vol. 3, no. 9). Published as the preface to *Men, Women and Pianos* by Arthur Loesser (Simon & Schuster, 1954). Reprinted in *Critical Questions,* edited by Bea Friedland (University of Chicago Press, 1984).

"On First Looking Into Our Own Chapman" (*The Griffin,* Sept. 1957, vol. 5, no. 8). Published as the introduction to *Selected Writings of John Jay Chapman* (Farrar Straus & Co., 1957).

"Two Letters" (*The Griffin,* June 1958, vol. 7, no. 6) in *Critical Questions.*

"The Playwright as Critic—of Music" (*The Mid-Century,* June 1961, no. 26) in *Critical Questions.*

Lionel Trilling

The following essays from *The Griffin* can be found in Lionel Trilling's *A Gathering of Fugitives* (Beacon Press, 1956):

"A Change of Direction" (1952, vol. 1, no. 3) and "American Portrait" (May 1954, vol. 3, no. 5). Reprinted as "Two Notes on David Riesman."

"Adams at Ease" (1952, vol. 1, no. 8).

"The Early Edmund Wilson" (1952, vol. 1, no. 9). Reprinted as "Edmund Wilson: A Backward Glance."

"The Measure of Dickens" (1952, vol. 2, no. 1). Reprinted as "The Dickens of Our Day."

"Zola's Quality" (Aug. 1953, vol. 2, no. 7). Reprinted as "In Defense of Zola."

"Art and the Philosopher" (Aug. 1954, vol. 3, no. 8). Reprinted as "Criticism and Aesthetics."

"The Novel Alive or Dead" (Feb. 1955, vol. 4, no. 2).

"A Ramble on Graves" (June 1955, vol. 4, no. 6).

"Profession: Man of the World" (Sept. 1955, vol. 4, no. 9).

"That Smile of Parmenides Made Me Think" (Feb. 1956, vol. 5, no. 2).

"Mr. Forster's Aunt Marianne" (Summer 1956, vol. 5, no. 7). Reprinted as "The Great-Aunt of Mr. Forster."

"Preface to *A Gathering of Fugitives*" (Sept. 1956, vol. 5, no. 9).

* * *

The following articles were reprinted in Lionel Trilling's *Speaking of Literature and Society,* ed. Diana Trilling (Harcourt, Brace, Jovanovich, 1980):

"Impersonal/Personal" (*The Griffin,* June 1957, vol. 6, no. 5). Reprinted as "The Person of the Artist."

"Proust as Critic and the Critic as Novelist" (*The Griffin,* July 1958, vol. 7, no. 7).

"The Last Lover" (*The Griffin,* Aug. 1958, vol. 7, no. 9). Also in *The Moral Obligation to be Intelligent,* edited by Leon Wieseltier (Farrar Straus Giroux, 2000).

"Paradise Reached For" (*The Mid-Century,* Fall 1959, no. 5).

"The Mind of an Assassin" (*The Mid-Century,* Jan. 1960, no. 8). Reprinted as "The Assassination of Leon Trotsky."

"An American Classic" (*The Mid-Century,* Sept. 1960, no. 16). First appeared in *Kenyon Review* (Winter 1942).

"Yeats as Critic" (*The Mid-Century,* Summer 1961, no. 27).

"A Comedy of Evil" (*The Mid-Century,* Nov. 1961, no. 32).

In addition:

"A Triumph of the Comic View" (*The Griffin,* Sept. 1953, vol. 2, no. 8). Reprinted as the introduction to the 1956 Modern Library edition of *The Adventures of Augie March.*

"Product of the Revolution?" (*The Griffin,* July 1955, vol. 4, no. 7). Published as the introduction to the *Collected Stories of Isaac Babel* (Criterion Books, 1955).

"An Investigation of Modern Love" (*The Mid-Century,* Aug. 1959, no. 2) and "Lawrence Durrell's *Alexandria Quartet*" (*The Mid-Century,* April 1960, no. 11) were reprinted in *The World of Lawrence Durrell,* edited by Harry T. Moore (Southern Illinois University Press, Carbondale, 1962).

ACKNOWLEDGMENTS

FOR PERMISSION TO reproduce certain materials in this book, I am grateful to the estates of W. H. Auden and Lionel Trilling, and their executors—respectively: Edward Mendelson and James Trilling.

I also owe thanks to the fine staff of the Rare Book and Manuscript Library at Columbia University, and especially Jennifer B. Lee, who bore the brunt of numerous inopportune requests.

My thanks extend also to Glen Hartley and Lynn Chu, who helped turn an idea into an idea that people could hold in their hands, and to Alys Yablon and Dan Freedberg of The Free Press, who wisely and capably handled the book and its editor.

Then there is Jacques Barzun. There is always Jacques Barzun.